Civil Justice Reconsidered

Toward a Less Costly, More Accessible Litigation System

Steven P. Croley

NEW YORK UNIVERSITY PRESS

New York

NEW YORK UNIVERSITY PRESS
New York
www.nyupress.org

References to Internet websites (URLs) were accurate at the time of writing. Neither the author nor New York University Press is responsible for URLs that may have expired or changed since the manuscript was prepared.

Library of Congress Cataloging-in-Publication Data
Names: Croley, Steven P., 1965– author.
Title: Civil justice reconsidered : toward a less costly, more accessible litigation system / Steven P. Croley.
Description: New York : New York University Press, [2017] | "Also available as an ebook." | Includes bibliographical references and index.
Identifiers: LCCN 2017003764| ISBN 9781479855001 (cl ; alk. paper) | ISBN 1479855006 (cl ; alk. paper)
Subjects: LCSH: Justice, Administration of—United States. | Civil procedure—United States. | Actions and defenses—United States. | Costs (Law)—United States. | Law reform—United States.
Classification: LCC KF8700 .C76 2017 | DDC 347.73/5—dc23
LC record available at https://lccn.loc.gov/2017003764

New York University Press books are printed on acid-free paper, and their binding materials are chosen for strength and durability. We strive to use environmentally responsible suppliers and materials to the greatest extent possible in publishing our books.

Manufactured in the United States of America

10 9 8 7 6 5 4 3 2 1

Also available as an ebook

To Bridget,

who knows something about Justice

CONTENTS

PREFACE

As a lawyer, I once represented a client who suffered significant but not permanent physical and emotional injuries. In the course of preparing the case, I called a well-respected plaintiff's lawyer whom a colleague recommended as a potentially useful source of advice. I described to him the basic facts and the legal claims I intended to bring on the client's behalf.

He asked me what my client's injuries were. I explained. They were straightforward enough, but he asked me again. So I explained again, trying to phrase differently what I thought was already made clear. We continued to discuss the case, and eventually he returned yet again to the subject of what harms my client had suffered. I explained once again.

He was not being dense or difficult. For some reason, he was just not able to track my explanation fully; we were somehow talking past each other. Over the course of our conversation, it became apparent why. His questions about my client's injuries were intended to ask what his/her permanent injuries were. That is, he viewed injuries and permanent injuries as much the same thing. He simply could not fathom—I mean to say, he literally did not understand at first—that I was undertaking to represent someone who had, by the time we spoke, recovered almost fully. Such a possibility was beyond the set of assumptions he carried into our conversation.

For this lawyer's practice involved representing individuals who suffered injuries that were permanent. He explained that in his extensive experience, the costs of litigating cases required permanent injury; prospective clients with non-permanent injuries would not stand to recover enough to justify the costs of their cases. He could not afford to litigate cases involving temporary harms, even if those harms had been substantial. So he did not.

On another occasion, I assisted in the legal representation of someone with whom I was very well acquainted, and whose attorney took the case in part because I was acquainted with the client. This client too—

hardworking, independent, a virtuous person in every way—suffered unexpected economic harm as a result of someone else's legal misfeasance. But in this case too, the client's harms were, although unquestionably substantial for the client, bounded. The attorney explained to me that his motivation to take the case reflected his own sense of justice, not a straightforward cost-benefit analysis of the likely return against the likely expenses of litigating it. In the absence of any larger sense of justice and injustice, considered purely in economic terms, such a case would be difficult to pursue.

These examples are not unusual. Anyone familiar with the civil justice system recognizes that litigation is difficult, time-consuming, and often prohibitively expensive. This means, in concrete terms, that individuals who suffer limited harms—though substantial harms from their perspective—are often unable to vindicate them through the legal system.

In fact, one could easily fill an entire book with examples of real-life individuals whose rights were in one way or another violated by the legal wrongdoing of others, yet who were unable to recover for their legal injuries (and not just personal injuries) given the costs of litigation. Such examples would highlight how justice is often beyond reach for ordinary citizens—sympathetic individuals who pay their taxes, mind their own business, and do right by their neighbors. Their stories would further illustrate, in powerful human terms, both how these individuals must absorb unexpected losses imposed by others' wrongdoing, and what the consequences of un-remedied legal harm look like for the average person. Such a book, by appealing to the reader's innate sense of right and wrong, might aim to demonstrate that the litigation system's promise of justice often remains unfulfilled.

This is not that book. At least that is not its mode of argument. This book *is* concerned with civil justice, centrally, and about how achieving justice requires a litigation system that accommodates not only those who can well afford the costs of litigation, but also those who cannot. But it takes up the subject in a more dispassionate way—in a more scholarly way—by parsing claims and arguments, considering alternative hypotheses, and marshaling available evidence. It does so not only towards evaluating the litigation system but also, and crucially, to propose ways to improve it.

Many commentators on the civil litigation system have taken the alternative path of argument-by-anecdote. The litigation system's most influential critics in particular, whose general contention is that the system is too accommodating to litigants who exploit it for selfish and socially harmful ends, have done so with considerable success. That contention has found effective voice in passionate though grossly embellished stories and misleading "facts," with few accompanying reform recommendations beyond very general calls to dismantle the justice system or at least to limit its relevance.

And here is the truth too: the critics are not off base completely. For one thing, anyone familiar with the practice of civil litigation understands that there are lawyers who bring cases of dubious merit. The critics are also right that the costs of litigation can be very burdensome, not only for those who are effectively prohibited from bringing it but also for those against whom litigation is brought, including small defendants certainly but even large defendants as well.

Sometimes defenders of the civil litigation system, for their part, may gloss over these realities and overstate their side of the argument too. Some defenders romanticize the system as if every plaintiff were deserving, or as if there were few unscrupulous lawyers seeking to profit from the system's high costs and other imperfections. Yet the civil litigation system does have its defects. What is more, high costs and limited access harm all potential litigants, defendants, and plaintiffs alike, and with undesirable social consequences at that.

There is very good news to follow clear-eyed assessment of the civil litigation system's promise and shortcomings, however: the latter conditions are surmountable. That is, the promise of civil justice can be better realized through achievable reforms beneficial to all who would engage it or be engaged by it. The litigation system can be rendered at once less expensive and—therefore—more accessible both for plaintiffs and defendants. These ends can be made possible by altering how familiar forms of civil litigation are conducted and by expanding the menu of procedures through which potential litigants can advance their claims in the first place. A combination of systemic and incremental reforms, targeting high costs and inadequate access, is entirely within reach. And such an improved litigation system becomes much more visible in the light of a sober analysis of the existing system's aspirations, features, and imperfections.

But to be clear from the start, such a project is important not in the abstract. Rather, a better litigation system matters only because of what is at stake for real people. It matters for potential plaintiffs otherwise priced out of the courts, for defendants otherwise required to bear excessive costs to defend themselves, and not least of all, for those who never encounter the civil litigation system directly but are nevertheless deeply affected by that system, which ultimately gives practical effect to the rule of law itself. The pages that follow call for reforming civil litigation in the interest of justice for all of these.

Introduction

This book seeks to provide a fresh perspective on a familiar subject—the civil litigation system. It aims to do so by synthesizing different perceptions of, and adjudicating among conclusions about, that system. "Civil litigation" refers here to the legal-procedural institution in which legal disputes might be brought, and through which they are resolved. Conventional wisdom holds that the civil litigation system performs poorly, although its critics are not unanimous in their identification of its largest defects, or in their recommendations for reform. Nor are observers always specific about what a well-working civil justice system would look like. On the way to proposing reforms of the litigation system, then, this book first addresses the question of criteria most useful for evaluating it, and in light of which desirable reforms might follow.

To generalize responsibly about civil litigation's standing, its most politically influential critics—associated loosely with the political right—portray a system of unscrupulous lawyers, undeserving litigants, unpredictable juries, and indifferent judges. According to these critics, civil plaintiffs prevail too often, and are awarded too much. Plaintiffs' lawyers are part of the problem, on this account. Motivated to file lawsuits because they stand to receive a substantial portion of the amounts their prevailing clients are awarded, lawyers often file cases of questionable merit. They need not win every such case, or even most of them. But if they receive substantial rewards often enough, they have an incentive to bring forth lots of cases.

Juries too are often part of the problem. Juries can be too quick to transfer substantial sums of money from blameless—but rich and impersonal—defendants to blameworthy (but poor and vividly hapless) victim plaintiffs, unaware of the adverse social consequences of doing so. And where jurors may be reluctant to provide Robin Hood–like justice, unscrupulous "expert" witnesses paid for their testimony might rationalize the result by testifying that the defendant before them was indeed responsible for the victim's harm.

So-called victims: undeserving plaintiffs are also to blame on this view. Seeking easy gain from civil litigation, they enlist lawyers to file lawsuits in bad faith. Sometimes, these undeserving individuals have caused their own injuries. Sometimes, they simply feign injury, or grossly exaggerate genuine but small injuries. Unfortunately, however, such litigants too often prevail; the civil justice system in effect rewards them.

The ills attributed to civil litigation are not at all limited to personal injury cases, however. According to influential critics, civil litigation of all types brings deleterious consequences: Plaintiffs lawyers file meritless suits under federal securities statutes, which increase corporate costs and ultimately harm stockholders. Class action attorneys recover handsomely in litigation brought under consumer protection statutes, in cases yielding no genuine benefit to consumers. Clientless "public interest" law firms bring expensive cases against state and local governments, costing taxpayers yet generating little or no benefit for their state or local community. Abusive litigation under the banner of civil rights and sexual harassment too often perversely discourages employers from hiring women and minorities, who if terminated or demoted are more likely to bring unwarranted litigation. Time-rich prisoners file frivolous, court-clogging cases concerning their conditions of confinement. Patent "trolls" bring extortionate intellectual property litigation, increasing the costs of business innovation. Ideologically driven environmentalists bring wasteful environmental litigation that undermines the public interest. In short, much civil litigation is not only wasteful, but also counterproductive.

All of this is possible, according to the critics, because—importantly—the rules and processes through which civil litigation is conducted work poorly. Here an important distinction must be made between *civil liability reform*, on the one hand, and *civil litigation reform*, on the other. Advocates for civil liability reform call for less legal liability as a matter of substantive law; they argue that the law should impose fewer duties and recognize fewer legal rights in the first place, reducing the breadth of activity that could give rise to a legal claim at all. Advocates for civil litigation reform, in contrast—the focus of this analysis—allege that the litigation system's poor handling of claims undermines and even perverts the intent of underlying legal rules. They therefore call for changes in the way that the litigation system administers claims, in order to avoid its mistakes. In short, liability reform focuses on the substantive law's reach, whereas litigation reform addresses the process through which legal disputes are resolved.

As it happens, some proponents of civil litigation reform also advocate for liability reform, and indeed some reform measures could be understood as either or both. For example, caps on the availability of monetary damages in civil cases can be understood as reductions in the degree of legal liability for wrongful conduct, or instead as a process corrective for civil juries who too often overcompensate civil plaintiffs because they do not calculate damages accurately. (Most proponents of caps on damages emphasize jury mistake—which results in excessive damage awards—as the main justification for caps.) But again the analysis here focuses on civil litigation reform, and brackets altogether debates about the proper scope of substantive legal liability generally.

Critics' concerns about the civil litigation system's costs and other process defects that reward bad faith litigation have, of course, led to many litigation reforms over recent decades at both the state and federal level. For example, many states have enacted legislation capping the amount of damages recoverable in civil cases, and some states have limited the availability of punitive damages or now require that punitive damages be paid to the state. At the federal level, civil litigation reform legislation has been introduced in every congressional session for well over a decade. Congress has meanwhile enacted limitations on the types of litigation that recipients of federal legal services funding can bring, and reforms addressing prisoner litigation, securities litigation, and class action litigation as well. Even the U.S. Supreme Court has contributed meaningfully to litigation reform, first tightening the standards for allowing expert witnesses to testify at trial, and then by substantially limiting punitive damages recoverable in personal injury lawsuits as well as recoverable attorneys' fees in civil rights litigation, and later by raising the pleading standards for civil cases.

And yet, this general critique of the civil litigation system is not the only one. It rather competes with another, very different perspective, which, though less frequently articulated and far less influential, is not unfamiliar. According to this alternative view—associated loosely with the political left—the litigation system is flawed because it is out of reach for many individuals who likely have suffered real injury. To put the contrast most starkly: whereas critics on the right allege that the civil litigation system often rewards undeserving parties, critics on the left argue that the system often fails to protect deserving parties. In particular, many individuals are unable to seek redress for their legal harms because, for them, civil litigation is not too easy but rather too difficult.

Critics of the civil justice system who highlight its prohibitive costs from this point of view often have in mind individuals who are poorly situated to defend themselves including those whose incomes are below the poverty line, victims of domestic violence, tenants, migrant workers, veterans, the elderly, consumers with substantial debt, and minorities. As a result, reform proposals accompanying this alternative critique call for increased financial support for legal aid, greater commitment to pro bono legal services by the organized bar, and new tools for individuals to bring their own claims to court without having to hire a lawyer. While these reforms certainly have not seen the sustained political traction associated reforms responsive to the excess-litigation critique, there is a general consensus among much of the organized bar and the judiciary that, at least for certain categories of civil claims, many would-be litigants are indeed effectively excluded from the civil justice system and thus greater access for those litigants would be desirable. Accordingly, many courts have implemented reforms to address the problem, such as simplified court forms, self-help kiosks, user-friendly case filing tools, and (in a few jurisdictions) even expedited procedures to make certain types of civil litigation easier.

While these two critical pictures of the civil litigation system tend to resonate with opposite sides of the political spectrum, and while the first empathizes mostly with civil defendants whereas the second highlights would-be plaintiffs, this book argues that they in fact share certain points of emphasis. This is not entirely surprising given that they are focused on one and the same litigation system—a system of common courts and common procedural rules, evidentiary rules, legal doctrines, traditions of civil pleading and practice, and a common set of potential remedies available to those bringing claims. The analysis here is motivated in the first place, then, partly by the question whether and to what extent these contrasting pictures of the same institution are exclusive, compatible, or reinforcing. It answers that although their policy reforms run in opposite directions, they share the concern that legally deserving parties are not always well served by the civil litigation system, and they both emphasize the broader threat that litigation costs pose to civil justice. This book is motivated also by fundamental questions both perspectives raise: What is civil litigation supposed to accomplish, and how is the civil justice system properly evaluated? Because any assessment of the civil litigation system requires some conception of how it should work, the analysis here provides a general framework for evaluating the civil litigation system in the course of bridging commentary about the need for "litigation reform," on the one hand, with calls for greater "access to justice," on the other.

Now for the preview. The analysis here advances four main claims. First, civil litigation matters most because of its consequences not for litigants themselves, but for the rest of society. Where the civil litigation system functions well, or poorly, important consequences are felt far beyond the litigating parties. Second, a well-working civil litigation system is accessible to parties who have suffered legal wrongs, and it adjudicates between competing parties' claims reliably in the sense that those with stronger claims tend to prevail over those with weaker claims. Third, while many of the most influential alleged failures of the civil litigation system are overstated, they are not wholly off base either; the system is not beyond improvement for reasons highlighted by its most influential critics. In particular, civil litigation often imposes excessive costs that, among other unfortunate consequences, impede access to the courts. Fourth, and not least of all, reducing the costs of civil litigation and promoting greater access are within reach. The analysis here accordingly proposes a number of feasible reforms to increase access to the courts and reduce litigation costs, in part by discouraging litigation that should not be advanced at all.

To anticipate these prescriptions in general terms, this book argues that existing rules and practices of civil litigation should be applied in ways to reduce certain "variable" costs, especially those that litigants impose on each other. A central point of this part of the argument highlights a distinction between the decision to initiate (or defend) a civil case in the first place, on the one hand, and marginal decisions to litigate further a case already underway, on the other. Parties to litigation should be incentivized to make better decisions about whether to incur, and to require their adversaries to incur, marginal litigation costs. Proposals to increase those incentives would accomplish the right kind of litigation reform.

At the same time, the civil litigation system requires new, less expensive processes that are accommodating to civil claims where less than millions of dollars are at stake. Traditional civil litigation often is too costly for parties with strong legal claims but only modest expected recovery. Courts should adopt innovative procedures with lower "fixed" costs, thereby reducing the unavoidable expenditures associated with bringing a civil case and making modest civil claims more economically feasible. Proposals in this vein would promote greater access to justice.

Through such reforms as specified below, the civil litigation system could simultaneously accommodate more claimants while discouraging excessive litigation. Indeed, these two sides of sensible reform are reinforcing. Accommodating more claimants requires curbing litigation costs, first because often it is litigation costs that impede access to the courts to begin with, and second because it will be important to keep litigation costs from overwhelming courts in a system accommodating to more potential litigants. Meanwhile, providing greater accessibility to the civil litigation system becomes more attractive if litigation costs are controlled, and so long as litigation costs are minimized to the extent feasible, it becomes harder to argue against providing more good faith litigants with an opportunity to advance their legitimate legal interests.

It is important to get a few matters straight at the outset, however—particularly with regard to what this analysis does not purport to do. One is that its recommendations are not intended to reinvent the civil litigation system wholesale. Instead, the effort here takes for granted the existing rules and institutions, offering practical, achievable ways to improve them. Most ambitiously, recommendations for courts to reallocate litigation costs in a calibrated way to discourage parties from imposing wasteful expenditures on their opponents will require judges to apply procedural rules in a somewhat new way. And new litigation procedures prescribed below, including a new "court of medium claims," would provide greater access to the courts for certain whole classes of litigants by creating a new mode of civil proceedings. But the focus here remains to identify how the existing civil litigation system can be realistically improved, not to imagine the implausible creation of some new system. Nor, moreover, does promoting civil justice require positing some alternative system anyway. The existing system is by no means defective to the core; it lends itself to improvements that would reduce costs and accommodate more litigants. In the analysis provided here, then, realism and optimism converge.

Second, the analysis here does not aim to join any side in the litigation debate; it aims instead to identify how and why the civil litigation system is imperfect and to suggest improvements responsive to its genuine shortcomings. As suggested above (and as demonstrated below), the dominant critique of civil litigation frequently overstates. But while the analysis here rejects strong versions of it, again that critique does yield some insights about the consequences of high litigation costs and the importance of requiring litigants in certain circumstances to internalize more of the costs of their litigation decisions. The approach taken here thus rejects any choice between a runaway litigation system, on the one hand, and one that is beyond cost-controlling improvements, on the other. The truth about civil litigation is found somewhere in between.

Finally, the analysis here does not target academic experts on civil litigation as its primary audience. To the contrary, it enlists them—relying on them in this effort to integrate literatures on litigation reform, access to justice, and civil procedure—in hopes of bridging social-scientific, normative, and doctrinal treatments of litigation. Key sources are acknowledged along the way, but several deserve introductory mention. For example, Haltom and McCann's (2004) important work on the role that rhetoric and anecdote play in many influential criticisms of litigation and tort law informs central parts of chapter 5. Similarly, Bogus's (2001) and Koenig and Rustad's (2001) related analyses inform key parts of chapters 2 and 5. Chapter 5 also draws on the work of Vidmar (1995) and Hans (2000) (and Vidmar and Hans (2007)) on the civil jury, as well as T. Baker's (2005) work on medical malpractice litigation. Chapter 6 draws on Miller's (2010, 2013) recent articulations of the inaccessibility of the civil litigation system and Kritzer's (2004) analysis of contingency fees. Eisenberg's invaluable empirical analyses of civil litigation (e.g., Eisenberg and Farber 1997; Eisenberg et al. 2005; Eisenberg and Heise 2009) inform chapter 5, as do Galanter's (e.g., 1993, 1996, 2001, 2006) and Hensler's (e.g., 1988, 1993). Rhode's (2000, 2004a) and Hadfield's

(2000, 2005, 2010) contributions to the literature on access to justice informs chapter 6, as does Rhode's work (2001) on the organized bar's proper role in promoting civil justice discussed in chapter 10. These examples are by no means exhaustive.

The analysis here does target thought leaders on the subject of civil litigation, and litigation reformers of all stripes. Drawing also on familiarity with the actual practice of civil litigation (a perspective missing from some treatments of the subject), it speaks to members of the bar and bench concerned with litigation reform, for sure, but also to policymakers generally, including non-lawyers. With respect to the latter, the opening chapter therefore supplies rather than assumes important background information about what the civil litigation system is and does.

The discussion maps like this. Part 1, "Foundations," provides an overview of civil litigation (chapter 1), explains its benefits (chapter 2), and specifies the features of a well-working civil litigation system (chapter 3). Part 2, "Evaluations," considers commonly alleged and actual shortcomings of the existing civil litigation system (chapter 4). It argues that the most influential criticisms of civil litigation do not find support from the available evidence (chapter 5). Part 2 further argues that the current litigation system is insufficiently accessible, most especially for those who have suffered genuine but small legal injury, and that all reformers' worries about excessive litigation costs seem well-placed (chapter 6). Accordingly, part 3, "Reform," prescribes a number of reforms both to reduce litigation costs, including mechanisms to filter out undesirable cases from the litigation system (chapter 7) and ways to require litigants to internalize more of the costs of their litigation decisions (chapter 8), and to promote the civil litigation system's accessibility, including new forms of civil litigation (chapter 9) and increased support for greater access (chapter 10). For reasons articulated in part 3, reforms along the lines proposed in this book would render the civil litigation system more just.

PART I

Foundations

1

The Civil Litigation System

An Orientation

Examining what is right or wrong with the civil litigation system requires some shared understanding of what that system does and what it is supposed to do. For example, when critics talk about the failures of the civil litigation system, what *exactly* are they talking about? And when civil litigation is said to produce just or unjust results, what is the benchmark against which those results are measured anyway? A broken civil litigation system cannot be fixed unless it is known how it is broken.

This chapter and especially the two that follow thus address these fundamental questions, starting here first with a basic description of the civil litigation system. While this chapter aims mainly to provide an introductory description of the object of study here, along the way it points out that initiating a civil case is more difficult than some commentary on civil litigation suggests, and it further observes that basic facts about the types of cases handled by the civil litigation system raise preliminary doubts about some of the system's most commonly alleged defects. Readers well familiar with the mechanics of civil litigation and the workload of the litigation system are warmly encouraged to skip ahead to chapter 2, however; the immediate discussion is intended as background for those not deeply acquainted with such topics.

A Civil Case

The paradigmatic civil case involves a dispute between private parties in which the government has no direct stake or role apart from umpiring the controversy neutrally. This is not to say the consequences of civil litigation are confined to the immediate litigants, however, as emphasized in the next chapter. But on the surface, a civil claim involves an allegation by one or more private-party plaintiff, that one or more other party defendant (treated throughout in the singular for each case of exposition) engaged in conduct, or perhaps failed to engage in conduct, resulting in some harm or injury to the claimant, and for which that party seeks some kind of redress—that is, "A versus B."

Not that the law recognizes every injury. Indeed, most of life's misfortunes, even those involving harm caused by others, do not give rise to legal liability at all. This is true even for parties who suffer indisputable physical injuries. Unless harm results from the violation of a duty or right that the legal system recognizes, the law provides no recourse. In short, not all harms are legal harms.

And rightly so, as the legal system is not designed to address all of life's adversities. Many injuries are best redressed by other institutions instead; certainly the *law* should not seek to redress all harms. And many more are simply best left un-remedied altogether; not every misfortunate requires some fix. It is also true that, for better or worse, the law does not seek to remedy all clearly contemptible conduct. But while questions about the proper scope of legal liability are fundamental to any understanding of the legal system, they are beyond the purposes here—assessing the civil litigation system in which claims about *recognized* legal harms are adjudicated.

To bring a legally cognizable claim, a plaintiff must allege the necessary factual and legal elements of the plaintiff's cause of action, articulated in the plaintiff's complaint. Filing a complaint triggers a larger process governed by rules of civil procedure, and requires some kind of response by the defendant. In response, the defendant might respond by arguing that the plaintiff's allegations do not state any injury recognized by the law and move that the court therefore dismiss the case. The defendant might also respond that the court in question lacks jurisdiction over the plaintiff's case. Or, the defendant might answer that even if the plaintiff's allegations are correct, other circumstances or factors require the conclusion that the defendant is not liable for the plaintiff's injuries—the defendant's affirmative defense to the claim.

A complaint that does not state a legally cognizable injury will be dismissed following an initial motion by the defendant. Two recent Supreme Court cases, discussed later in chapter 4, require a civil complaint to contain allegations that plausibly establish some right to legal relief as a condition of avoiding dismissal of the case by initial motion.[1] These cases to some extent heighten the pleading standard a would-be plaintiff must satisfy. Such allegations must show that it is not merely possible the plaintiff is entitled to relief, but plausibly so. Motions to dismiss a complaint for failure to allege a legally cognizable injury can be filed quickly and cheaply.

Civil defendants routinely file motions to dismiss a case as their first response to a lawsuit, often successfully. This mechanism to filter out cases that present no legally recognized harm constitutes an important part of the civil litigation process, and the ease with which defendants can file motions to dismiss is not underestimated by plaintiffs' attorneys, who therefore lack incentives to file cases not likely to survive initial motions. Parties without legally recognized injuries will therefore find securing legal representation difficult.

In addition to stating a legally cognizable injury, would-be plaintiffs must also satisfy certain procedural requirements incident to civil litigation. For example, cases must be brought within the applicable statute-of-limitations period following an alleged injury. Otherwise, even recognized claims may be barred, as the civil litigation system righty does not welcome aged allegations or dated evidence. But this means that statutes of limitations provide another constraint on initiating a claim. Sometimes, that limitation can be substantial. In one well-known example, the U.S. Supreme Court in *Ledbetter v. Goodyear Tire & Rubber Co.* held that a plaintiff filing a claim of employment discrimination must initiate a case within 180 days of the alleged act of discrimination.[2] In that case, the plaintiff's suit was predicated on years of intentional gender discrimination in the form of unequal pay, and she had no way of knowing when the discrimination began, given that the compensation of her co-workers was confidential. Nevertheless, the Supreme Court's holding (subsequently undone by federal legislation) effectively prohibited the plaintiff from recovering for past discrimination, on the grounds that her claim was too late.

Several states have recently seen litigation reform proposals that would have the effect of reducing statute-of-limitations periods. These proposals provide that the statute-of-limitations clock begins at the time of injury, rather than at the time the potential plaintiff discovers the injury or has reason to discover it. In cases where a prospective plaintiff learns of the injury after having initially suffered it, as in some toxic torts and medical malpractice cases, for example—as well as in civil rights cases like the *Ledbetter* case—this reform has the practical consequence of shortening the time period in which a plaintiff can file suit. In any event, statutes of limitation govern all civil claims, and thus they provide another practical constraint on potential plaintiffs' ability to find representation and initiate litigation. Lawyers simply will not take cases of long-injured parties where the statute of limitations has run.

Identifying a legally recognized wrong and satisfying relevant procedural requirements are necessary—but not sufficient—conditions for bringing a civil claim with any chance of success. The legal wrong alleged must also be proven. That is, a potential plaintiff must provide credible evidence that the would-be defendant committed a legal wrong that harmed the plaintiff. Without *evidence* of a wrong and resulting harm, a plaintiff cannot satisfy the burden of proof required to prevail. Indeed, the civil litigation process writ large can be well understood as a process for developing and testing evidence of legal wrongdoing.

Assuming there are factual disagreements between the parties after both sides have stated their initial positions, the typical civil case then proceeds to the fact-finding or discovery phase of the litigation (otherwise, the court can decide the case, based on uncontested facts, by applying the relevant law). In many cases, discovery can be the most costly phase of litigation, as fact-finding can be time-consuming and document-intensive, and often leads the parties to enlist outside experts to support their factual allegations. In response to the fact-finding stage, the parties may refine their factual allegations and the legal positions on which they depend in light of what they have learned. For example, plaintiffs might drop or possibly amend certain claims.

Following the close of discovery, the parties may ask the court to resolve the case on the law—that is, without the need for trial—on the theory that the facts gathered through the discovery process clearly support a legal conclusion in favor of one side or the other. Typically, it is the defendant who moves the court to grant "summary judgment" in its favor, which, if granted, ends the case (subject to possible appeals or other developments). Summary judgment in fact disposes of a significant number of civil cases that get even that far (Burbank 2004; Hadfield 2004; Bronsteen 2006).

Plaintiffs bear the persuasive burden in a civil case. That is, the plaintiff must show that it is more likely than not that the defendant committed a legal wrong that harmed the plaintiff, and must do so moreover through legally admissible evidence—that is, evidence that the court deems sufficiently probative and non-prejudicial to warrant its admissibility. The rules of evidence thus provide a separate set of filters on civil claims. Furthermore, civil plaintiffs bear the burden with respect to each legal element of a plaintiff's claim. Defendants, in contrast, can defeat a claim by calling into probable question any element of a plaintiff's claim. And procedurally, defendants commonly have the last word in litigation, as the litigation process allows for defendants to rebut plaintiffs' allegations. For these reasons, many civil litigators consider "offense" more difficult than "defense."

To satisfy evidentiary standards, plaintiffs must produce witnesses, documents, or other materials corroborating a plaintiff's factual allegations, a burden that can prove more difficult for certain types of civil cases than for others. For instance, sometimes civil rights plaintiffs must prove discriminatory intent, fraud plaintiffs must prove intent to deceive, and antitrust plaintiffs must show collusion. None of these is easy. But the larger point is that questions about the practical demonstrability of a potential claim will constitute any attorney's first considerations about the viability of a case. Unless the litigation process is likely to produce credible admissible evidence supporting a claim, again potential plaintiffs will be unlikely to find legal representation.

Evidentiary standards and the allocation of the burden of proof in civil litigation also call into question some critics' casual claims about the ease with which plaintiffs, including bad-faith plaintiffs, can initiate litigation. For evidence of legal wrongdoing and harm often can be difficult to marshal. Sometimes, the harms resulting from wrongdoing can be hard to demonstrate or measure, even when there is little question that some level of legal injury occurred.

In the unusual civil case that goes all the way to trial, a jury—or in certain cases, a judge—resolves the remaining contested factual questions. Indeed, that is the core purpose of the civil trial, to resolve open factual questions not answered through the litigation process up to that point. At trial, the plaintiff puts on its case, after which the defendant typically puts on its case in rebuttal. Along the way, the court may resolve evidentiary and other legal questions that arise during the trial. At the end of the process, the fact-finder resolves contested issues, and the court enters a judgment on the legal case corresponding to the resolution of factual issues. Following trial, either side may seek to appeal certain legal rulings made along the way.

This process seldom plays out in full, however; only about 5% of all civil cases proceed through trial (e.g., Galanter 2004; Hadfield 2004; Schlanger 2006).[3] Many cases are adjudicated before trial, whether early in a case, because the plaintiff failed to identify a legal injury, for example, or later in the case because for instance the court determined the evidence developed during pretrial litigation requires a summary judgment in the defendant's favor (or, rarely, in the plaintiff's favor) without trial. Though estimates vary widely, according to some, two-thirds or more of all civil cases settle, a rate that depends in part on the legal subject matter and on the type of litigants in question (e.g., Galanter and Cahill 1994; Hadfield 2004, 2005; Eisenberg and Lanvers 2009). (The settlement "rate" also depends on whether the denominator is taken to be all cases filed, as opposed to only cases that survive initial motions and progress further into the litigation process.) In addition, some cases are dismissed because they are abandoned by the plaintiff, and a few percent are resolved by default due to the defendant's inaction or because the defendant does not appear.

Types of Civil Litigation

The civil litigation system handles various types of cases, owing to the variety of legal duties, rights, and obligations embodied in law. Notwithstanding this subject matter variation, though, civil cases share common rules, processes, and procedural norms; thus, it is possible to generalize about civil litigation even while the substantive legal doctrines applied vary from case to case. As detailed shortly, contracts and torts cases, respectively, constitute the two most common types of "general civil cases" ("general" commonly refers to non-specialized cases). In a contracts case, the plaintiff alleges that the defendant injured the plaintiff by failing to live up to the obligations of a binding contract between them. The plaintiff thus seeks a remedy for the harm resulting from the defendant's breach. That remedy usually takes the form of monetary damages measured by what gain the plaintiff would have gotten as a result of the contract if the defendant had honored it, though different remedies may be available under certain circumstances.

In a torts case too, the plaintiff alleges that the defendant injured the plaintiff by failing to live up to a legal obligation. But whereas in a contracts case the defendant's obligation is created by a contract, in a torts case the defendant's obligation stems from duties that the law imposes, including duties not to create unreasonable risks for others. Automobile accident cases constitute a classic example. Medical malpractice cases are another—frequently mentioned by critics of the civil litigation system—in which patient-plaintiffs seek compensation for injuries resulting from alleged violation of standards of medical care. Products liability cases, where consumers injured by defective products seek compensation for injuries caused by those products, and premises liability or "slip and fall" cases provide additional paradigmatic examples of tort litigation.

Both contracts and torts cases traditionally constitute common law suits, meaning that judge-made law is the original source of the defendant's legal obligation, as opposed to legal rules created by legislatures or administrative agencies. Property cases, concerning contested claims towards land or at times other forms of property, are another familiar type of common law case; traditionally, rules governing property ownership and the scope of property rights were rooted in the common law as well.

Not all civil cases are common law cases, however. To the contrary, many types of civil cases are premised on the violation of requirements created by statute or regulation. In these cases, the plaintiff is seeking redress for the defendant's alleged violation of an obligation created by an act of a legislature or a requirement established by an administrative agency charged with implementing a statute. Examples include cases alleging violation of the antitrust laws, civil rights laws, consumer protection laws, environmental laws, or securities laws, to name only a few. In an environmental case, for instance, the plaintiff might allege that the defendant violated an environmental statute or regulation, for which the plaintiff would likely ask the court to order the defendant to comply. In a securities case, the plaintiff might allege that the defendant's violation of securities laws harmed the plaintiff economically, and as a result the plaintiff would seek monetary compensation, often along with other plaintiffs joined together in the same lawsuit. Civil rights cases allege violation of discrimination laws, and typically seek to enforce those laws and, where appropriate, to provide compensation to the plaintiff as well.

Civil litigation could also be understood to encompass broadly various proceedings such as those related to probate matters, family matters, immigration status, and actions to commit a person for involuntary hospitalization. All of these constitute "civil cases" in the sense that they are not criminal proceedings. But they fall outside of the scope of the present analysis, which considers (the vast) categories of civil litigation not brought in specialty courts or that involve their own sets of rules and procedures. The focus here, in other words, is on what is referred to as traditional "general civil litigation"—civil cases that share a common set of longstanding procedural rules and common stages of litigation that transcend different legal subject matter, brought in courts of general jurisdiction as opposed to specialty courts.

That said, small claims cases are closely related to the type of litigation of interest here, as part 3 will later make clear. Like general civil litigation, small claims also involve an allegation by the plaintiff that the defendant violated a legal obligation causing harm to the plaintiff, and may involve a variety of legal subject matter. By definition, however, small claims actions have maximum amounts in controversy, and are therefore brought in small claims courts in which the plaintiff seeks a monetary remedy below some threshold amount. Small claims cases also relax the procedural and evidentiary rules characterizing traditional general civil litigation, a topic explored further in part 3.

Multiple Jurisdictions

While general civil cases share certain basic procedural rules and practices, those cases might be brought in different court systems, each with its own jurisdiction. The federal courts have jurisdiction over two general classes of civil cases, those posing questions of federal law ("federal-question jurisdiction") and cases involving questions of state law where the litigants on opposing sides of a case happen to come from different states ("diversity jurisdiction," because the litigants come from diverse states). Diversity suits must involve a claim over a certain dollar amount, however—called the "amount-in-controversy" requirement—or otherwise the stakes are not considered high enough to warrant federal adjudication. In addition to federal-question and diversity jurisdiction, the federal courts also have "supplemental" jurisdiction to hear state-law claims even between citizens of the same state if those state-law claims are part of a case that also presents one or more questions of federal law. That is, to relieve litigants whose disputes involve questions of both federal and state law of the burden of litigating twice, once in federal court concerning their federal issues and once in state court concerning their state-law issues, the federal courts may exercise jurisdiction over such disputes as well.

But most of the action is found in state courts by far: among all civil cases, over 90% are brought in state court. (Thus the analysis offered throughout applies most especially though not exclusively to state litigation, although federal rules of procedure, on which state rules are most often based, are mentioned by way of general illustration.) Whereas the U.S. Constitution creates "limited" jurisdiction for the federal courts—jurisdiction limited by the Constitution and limited to cases that Congress has specifically authorized—state constitutions create instead "general" jurisdiction for their state judiciaries. In other words, state judiciaries have expansive jurisdiction extending to the subject matter of most any type of civil case, including disputes involving only questions of federal law, though the state courts are obligated in such cases to interpret federal law faithfully. But one implication is that a prospective litigant considering filing a lawsuit involving a question of federal law might file either in federal or in state court, depending on a variety of considerations, including the familiarity of the litigant's attorney with federal or state legal practice, geographical convenience, the perceived quality of the federal and state benches in question, expectations about how long the case would take in the federal and state systems, predictions about whether one forum or the other would be more friendly towards the case, and other considerations.

Civil litigation does not present a choice only between federal courts and state courts, however. As every state has its own court system, there are really fifty-one separate civil litigation systems (plus the local courts of Washington, D.C. and the U.S. territories). Moreover, within a single state, judiciaries are typically organized by county, and different counties and regions of different states often have their own specific norms and reputations, just as different federal courts may have their own philosophies and orientations.

To highlight one distinction among states courts that will prove relevant later (and relevant to measures of the volume of civil litigation that will be discussed in this chapter), some states have "uniform" or "single-tiered" judiciaries, in which *any* kind of case can be brought in the trial courts. Other states have, instead, what are known as "courts of general jurisdiction," to be distinguished within those same states from courts having limited jurisdiction. Courts with limited jurisdiction are authorized to hear only certain types of cases, whereas general jurisdiction courts hear all other cases not brought in limited-jurisdiction courts. In other words, in these states, the courts are not uniform, but are instead divided into limited- and non-limited-jurisdiction (i.e., general) courts.

To complicate things still further, a litigant from one state might well file a case in the courts of another state. That is, while the separate state judicial systems exist physically within state borders, under appropriate circumstances their reach can nevertheless potentially extend—just like the federal courts—throughout the country. State courts have authority to reach beyond their own state borders to the extent that they have valid "personal jurisdiction" over a party outside of their state. As its name suggests, personal jurisdiction means jurisdiction over the party sued, in contrast to a court's "subject matter" jurisdiction over the legal question presented in the suit. Both personal jurisdiction and subject matter jurisdiction must be satisfied for a lawsuit to go forward. Very generally speaking, state courts have personal jurisdiction over out-of-state parties to the extent out-of-staters have some degree of "fair notice" that they may be subject to the jurisdiction of other states' courts.

Such complications go beyond present purposes, however. And yet, the fact that the civil litigation system consists of a complex network of partially interlocking federal and state jurisdictions does lead to one crucial preliminary observation: when critics claim "*the* civil litigation system" is broken, they are really indicting a large number of separate though connected court systems alleged to suffer from the same basic defects—a broad critique indeed.

The Volume of General Civil Litigation

An orientation to the civil litigation system also requires some understanding of how many cases are brought within it, and which types. According to data from the Court Statistics Project of the National Center for State Courts (NCSC), and excluding civil matters brought in specialty courts, the civil litigation system sees over 7 million general civil cases—common law cases as well as cases brought under various statutes—across federal and state jurisdictions per year.[4] Among these, contracts cases are the most common by far,[5] many of them routine actions by creditors alleging that a debtor has not made payments necessary according to a loan or other credit agreement. Contracts cases are small with respect to the total dollars at stake, though with important exceptions. Beyond contracts cases, tort and property cases constitute the somewhat distant second and third most common types of general civil cases. As noted above, the vast majority of all of these are brought in state courts. According to the Administrative Office of the U.S. Courts (AOUSC), the federal courts see roughly 65,000 to 75,000 tort cases annually, 30,000 to 35,000 annual contracts cases, and 5,000 to 10,000 property cases per year over the last decade. While federal courts see roughly one-quarter million civil cases annually in total, most of those are brought under a federal statute.[6]

The fact that the modal civil case is a contracts case raises noteworthy initial questions about allegations by some critics of a litigation epidemic (accord Galanter 2001). For critics of the civil litigation system curiously do *not* generally identify contract disputes as litigation emblematic of the system's problems, which perhaps suggests that, in fact, the system handles its most common type of case reasonably well. Instead, many critics of civil litigation highlight tort litigation, even while they expressly target other types of civil litigation as well. The undeserving but successful tort plaintiff, aided by the unscrupulous tort lawyer, epitomizes what is allegedly wrong with civil litigation.

Tort cases are not as common as might be expected, however, relative to the policy attention tort reform has attracted over the years. Among uniform-jurisdiction states whose trial courts are authorized to hear all types of cases—including small claims cases, probate cases, and other specialty cases—tort cases constitute a median 3 to 4% of all civil cases.

Among states with general jurisdiction courts—courts authorized to hear cases excluding those brought in small claims courts and other specialty courts—the median percentage of tort cases out of all civil cases is 14 to 17%.[7]

Torts cases themselves vary widely, ranging from small slip-and-fall cases, to medical malpractice cases, to complex products liability suits. Although the latter are emphasized most by litigation reformers, automobile cases constitute a majority of all state tort litigation. Extrapolating from sample states, the National Center for State Courts estimates that automobile cases constitute about 52% to 66% of all tort cases.[8] Slip-and-fall cases, intentional torts, and other routine tort actions together comprise nearly 40% of all tort actions. Medical malpractice and products liability cases, in contrast, constitute a very small percentage of all torts filings, approximately 3% and 4% respectively.[9]

Based on another sample, the National Center for State Courts also computes that medical malpractice cases constitute a small percentage (2.1% to 7.9%) of all tort cases, and thus a miniscule percentage of all civil cases. In absolute terms, annual medical malpractice actions number from a low of several dozen in small states like Hawaii and Rhode Island, to over one thousand in states like Michigan and New Jersey, to a high of some four thousand in New York.[10] At least on the surface, none of these numbers suggests an especially burdensome medical malpractice litigation docket or runaway medical malpractice liability.

Such findings comport with older data reported by the Bureau of Justice Statistics (BJS) in conjunction with the National Center for State Courts. Medical malpractice, products liability, and toxic tort cases taken together comprised 10% of all torts cases in a sample of the country's seventy-five largest counties (in which approximately half of all tort suits are filed) for sample year 1992. Of those, medical malpractice claims constituted 5% of the cases, while products liability cases and toxic substance cases constituted 3% and 2%, respectively. According to BJS, 60% of all torts cases arose from automobile accidents, while 17% were premises liability cases. The BJS data too show that tort litigation constitutes a small percentage of all civil cases filed in general jurisdiction state courts (10% of all civil cases), and furthermore that the kinds of tort cases reformers emphasize the most constitute only a small percentage of overall tort litigation.[11]

On the other hand, snapshots of the incidence of tort litigation in re-cent years may not capture the possible consequences of tort reform long undertaken in many states. That is, if tort cases—and perhaps medical malpractice and products liability cases in particular—are not very common in recent years, that might cast doubt only on some critics' claims about the *continuing* need for reform, but not about the need for reform in years past. Over recent decades, many states enacted various tort and civil litigation reform measures, reflecting the belief that there was too much litigation. Current litigation levels, if lower than in pre-reform years, may thus simply illustrate the efficacy of those earlier reforms.

In one effort to test the effects of tort reform, the National Center for State Courts examined medical malpractice and products liability cases in Mississippi over a ten-year period (1997 to 2006) that spanned the enactment of several substantial reform measures in that state tar-geting both medical malpractice and products liability suits. This study concludes generally that "most tort reform measures appear to result in short-term fluctuations in caseloads," and that Mississippi's legislative reforms in particular "appear to have exerted at most a brief influence on medical malpractice and product liability caseloads" in that state.[12] One reform in particular, a state supreme court rule change barring joinder of claims by similarly injured plaintiffs against a product manu-facturer, may have increased the number of cases, as now plaintiffs must each bring their own suit rather than a combined case.

While one cannot generalize from the experience of a single state, Mississippi might not be unique. According to NCSC data, the number of tort cases filed in a large sample of states increased by almost half between 1985 and 2003, years spanning most tort reform initiatives.[13] Taking the period more closely surrounding the first wave of state tort reform measures in the late 1980s, NSCS sample data from sixteen states show a leveling but no decrease in tort litigation from the mid-1980s through 1993.[14] Of course, there is no reason to believe that tort reform in the long run encouraged litigation—undoubtedly the opposite is true given the purpose and substance of tort reform, particularly with respect to certain reforms such as damage caps. Still, for independent reasons (such as possible increases in the incidence of legal misfeasance), tort litigation is more common post–tort reform than it was prior to reform, yet it still remains a small fraction of overall civil litigation.

That leaves tort litigation brought in federal court, which for reasons previously suggested (that is, in federal "diversity" cases, the federal courts apply the state law) might be expected to reflect state trends. In contrast to state tort litigation, products liability cases make up a majority of federal tort suits. A typical federal tort case involves an individual plaintiff bringing a claim against an out-of-state defendant, such as the maker or seller of some product that allegedly caused the plaintiff personal injury. As noted, according to AOUSC data, the volume of federal tort and federal products liability cases fall in the range of several dozen thousand cases per year. Furthermore, the numbers of federal tort, and specifically products liability, cases have risen over the past four decades (since 1970)—that is, for a period spanning both sides of state tort reforms—with peaks in 1991 and 1999, each followed by valleys in 1995 and 2001.[15] In other words, trends in federal tort litigation do not seem to map state tort reform initiatives in any obvious way—again suggesting that the data may reveal more about other dynamics than they do about the consequences of state-level reform. Or, in other words, the fairly modest amount of federal tort cases does not appear to reflect any dramatic consequence of state tort reform, as the total volume of federal tort cases has increased some since the 1980s. Nor does the absolute volume of federal tort cases reveal an obvious problem of excess tort litigation.

Litigation reformers often point also to class action litigation as another area requiring reform. According to these critics, class actions frequently involve lawyers seeking to extract a settlement from a defendant corporation that enriches the lawyers but not their nominal clients. That is, in contrast to an individually litigated tort claim, where at least the plaintiff benefits from a successful case, in many class actions the plaintiff class receives little of value even when the class prevails or secures a settlement. Indeed, many view class action litigation as "clientless" litigation, underscoring the case for reform. The critics of class action litigation have advocated for reform with considerable legislative success, as chapter 3 explains, although calls for further reform continue to the present.

Such reforms raise the question how common class actions are and, again, how common they were before recent legislative reforms. According to AOUSC data, federal class actions number between two thousand

and three thousand annually.[16] Of those, tort class actions number in the several hundreds per year, while contract class actions number a couple hundred per year for recent years. Most federal class actions, by far, are not aggregated tort claims, but rather suits brought under federal statutes. Among those latter, about two hundred or so class actions under federal civil rights laws are brought each year, as are class actions under federal labor laws, while class actions brought under federal antitrust statutes number between about one hundred and two hundred annual cases. Such numbers—a few hundred cases per year—seem unlikely to ground a powerful case for reform, again at least at first glance. Class action reform would seem necessary only if class action abuse was common, and common class action abuse would seem possible only where class actions themselves were common. Put differently, it is not clear that there are enough cases for abuse to constitute a serious problem. A couple hundred civil rights and labor class actions per year is just not enough volume to make reform urgent, especially without information about how these relatively infrequent cases are abusive.

That leaves the largest category—class actions brought under federal securities laws—which represent one-fourth to one-half of all annual federal class actions. Securities cases have proven especially controversial in recent decades, leading to legislative reform. AOUSC data show, however, that federal securities class actions number from about seven hundred to about sixteen hundred per year since 2000, and about halfway between those figures for recent years.[17] Taking fifteen hundred cases a year as a rough average yields about thirty cases per state, though federal securities class actions are not evenly distributed either among states or among federal districts. While strong inferences cannot be drawn from this data, again it seems fair to question why, if securities class action litigation were an easy way to recover undeserved gains as a result of a defective litigation system, more litigants would not take advantage.

Some critics identify civil rights claims as another category of excessive litigation. On this account, many civil rights cases (setting aside prisoner cases, to be considered separately later) constitute attempts by disgruntled former employees to misattribute adverse employment actions to discrimination, or attempts by self-appointed civil rights lawyers to fashion society in their own image. But the volume of federal civil rights litigation seems rather modest, for reasons considered later. Because many civil rights cases implicate federal law and thus give rise to federal subject matter jurisdiction, as explained earlier—and also because federal courts are sometimes viewed to be more friendly to civil rights cases than some state courts are—civil rights plaintiffs often bring their claims in federal court. To be sure, state courts hear civil rights claims too, including both suits brought only under state civil rights laws and cases involving federal law where parties prefer state jurisdiction. But because civil rights plaintiffs often file cases in federal court, federal court data provide one meaningful gauge of the volume of civil rights litigation. According to BJS, federal civil rights cases total a few dozen thousand cases per year, across the entire country.[18] Of those, employment-related claims, in which an employee or former employee alleges some kind of discrimination against an employer, constitute the largest share. Even those, however, vary from some eight thousand to twenty-three thousand per year over recent years. Perhaps the critics are right that civil rights litigation is excessive, often brought by undeserving plaintiffs, but such modest numbers (among a population of roughly 300 million people) alone do not make that case. That possibility is not ruled out by the volume of employment discrimination cases, but here again, any type of litigation providing undeserving parties with an easy opportunity to recover might be expected to generate more cases.

While illuminating as a descriptive matter and useful in understanding just what the civil litigation system does, data about the volume of litigation do not answer fundamental questions about the purposes of civil litigation, much less whether the litigation system performs them well or poorly. Even if the volume of litigation does not at first glance seem large enough to suggest that the civil litigation system is overwhelmed, and in particular by the types of cases most often mentioned by litigation reformers, still that leaves open the question whether there is too much, or perhaps too little, civil litigation of various types. Separately, descriptive data also leave unanswered the question about whether the litigation system resolves cases in the right way, a topic to come.

Summary

Civil litigation is the institution through which disputes about legally recognized wrongs are resolved through processes designed to test the strength of competing factual and legal contentions. Most civil cases are resolved during stages of litigation before trial; only some 2% to 6% of civil cases are tried, depending on the type of case. Many are also settled between the parties sometime after they are filed. Civil cases are brought in various jurisdictions, mainly in state courts but also in federal courts. General common law claims are brought most frequently in state courts, whereas federal courts see many cases involving federal statutes as well as some common law claims. Contract cases far outnumber all other types of general civil cases, whereas the types of cases highlighted by civil litigation reform are significantly less common. To generalize very broadly, over recent decades the volume of civil litigation has been fairly stable, with modest year-to-year variation.

Such an orientation to the civil litigation system is necessary for the purposes of evaluating assessments of its performance, but not sufficient. For of course no simple description can answer the interesting normative questions about whether civil litigation is excessive, or whether the system resolves cases in desirable ways. Addressing those questions also requires an articulation of how the litigation system *should* resolve cases, and thus the identification of criteria marking a well-working civil litigation system. These issues are explored in the next two chapters, and they motivate all that follows.

2

The Benefits of Civil Litigation

The Premise

On next to the purpose of civil litigation. For without some understanding of what litigation is supposed to accomplish, diagnosis and sensible reform are not possible. And, whatever its shortcomings, there is no gainsaying the benefits of civil litigation. Indeed, it is difficult to imagine a legal system without it. For litigants themselves, its benefits include the satisfaction that comes with having their legal claims considered—their "day in court"—and not least of all from the remedies successful litigants secure or the sanctions they avoid. These private benefits drive much civil litigation.

Civil litigation yields public or social benefits too—benefits realized by those who are never party to any civil case. These social consequences constitute civil litigation's most important consequences, and are of primary concern here. The observation that litigation generates social benefits is not new, to be very sure (e.g., Pound 1906). But it is overlooked, misplaced, and outright denied frequently enough to warrant re-articulation here.

As chapter 4 will explain, civil litigation—according to its most influential critics—benefits some self-interested parties, but is otherwise socially harmful, *not* socially beneficial. Even among those who do not fully embrace that critique, litigation is commonly viewed as a necessary inconvenience, not a beneficial activity. This latter perspective is limited neither to litigation's loudest critics nor to the policymakers they influence, but extends also to some members of the bench, who view litigation as the manifestation of some kind of failure. It also extends to broad segments of the public.

But that perspective is deeply puzzling. For the obligations imposed by the law are not self-enforcing. To the contrary, legal obligations— embodied in the law's substantive rights, duties, and prohibitions broadly understood—are given force through litigation or the possibility of litigation. In other words, litigation provides the occasion for the enforcement, application, interpretation, and indeed modification of legal requirements. Legal duties, for example, might come with some moral obligation to obey, but such obligation is hardly sufficient to ensure compliance with them. The law therefore imposes various sanctions and remedies for their violation. Indeed, the nature of legal rights is commonly characterized precisely in terms of the remedies available for their violation.

In this light, civil litigation is properly seen as the institution that operationalizes the law's rights, duties, and prohibitions. Without the mechanism of civil litigation, legal obligations would mean little indeed. Yet, widespread respect for the law, or at least wide recognition of the law's legitimate purposes, is oddly not accompanied by corollary recognition of the importance of the system through which legal requirements find concrete application. But unless legal obligations command their own obedience, and they do not, civil litigation to enforce them is necessary. From this point of view, civil litigation is entirely desirable (because necessary), at least to the extent that the litigation system performs reasonably well. This claim is developed shortly below.

The Private Benefits of Civil Litigation

As a state-enforced mechanism for resolving disputes, civil litigation often is an attractive alternative to other forms of conflict resolution. As chapter 1 briefly observed, by providing some corrective for legal wrongdoing, civil litigation vindicates the law's obligations. It is safe to say that most parties initiating litigation are motivated principally by the remedies available to them, however, and not by the resulting vindication of legal obligations more generally. It is also safe to say that the private benefits of litigation are more modest than is commonly understood.

Monetary damage awards provide the primary economic incentive for much litigation. Monetary payments may or may not compensate a plaintiff perfectly, depending on the nature of the plaintiff's harm. In commercial cases, for example, where legal harm results in lost profits, money damages might compensate the plaintiff completely, restoring the plaintiff to the same position as had the defendant committed no wrong. In a torts case, in partial contrast, money damages can compensate a plaintiff fully for the economic aspects of an injury—the costs of medical bills and lost income due to injury—but provide imperfect compensation for the non-economic aspects of the harm—the pain and suffering resulting from the tort. Even so, monetary payments constitute the law's attempt to make the plaintiff whole.

Because non-economic harms can be hard to verify and to quantify, however, damages to compensate for non-economic injuries are available only in certain circumstances—typically in personal injury cases where the plaintiff has also suffered a more palpable injury. In such cases, though, much of the harm resulting from legal wrongdoing may be non-economic in nature. Thus, potential damage awards for non-economic harms, where they are demonstrable, can be much of what prompts those suits. On the other hand, the burden of proving them, which often requires expert testimony, sometimes can prove prohibitively costly.

Moreover, for many potential litigants, recoverable economic and non-economic damages are modest, as a result of natural limits on both. For example, in employment cases, economic damages (most damages in employment cases are economic) are bounded by an employee's salary. In an employment case alleging discriminatory termination, all the employee might hope to recover is an amount equal to the employee's salary during the time period following the termination. In many jurisdictions, employees have a duty to mitigate, which means to find another job. In that case, the employee might hope to get, at most, the pay differential between the employee's original job and the job taken to mitigate damages. In any event, compensation following a successful employment discrimination claim will be a function of the plaintiff-employee's lost salary.

And the time period relevant to that calculation may be small. Most employees who are both discriminated against and motivated to bring suit do so shortly after the alleged discrimination. In that event, not much time has elapsed, and thus damages calculated in terms of lost wages are modest. Even if the employee is content to wait, or decides to seek administrative remedies before filing a case, the relevant statute of limitations, typically two or three years, will in effect limit the amount of lost compensation the employee may allege. Compared to the costs of litigation, the expected net benefits from employment discrimination litigation can be very low, especially as the employee must show some kind of nefarious treatment, which may require substantial discovery.

Economic damages are limited in other types of civil cases as well. In torts cases, for example, economic damages cover lost wages and medical expenses. Only in cases involving the most serious injuries, where lost wages and medical expenses accumulate over a long period of time, do such damages become substantial. In the ordinary slip-and-fall or minor auto accident case, plaintiffs eventually get back on their feet, and thus their economic losses are contained.

The same is true for non-economic damages: unless a plaintiff suffers permanent injury, the pain and suffering caused by personal injury eventually recedes. Thus, non-economic damages will be limited by natural recovery. One would therefore expect to see costly litigation only in instances where the plaintiff is seriously and permanently injured. Otherwise, the compensation for what proves to be only temporary pain and suffering, even if that pain and suffering is great, is unlikely to offset the high costs of pursing such a case.

Legislated damages caps for pain and suffering, discussed in more detail later, impose another upper boundary. They discourage litigation wherever the costs of litigating begin to approach the caps. Ironically, this can mean that the most egregious injuries, often among the most expensive to litigate given the need for expert testimony, will not be litigated because it is for those cases that litigation costs can quickly approach or exceed the caps.

By contrast, high damage awards will be more common in commercial cases involving large enterprises. There, the economic stakes of legal misfeasance can be substantial, owing simply to the scale of many commercial parties' operations; being large, they are inherently susceptible to "larger" (that is, greater) legal harm. Thus, for example, expectation damages for large entities in contract litigation can easily outweigh the costs of litigation, even when those costs are high. One would therefore expect to find high monetary damage awards most often in large commercial cases between litigants with significant resources.

In addition to compensatory damages, in limited circumstances the law also provides for the possibility of punitive damage awards, amounts beyond that which is necessary to compensate an injured party but deemed necessary nevertheless in order to punish the legal wrongdoer. In the exceptional case where punitive damages are available, because the defendant's behavior was egregious, they too provide an incentive for litigation, though potential claimants cannot usually count on receiving a punitive damages award. Although juries on rare occasion give exceedingly high damage awards, judges can correct for outlier cases. Punitive damages are, moreover, generally modest, as detailed later—a finding likely to prove stable due to constitutional limits on the availability of punitive damages. For example, in *State Farm v. Campbell*, the U.S. Supreme Court ruled that punitive damages should not generally exceed a certain multiple of compensatory damages.[1] Punitive damages therefore may be expected to fuel some, but little, civil litigation.

For certain types of civil cases, monetary damage awards may not provide the primary private incentive for litigants to initiate litigation at all. In such cases, including much civil rights litigation and environmental litigation for example, plaintiffs often seek injunctive or declaratory relief—asking courts to order the opposing party to do or refrain from doing something or simply to declare that the legal rights of the complaining party have been violated. In cases where recoverable monetary damages are low or a plaintiff has not suffered any economic harm, the recovery of attorneys' fees are necessary to help incentivize such litigation, without which such litigation may not be brought at all. For otherwise, unless a plaintiff can pay attorneys' fees out of pocket and is prepared to do so, it is not clear how the attorney would be compensated.

But attorneys' fees are recoverable only when specifically provided for by statute.[2] Statutory fee awards, even where available, are generally modest as well. First, they are capped at local market rates. In addition, prevailing attorneys seeking fee awards must submit evidence justifying their fees. In the face of any objection, courts hold evidentiary hearings and render judgments on the appropriate size of an award. Even in the absence of any objection, fee awards must generally be approved by the court. Finally, statutory fees are not available where the plaintiff loses. In fact, in certain circumstances (such as cases against the federal government), the availability of fees for successful litigants is conditioned not only on success, but also on a lack of substantial justification for the defendant's position.[3]

In addition, the U.S. Supreme Court has limited the availability of statutory attorneys' fees over recent decades. For example, in *Buckhannon v. West Virginia*, the Court held that statutory attorneys' fees are not available to plaintiffs when the defendant modifies the very behavior that the plaintiff intended through litigation to enjoin.[4] In other words, if a plaintiff brings a civil rights case seeking injunctive relief against the defendant, and the defendant subsequently undertakes to discontinue the behavior that prompted the plaintiff to sue, but does so before a court issues an injunction requiring the defendant to do so, the defendant renders the plaintiff's case "moot," and the plaintiff then may not collect attorneys' fees.

Prior to *Buckhannon*, the federal appellate courts had adopted what was known as the "catalyst theory," according to which civil rights plaintiffs were entitled to attorneys' fees if their lawsuit was the catalyst for the defendant's change in practice. Without the catalyst theory, civil rights defendants could easily moot out a plaintiff's case, and avoid paying attorneys' fees. With *Buckhannon*'s rejection of the catalyst theory, civil rights defendants often can now do just that. Although *Buckhannon* itself involved a specific federal housing statute, the fee provision in that statute is typical of those in other statutes, and lower courts have applied its logic to civil rights cases brought under other statutes as well.

For an earlier example, the Supreme Court in *Evans v. Jeff D.*, a civil rights case brought by the Idaho Legal Aid Society on behalf of mentally handicapped children, held that federal district courts could approve class action settlements in which the defendant offered to grant class plaintiffs their requested relief on the condition that the plaintiffs waive their attorneys' fees, to which they would otherwise be entitled.[5] The plaintiff class's lawyer concluded that, as an advocate for his clients, he was ethically bound to advise them to accept the defendant's offer, putting their interests above those of his own employer, Idaho Legal Aid, even though statutory attorneys' fees were what made it possible for him to represent such plaintiffs in the first place. He then argued in court that the defendant's end-around attorneys' fees—requesting a waiver of fees as a condition of settling the litigation—should not have been allowed by the court when the district court approved the settlement. On appeal, the Supreme Court disagreed, holding that the court did not improperly approve the settlement conditions on waiving attorneys' fees.

Both *Buckhannon* and *Evans v. Jeff D.* thus illustrate the potential difficulties of recovering attorneys' fees. While important for certain types of cases which would otherwise be seldom brought at all, attorneys' fees, like punitive damages, are not common enough or large enough to fuel a great deal of civil litigation outside of select areas.

In sum, the expected private gains resulting from damage awards, injunctions, or an award of attorneys' fees motivate most civil litigation. On the defense side, litigants are privately motivated—to defeat claims and to avoid adverse judgments and unfavorable settlements—while their attorneys too are motivated by the expected benefits associated with their compensation, which typically takes the form of hourly fees. Chief among the private benefits motivating civil plaintiff and their lawyers are monetary damage payments resulting from a successful case or settlement. But monetary damage awards are often limited, if not by legal caps then by the natural circumstances surrounding a case. This is especially true for smaller litigants who, as explained, are capable of sustaining economic and even non-economic losses only up to some extent. On the other hand, larger potential litigants, including commercial enterprises, are capable of sustaining larger losses; for them, the expected private returns on litigation may justify substantial costs. But the key point for now is that potential litigants, of any size, will be inclined to litigate only where their expected costs are exceeded by their own expected benefits. Of course, the expected benefits and costs of litigation will in many cases be reflected in parties' decisions to settle litigation as well as to initiate it. In any event, for the reasons identified above, the expected private benefits of litigation are often fairly modest.

The Social Benefits of Civil Litigation

As already noted, civil litigation also generates social benefits—a happy byproduct of private parties' decisions to litigate—although defenders of litigation are not consistently articulate or emphatic on this point. An analogy to the criminal law may be helpful here. The law's criminal obligations, like its civil obligations, are enforced to a large extent through litigation and the prospect of litigation. That is to say, criminal law is enforced through criminal litigation (i.e., prosecution), which includes the risk of prosecution for those who violate the criminal law's obligations—a risk considered to deter violations of the criminal law. Of course, given the many imperfections of criminal investigation and criminal proceedings, false positives (erroneous convictions) and false negatives (erroneous acquittals) characterize criminal litigation. Criminal litigation's efficacy thus requires ongoing assessment and reform. So too the rules of criminal procedure, including the practices of criminal investigations, criminal discovery, plea bargaining, and criminal trials, warrant regular revision towards ensuring that those who commit crimes are brought to justice, that only those who violate criminal prohibitions are convicted, and that criminal litigation is conducted at manageable costs. Imperfections in criminal procedure and criminal litigation inspire, as they should, various criticisms both from those who worry that the criminal law's obligations go under-enforced, and from those who worry about excessive criminal liability.

Yet few doubt that the enterprise of criminal litigation, warts and all, is fundamentally socially beneficial. While important arguments about the proper scope of substantive criminal liability, the nature of criminal responsibility, and the efficacy of some forms of criminal punishment (especially for certain offenses) continue, there is little question that, on a very basic level, the enforcement of criminal law through prosecution advances important social aims. Indeed, it is difficult to imagine how criminal law might otherwise be enforced, and very few reformers of criminal law or criminal litigation, if any, would call for the outright elimination of criminal liability or prosecution. This is because the enforcement of the substantive criminal law—through litigation—is widely taken to generate important social benefits, including, among others, specific and general deterrence, restorative justice, social order and stability, and the affirmation of certain social values embodied in the criminal law.

Nor is there any question that these social benefits extend beyond whatever benefits the immediate victims of crime and those who prosecute crime experience as a result of criminal litigation. In other words, criminal litigation brings social benefits not because society happens to be populated by victims of criminal wrongdoing, but rather because its beneficiaries include, most of all, non-victims as well. This includes those whom the criminal law deters and especially those who never become victims of crime at all. Put differently, the beneficiaries of criminal litigation extend far beyond the parties associated with criminal cases.

So too with civil litigation. Legal obligations imposed by the common law, statutes, regulations, and indeed even the Constitution also are enforced by litigation and the possibility of litigation. And just as it is difficult to imagine upholding the obligations imposed by the criminal law in a world without criminal prosecution, so too it is difficult to see how civil legal obligations could be upheld in a world without civil litigation. But if they would not be enforced, neither would they be meaningful. Thus, the law's commands would matter little. It is not too much to say, then, that the rule of law itself requires civil litigation.

And here too, the beneficiaries of litigation extend far beyond the parties to particular civil cases. As legal misfeasance is deterred by civil litigation and the possibility of litigation, the deterrence of legal misfeasance is beneficial to those whose legal rights are never violated at all. And, in addition to the social benefits of "deterrence" narrowly conceived, vindicating legal obligations also reinforces important social values and commitments underlying and expressed through the law—among others, commitments to justice, fairness, and the preservation of legal rights—which reinforcement is of course socially beneficial in larger ways. Like criminal litigation, civil litigation's social benefits are broad.

This is not to say, however, that every civil obligation necessarily yields social benefits. There is no question that the substantive law is far from perfect. And while legal obligations that yield no social benefits tend to be unstable in the long term, still the substantive law is always susceptible to improvement that would be socially beneficial, more desirable from a relevant policy perspective, or indeed more just. Much less is the suggestion here that every civil *case* generates social benefits—of course not. The point is at once more general and modest: because upholding legal obligations *generally speaking* is socially beneficial, the litigation system that is indispensable for doing so is too.

It follows from this perspective that civil litigation will tend to be under-supplied. That is, potential litigants will initiate litigation mainly only when their own private benefits exceed their costs; most decisions whether to litigate will not reflect considerations of litigation's social benefits. Some of those potential social benefits will therefore go unrealized, once a litigant's private costs come to offset private benefits, though considerations also of a case's social benefits may have made litigation, all things considered, worthwhile. Like any activity generating positive social externalities, then, civil litigation will tend to be initiated at socially suboptimal levels (cf. Rubenstein 2006). Indeed, some of civil litigation's process rules recognize this, and therefore allow individuals to bundle their claims into one case in order to economize where the benefits of separate cases would be too small to be practical. Thus class action litigation is premised on the observation that litigation initiated by some will generate benefits for many others—not inevitably or in every case, but rather as a general proposition that justifies class litigation as a form of civil process (Hensler et al. 2000).

That said, perhaps alternatives to civil litigation brought by private parties seem feasible for enforcing the law, thus making civil litigation in that sense distinguishable from criminal enforcement through individual cases brought by prosecutors on behalf of the state. In other words, criminal law aside, maybe enforcing the law without litigation, or at least with much less civil litigation, is somehow possible. In fact, some critics of civil litigation call for increased reliance on administrative agencies as an alternative to private litigation. The idea is that government agencies might largely displace litigation by private parties, in order to ensure compliance with the law and thus to promote the social benefits associated with compliance.

Indeed, "regulation not litigation" is a frequent theme of some of civil litigation's critics. They suggest that regulation might supplant civil litigation in a variety of areas: administrative regulation of food, drugs, and other consumer products and services could displace much of tort law. Antitrust agencies might displace private antitrust suits. Environmental regulation could obviate the need for litigation by environmentalists. Government agencies instead of private litigants could enforce securities laws, consumer protection statutes, and the civil rights laws. In all such cases, compliance with the law's substantive obligations could be enforced by agency experts in place of private litigants.

This view is simplistic, however. For one thing, agency regulation itself depends upon civil litigation. That is, where agencies enforce legal obligations, they too do so ultimately by filing civil lawsuits against legal wrongdoers. In other words, administrative agencies become civil plaintiffs. In fact, federal administrative agencies bring thousands of civil cases every year. Likewise, state administrative agencies are frequent civil plaintiffs. Federal and state agencies also bring many more cases in administrative courts. To be sure, agencies possess other tools to promote enforcement of the law—inspections, citations, injunctions, and so on—but ultimately these tools too largely depend upon civil litigation and the threat of litigation. The dichotomy between "regulation" and "litigation" is thus false. The former depends upon, and frequently results in, the latter.

More importantly, the extent to which administrative agencies are equipped to enforce the law's commands is limited. Agencies simply lack the institutional capacity to monitor and investigate all possible instances of wrongdoing, much less to enforce all legal obligations. While agencies commonly have complex regulatory missions, they also have limited budgets and finite human resources with which to pursue their missions. As a result, the legal jurisdiction of administrative agencies virtually always outpaces their institutional capabilities. Indeed, agencies are often sued by private parties seeking to compel them to enforce the laws and regulations that agencies administer. Moreover, their jurisdiction does not extend to righting the kinds of private injury that give rise to most civil cases, such as contractual wrongs (as explained in chapter 1). Thus, increased reliance on administrative agencies in lieu of private civil litigation would require an expansion of their jurisdiction that is wholly unrealistic.

Furthermore, a longstanding wariness towards bureaucratic institutions is part of the U.S. political tradition, in which strong centralized agencies are considered antithetical to the American system of government with its emphasis on private incentives and localism. Consequently, relative to other modern democracies, the U.S. has a small central government, certainly with respect to its regulatory capacity. In other words, in a very real sense, limited administrative government reflects an American preference for decentralized litigation over centralized bureaucratic authority, as Kagan (2001) and Burke (2002) have well demonstrated. Relying on administrative agencies large enough to displace enforcement through private litigation would require an altogether new conception of the proper scope of bureaucratic power.

Nor is bureaucracy free. Increased reliance on administrative agencies to enforce legal obligations would also require larger agencies, bigger public budgets (and thus increased demands on taxpayers), and in general a greater commitment to the regulatory state. One advantage of a smaller centralized government is that social resources are spared for the pursuit of other public and private ends. Even if, as an abstract proposition, agency regulation could displace some private litigation, it would come at significant cost.

Moreover, agencies are not perfect either. While the flaws and limits of government regulation can be overstated, at the same time the decision-making processes of agencies can lead to error. Poor or mistaken agency decisions can, given their general applicability, bring undesirable consequences with broad effects. Thus, supplanting litigation with larger administrative agencies would amplify existing concerns about excessive bureaucracy and the social costs of bureaucratic error.

In this light, administrative regulation is best understood as a complement to, rather than a substitute for, private litigation. Privately motivated plaintiffs, seeking to vindicate legal injuries they themselves have suffered, do much of the legal enforcement work that administrative agencies would otherwise have to do. As others have pointed out, the real question is not litigation "or" regulation, but rather under what circumstances greater reliance on administrative agencies is more desirable, and when greater emphasis on litigation brought by private parties is advantageous (e.g., Carlton and Picker 2014). In reality, the enforcement of legal obligations depends upon varying combinations of both.

In any event, the argument that civil litigation creates not only private benefits but also social benefits extending well beyond the litigants involved becomes easier to see with concrete examples. Consider first the two most common types of general civil litigation identified in chapter 1: contracts and tort cases. Contracts litigation may be viewed as the most private of private litigation; contracts cases usually involve zero-sum, fact-intensive disputes between the opposing parties to a private deal. From one perspective, who cares whether a contracts plaintiff prevails to recover damages against a breaching defendant, or whether the defendant prevails because the court rules that there was no contract, no breach, or no harm? The *social* significance of a routine contracts case may seem attenuated.

Yet private contracts litigation generates crucial social benefits. These include the stable enforcement of contracts, clarification of contract law, and the specification of conventional contractual terms (e.g., Baker and

Griffith 2009). In the language of contracts scholars, contract litigation yields "network externalities," the socially beneficial development of a predictable contracts regime, available to all participants in it. These network externalities are positive externalities. Through contracts litigation, parties to a case create benefits to others who will employ better-developed contract terms in the future. In this way, contract litigation advances society's interest in preserving a regime in which its citizens and businesses know what contracts mean and how they will be respected and enforced. The socially invaluable institution of stable contract enforcement, and in turn the stability and efficiency of markets that that institution promotes, is advanced by privately motivated litigation. Market participants never party to any contracts lawsuit benefit.

Indeed, the beneficial externalities created by contracts litigation motivate calls for the development of stable contracts regimes in legal systems around the world that lack them. Law reform in under-developed legal systems commonly emphasizes the importance of a mechanism for contracts adjudication. Likewise, a well-functioning contracts system is a common good-governance condition for development loans by market-promoting organizations such as the World Bank and the International Monetary Fund. This is so because a legal infrastructure that ensures the stability of contracts is well understood to be broadly beneficial.

Tort litigation—the second most common type of general civil litigation and the favorite target of many litigation reformers, as noted in chapter 1—likewise generates considerable social benefits (e.g., R. Abel 1987; Bogus 2001; Koenig and Rustad 2001; Galligan 2005). First of all, the prospect of tort liability deters unreasonably risky conduct (Landes and Posner 1987). When those positioned to create risks for others anticipate the possibility of legal liability for their actions, they will be inclined to be more careful. As is also well understood, if tort law never imposed liability for unreasonable conduct, there would be more of it, with resulting harms that society would be forced to absorb. Society's interest in avoiding the harms associated with unreasonable behavior is therefore advanced by the possibility tort litigation. In short, tort litigation promotes safety.

Medical malpractice litigation, in particular, also often mentioned by litigation's critics, creates positive externalities as well, in part because investments in care often are not patient-specific but rather require measures that benefit patients collectively (e.g., Arlen 2010). Indeed, while many critics charge that tort liability is excessive, that very complaint highlights the deterrence benefits of tort litigation. That is, the critics worry that excessive liability discourages parties from engaging in productive activities too much, for fear of tort liability. But this worry (addressed later in part 2) assumes that tort liability and thus tort litigation affect those not party to a case. While the question whether tort litigation's deterrence effects are too great, too small, or about right might be subject to debate, the point is that very debate recognizes the social consequences of tort litigation. To the extent that tort cases on the whole deter undesirable activities, then, tort litigation creates social benefits.

Tort litigation creates social benefits beyond deterrence, however. Importantly, tort cases provide a mechanism for compensating legally injured parties, an important benefit independent from deterrence. In the absence of tort litigation, such parties often would be compensated through other private or public means (or perhaps not at all). This means that private or government resources are taxed less, where tort litigation instead provides compensation for injured parties. Beyond deterrence and compensation, tort litigation provides other collective benefits as well, including social stability, the articulation of community norms of reasonableness, and the protection of conceptions of fairness. Like contracts litigation, private tort litigation generates various positive externalities.

Contracts and tort litigation by no means exhaust the types of litigation that generate significant social benefits, however. For another example, much of the litigation brought by legal services organizations—another frequent target of some critics of the litigation system—yields significant public benefits. Cases brought by legal services lawyers commonly aim to vindicate the rights of individuals where the economic stakes in absolute terms are modest. Even so, as in the case of tort litigation, the pursuit of small individual claims can, in the aggregate, carry with them broad social benefits, as recent work has shown (e.g., Abel and Vignola 2010). In fact, evidence shows that legal representation for the impecunious advances socially beneficial purposes, including reducing homelessness, poverty, and even crime. Indeed, some argue that expenditures on legal services not only are negatively correlated with homelessness and domestic violence (e.g., Murphy 2002; Farmer and Tiefenthaler 2003; Elwart et al. 2006; cf. Scherer 2006), but that the social returns on legal services expenditures exceed those expenditures. Several studies conclude that increases in legal services funding for the poor increases state revenues and alleviates drains on state and local budgets (Boyle and Chiu 2007) by greater amounts (Feelhaver and Deichert 2007; L. Abel 2009; Florida TaxWatch 2010; Iowa Legal Aid 2013; Maryland Access to Justice Commission 2013; Boston Bar Association 2014; Smith and Thayer 2014).

This is no small matter. Homelessness, poverty, and crime are costly not just for their individual victims, but for society generally. Put in economic terms, they create substantial negative externalities. Policymakers aim to reduce such problems, relying on various policy tools, precisely because of their undesirable effects on families, neighborhoods, and cities. To the extent litigation brought by legal aid organizations also helps some to reduce these social ills, that litigation generates social benefits.

Consumer cases provide another example of civil litigation generating social benefits. By discouraging deception, misinformation, and other practices that create or exacerbate market failures, consumer protection statutes seek to preserve the integrity of consumer markets, promote market efficiency, and thereby advance social welfare. Consumer protection laws thus often contain private rights of action authorizing litigation for their violation, which is to say that can be enforced through private litigation. Private parties bringing consumer cases confer social benefits by discouraging fraud and promoting the efficiency of consumer markets.

Private antitrust litigation likewise promotes market efficiency (e.g., Leslie 2012). Excessive market power undermines social welfare for reasons that are well understood, and thus litigation to enforce the antitrust laws promotes social welfare. Similarly, civil litigation to enforce the securities laws also enhances the integrity of securities markets, promotes efficient market transactions, and thereby reduces the cost of capital (e.g., Choi 2004). Private civil rights litigation generates social benefits by discouraging discrimination and vindicating core social and political values. Here again, the point is not simply that civil rights litigation deters potential future wrongdoers, which it does, but more generally that such litigation is the institution for articulating and preserving society's commitment to the preservation of rights. For another example, civil litigation under the Freedom of Information Act promotes the public's interests in government transparency and accountability. Whistleblower litigation protects the integrity of government programs and thereby conserves resources for the government and in turn for taxpayers (e.g., Engstrom 2012). First Amendment litigation ultimately safeguards all citizens' rights to free speech and religious freedom. And so on. These examples are of course not exhaustive, but they suffice to show that the institution of civil litigation often generates social benefits.

The law itself recognizes this, especially but not only in the context of litigation that commonly leads to injunctive rather than monetary relief. For example, provisions on attorneys' fees in certain statutes reflect consideration of the socially beneficial consequences of certain types of litigation. Because the enforcement of the environmental laws advances social interests in environmental protection, for instance, certain environmental statutes provide attorneys' fees for successful private litigants. To the extent parties bringing environmental litigation can recover some of their costs, they will be more inclined to bring it, especially given that such litigation does not generally lead to monetary damage awards. And environmental litigation brought by private parties has been recognized as an indispensable element of environmental enforcement (e.g., J. Miller 1987). Although some may argue that some environmental laws go too far, while others argue to the contrary that environmental laws fall short of protecting the environment sufficiently, that debate over the proper boundaries of environmental protections raises a different issue. Given that properly balanced environmental laws are beneficial, it follows that environmental litigation, the mechanism for enforcing environmental laws, is socially beneficial. Again, not all environmental enforcement can feasibly be done by the government, and thus harnessing the private (including ideological) motivations of those engaged in litigation to enforce environmental protections advances important social aims.

Same for the fee provisions available under various civil rights laws. As previously noted, successful civil rights plaintiffs might recover attorneys' fees when they prevail. Without such fees, much civil rights litigation would be very difficult given that plaintiffs often seek declaratory or injunctive relief or otherwise bring cases with substantial legal but minor economic harms. This makes hourly representation as well as representation where an attorney's compensation is contingent on the recovery of monetary damages impractical. Here again, the availability of attorneys' fees encourages socially important litigation.

In private antitrust cases, successful parties often are entitled to recover treble damages. As with recoverable attorneys' fees, the purpose of treble damage awards is well understood to encourage litigation that yields socially beneficial externalities and is thus not brought often enough. Enforcement of the antitrust laws promotes market efficiency and protects consumers. Treble damage awards for successful private antitrust plaintiffs reflect the understanding that such private litigation advances broad consumer interests, and that without the incentives created by the prospect of treble damages, such litigation would not likely be initiated often enough.

All of this said, it might be useful to reiterate an important qualification. The argument here is emphatically not that every civil case generates beneficial externalities, much less that every civil plaintiff nobly advances some important social cause. As explained later, some plaintiffs may bring cases in bad faith, just like some litigants may in bad faith deny they have committed legal harm. Furthermore, the civil litigation system, like every other complex institution, is of course not immune from error. Sometimes courts and juries make mistakes. Sometimes those mistakes are very large. And in cases where that happens, the consequences certainly can be socially undesirable, as well as unjust for the litigants themselves.

But these observations do not call into question the more general point that the enterprise of civil litigation is socially beneficial in the specific sense that it advances important interests of those who are never party to a civil case. It does so, at bottom, by operationalizing the law's substantive commitments—enforcing legal rights and obligations. And for that reason, it is difficult to imagine a well-working legal system without civil litigation. From this perspective, the social benefits of privately motivated litigation seem beyond question, an observation too often misplaced in influential discussions of the need for litigation reform.

Nor does the analysis here assume away the social *costs* of civil litigation. Just as the private benefits of litigation are offset, and often outweighed, by the private costs that would-be litigants have to incur in order to bring a case, so too the social benefits of litigation come at some social cost, including, among others, the overhead social costs of administering the civil litigation system, though taxpayer costs associated with funding the courts are rather modest. Those social costs should be minimized to reasonable extents, and litigants should be encouraged not to generate them wastefully. Later, chapter 7 will propose procedural changes that would reduce both the social and the private costs associated with civil litigation for cases involving low stakes, with the fortunate consequence of reducing society's cost of administering civil justice.

The civil litigation system imposes a different set of social costs—and regrettable private costs on litigants as well—when it resolves cases incorrectly, distorting rather than reinforcing legal obligations. As chapter 4 will show, this is a major theme of the most influential critique of civil litigation. But while the claim that civil litigation routinely resolves cases incorrectly remains unsubstantiated (certainly in its exaggerated form, as chapter 5 will show), still civil litigation inevitably generates some level of error, and where it does so it generates costs likely felt beyond the parties to a given case. A civil litigation system that resolves cases in the right way and at a reasonable cost is, therefore, a requirement of civil justice, even though reducing error can itself can be a costly project (as chapter 3 will emphasize). But all told, the fact that civil litigation is in some ways socially costly does not call into question the observation that it is fundamentally socially beneficial as well.

Desirable Levels of Litigation

But even if civil litigation generates social benefits, how much of it is necessary or desirable? For example, while chapter 1 noted that tort cases are far less frequent then contracts cases, might there be too many torts cases even so?

Unfortunately, identifying the right amount of civil litigation is not easy, except perhaps in the abstract. In principle, and barring some system not dependent on those legally wronged to discourage legal wrongdoing (see Gilles and Friedman 2012), a desirable amount of litigation would be generated if only parties with genuine, legally recognized harms brought cases. In other words, the denominator for calculating the right amount of legal claims is defined with reference to the number of legally cognizable wrongs, with the numerator as the number of cases necessary to vindicate those legal wrongs. Ideally, the resulting fraction should approximate, or certainly not exceed, 1. If instead the number of cases brought exceeded the number of underlying legal wrongs, the frequency of litigation would plainly be excessive—too many cases against the background incidence of real legal wrongdoing. If, on the other hand, the number of cases brought were far less than the number of underlying legal harms, there might be too few cases—too many legal injuries never remedied.

Of course, it would be preferable if legal wrongdoing were avoided completely in the first place—that is, whenever it could be avoided at reasonable cost. To that extent, the fewer legal wrongs committed, and thus the less litigation, the better. Avoidable harm wastes resources and causes legal injury unnecessarily. In any event, the central question here asks about the desirable level of litigation *against some backdrop of legal wrongdoing*. Given some underlying incidence of legal misfeasance, civil litigation to remedy legal wrong is desirable, both for the injured party's benefit but also to reinforce substantive legal obligations.

To be sure, great uncertainty often surrounds the question whether a legal harm was committed: often it is not possible to say, prior to initiating litigation, whether a party has a meritorious legal claim to be remedied. Indeed, the very purpose of litigation is to resolve *that* uncertainty. But the point stands that some potential litigants are well justified in bringing their cases initially—because there is a substantial chance that a court or jury will properly conclude they suffered a legal injury at the hands of the defendant, even if ultimately they lose their case—while other potential litigants have no business bringing suit in the first place because their cases lack merit, even though in an imperfect civil litigation system they might prevail. The former should litigate and the latter should not; the former should be encouraged to litigate, and the latter discouraged.

One problem, however, and a large one, is that only the latter are easy to identify. Litigation, the very act of filing a claim, itself provides one way to identify parties who should not bring suits but do; bad-faith plaintiffs show up at the courthouse door. But knowing whether on the whole there is too much litigation, or too little, requires identifying *also*

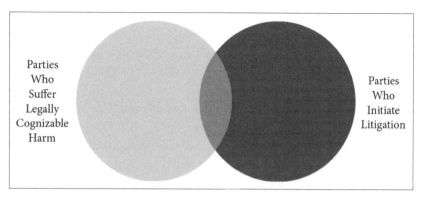

Figure 2.1. Suffer Genuine Legal Harm vs. Initiate Civil Litigation

Parties Who Suffer Legally Cognizable Harm

Parties Who Initiate Litigation

those who would have strong legal claims but nevertheless never file cases—"absent plaintiffs," so to speak. Figure 2.1 exaggerates the distinction between those who have suffered a harm that the legal system recognizes, and thus who in good faith might initiate litigation, on the one hand, and those who in fact bring litigation, on the other hand, whether or not they have suffered legal injury at all. The more those who litigate correspond with those who have suffered legal harm, the better; hopefully, the groups represented by the circles in figure 2.1 mostly overlap. But again, unfortunately, some parties who bring litigation have not suffered any legally recognized harm, a major theme of litigation reformers, as part 2 will explore. A subset of those inevitably bring suit innocently on the mistaken, good faith understanding that they have suffered legal harm, when they have not. Where the civil litigation system works well, these parties will tend not to prevail. Another subset instigates litigation in bad faith, seeking unwarranted legal recourse. The civil litigation system should disincentivize them, as later chapters will propose. The more the civil litigation system can discourage these litigants, the better.

At the same time, for a number of reasons including especially the costs of litigation, relative to its expected benefits, some parties who have suffered genuine legal injury will never bring a case at all, even though they would tend to prevail were they to do so. These absent plaintiffs are harder to quantify. Unlike parties who are identifiable by the cases they file, non-litigants are not identifiable through the cases they do *not* bring—obviously but importantly. By definition, absent plaintiffs leave no tracks. They must be identified or estimated, if at all, through some mechanism besides civil case filings, a most difficult task. But whether or not susceptible to estimation, the point is that not all genuine legal injuries lead to litigation, which is to say that the law's substantive obligations to some extent go unenforced.

Not that every legal harm must generate a lawsuit, however. So long as legal wrongs are vindicated frequently enough to reinforce the substantive law's obligations, the social benefits of litigation might be largely realized even if some legal harm, here and there, is never remedied. On the other hand, that point could be taken too far: too many absent plaintiffs lead potential legal wrongdoers to discount the risk that their legal misfeasance will subject them to liability, and therefore the law is likely to remain under-enforced. No less, absent plaintiffs also mean that legal injuries go un-remedied, or else must be absorbed by other institutions. Meanwhile, legal harm never vindicated also erodes the broader social commitments embodied in the law. At least to some extent, then, the more often that potential litigants determine that vindicating their bona fide legal harms is worth the costs, the better.

Absent medical malpractice plaintiffs just so happen to leave tracks in the form of their personal medical files, making rough estimations about the propensity to bring litigation over incidences of potential legal injury possible. That is, it is possible to sample medical records to measure the frequency of medical malpractice litigation against the background incidence of apparent underlying medical malpractice, tracing the extent to which patients who received unreasonably poor medical care, as revealed in their sample records, filed a medical malpractice claim. Several ambitious studies have undertaken that laborious task. Taken together, they show that medical malpractice is very often under-litigated, in that peer-reviewed cases of medical misfeasance often do not lead to any legal claim (see generally T. Baker 2005; Hyman and Silver 2006). Given the costs of medical malpractice litigation, one might expect that malpractice resulting in non-permanent—or permanent but not serious—injuries might be litigated infrequently, especially when considering the low volume of medical malpractice noted in chapter 1.

Beyond sampling medical files, in any instance where legal harm results in personal injury, it might be possible to compare the incidence of litigation against available data on product accidents, adverse drug reactions, or workplace injury likely to result from legal misfeasance. Agencies such as the Centers for Disease Control, the Consumer Product Safety Commission, and the Occupational Safety and Health Administration maintain potentially useful data. Likewise, the Federal Trade Commission collects data on the incidence of consumer fraud, while the Equal Employment Opportunity Commission (EEOC) maintains some information about individuals who believe that their civil rights have been violated by employers. In fact, consultation with the EEOC is often a requisite for bringing certain employment claims. Thus it may be possible to generate estimates of the incidence of non-frivolous employment claims, for example, to be compared against the incidence of actual litigation, as the EEOC cannot take every deserving case.

While some important and groundbreaking work along these general lines has been done (see Studdert, Brennan, and Thomas 2000 (collecting example)), much work remains; additional studies are necessary to determine how many potential litigants who would have had strong legal claims never initiate litigation. In the meantime, as others have concluded (e.g., Galanter 1993; Eisenberg and Farber 1997; Hadfield 2000; Haltom and McCann 2004; T. Baker 2005; Nockleby 2009), it seems entirely likely that *some* amount of genuine legal harms are never vindicated through litigation. In such instances, the private benefits of litigation are never realized (again, in some cases because the expected private costs are greater) and potential social benefits remain unrealized as well.

Summary

Civil litigation by private parties is motivated by litigants' anticipated benefits. Money damage awards are the paradigmatic form of benefit, but litigants and their lawyers may be motivated by other civil remedies, including injunctions to enforce legal obligations, as well as by attorneys' fees in certain areas where traditional remedies are considered unlikely to motivate desirable levels of litigation. Because litigation is costly, however, generally speaking litigants will be motivated to bring it only where their own expected benefits exceed their expected costs.

Yet the benefits of litigation extend beyond those potentially realized by litigants themselves. While not every civil case advances some social purpose, as a general matter the law's substantive obligations find concrete application only through the enterprise of civil litigation. By enforcing legal obligations—necessary to promote economic activity, foster social stability, provide compensation, and safeguard fairness, among the law's other purposes—civil litigation advances important social interests.

That civil litigation generates social as well as private benefits is not to say that it does so at the lowest possible cost, however, or that the litigation process could not be improved. Improvements that might lower both the social and the private the costs of litigating may well be possible. To be slightly more specific: accommodating more parties who suffer legal harms to bring suit may be in order, as may measures discouraging undesirable and excessive litigation. The following chapter explores such issues by identifying the central features of a well-working civil litigation system.

3

Features of a Well-Working Civil Litigation System

A Framework

Chapter 2's contention that civil litigation advances important social interests by operationalizing the rule of law leads quickly to questions about how well or poorly it does so. If civil litigation generates social as well as private benefits, a well-working litigation system seems especially important. And if the litigation system might be improved—in particular if it is feasible to reduce the costs of litigation in order to realize still more benefits—reasonable reform seems warranted. So: When the civil litigation system functions well (or poorly), what does *that* look like? This chapter supplies a conceptual framework essential for evaluating the civil litigation system, considering criticisms often made of it, and identifying possible ways to improve it.

Civil Litigation for Civil Justice

Courts are supposed to administer justice, an uncontroversial if abstract claim. "*Civil* justice" conveys the aspiration to achieve justice through the outcome of civil cases—that is, to resolve civil disputes in the right way. Where the civil litigation system works well, that aspiration tends to be realized. This in turn requires identifying criteria for assessing the civil litigation system's performance. If civil litigation yields just or unjust results—if it advances civil justice or falls short—it does so relative to criteria that require identification.

Two such criteria recommend themselves, at the very least as minimal conditions, although some might advance a much broader conception of justice (Blasi 2009). First, civil justice requires *access* to the civil litigation system in the first place (e.g., Nockleby 2009 (collecting sources)). That is, as the purpose of civil litigation is to vindicate the violation of legal rights and duties, civil justice is possible only to the extent that legally injured parties can mobilize the civil litigation system seeking redress of their wrongs. To paraphrase a famous argument, legal rights without corresponding remedies do little good; unless rights are supported by legal remedies to address their violation, rights in the abstract offer little protection. Likewise, legal remedies are hollow without some means of triggering their availability; unless legal remedies are indeed available from the courts, remedies in the abstract mean very little. Civil justice may be satisfied, then, only if those legally wronged have some meaningful opportunity—and, crucially, at a reasonable cost (more on that later)—to resort to the civil litigation system at all. Put simply, civil justice requires access to the courts.

Access likewise requires that those defending against claims have access at reasonable cost as well. In other words, access is a bilateral proposition. It requires in the first instance the ability of good-faith plaintiffs to have their claims heard, and at the same time that good-faith defendants the ability to have their day in court as well. So although the term "access to justice" is used most often to refer to the ability or especially inability of impecunious individuals to bring their claims to the courts, and while that aspect of access is certainly encompassed here, access for present purposes is a broader concept. Here, access requires that litigants on both sides of the "v." in a civil case have a reasonable opportunity to advance their legal interests.

Because plaintiffs are the "first movers" in a civil case, as chapter 1 explained, a defendant's access becomes relevant for practical purposes only once a corresponding plaintiff has sufficient access to initiate a claim. It is for this reason that potential plaintiffs rather than potential defendants are often the focus of discussions of access to the courts. But where plaintiffs do enjoy access, the concept as employed here requires that defendants, as well, have an opportunity to advance their interests at some reasonable cost.

Access is of course not sufficient to satisfy civil justice, however. Civil justice also demands that the outcomes of civil cases yield the correct results on the merits—that courts and juries get it right—or in other words that the litigation system is *reliable*. The civil litigation system is reliable to the extent that litigants with legally strong positions tend to prevail, and litigants with legally weak positions tend not to prevail (cf. Silver 2002). Just as the criminal justice system is reliable to the extent that those who have committed crimes are determined to be guilty while those who have not are acquitted, civil justice requires giving legally wronged parties their due (Solomon 2010). This element of civil justice takes all underlying legal rights and obligations as given, as if they are worthy of application and enforcement. Of course, as previously noted, they may or may not be. But when and whether underlying legal rights and duties are themselves just is a topic far beyond the scope of the analysis here. The central question here considers instead whether—*given* existing legal duties and entitlements—civil litigation enforces them properly. If litigants win when their legal claims are weak (and their opponents' are relatively strong), or lose when their claims are strong (and their opponents' relatively weak), civil justice is thwarted.

Civil justice is, then, a function of the extent to which the litigation system is both accessible and reliable. The question now becomes whether access and reliability are sufficient, as opposed to necessary, conditions of civil justice. It might be argued that civil justice also requires, for example, that cases be resolved reasonably quickly; a hopelessly slow civil litigation system might be considered, for that reason, unjust—paralyzing litigants with unacceptable delay. For another example, it could be argued that civil justice also requires some element of procedural fairness, such that a litigation system not considered procedurally fair would, for that reason, not satisfy the demands of civil justice. (For an example of empirical findings that illustrate how individuals place importance on perceived procedural fairness of legal institutions, see Tyler 1988.)

As important as such other considerations may be, however, they seem largely if not entirely encompassed by the requirements of access and reliability. For example, access encompasses the speed at which the civil litigation system resolves cases, in that a hopelessly slow system at some point becomes, for practical purposes, inaccessible. Similarly, access and especially reliability probably cover procedural fairness as well: a broadly accessible system in which those with stronger legal claims regularly prevail over those with weaker claims is likely to be regarded as procedurally fair. Or put differently, it is not clear in what sense an accessible system that consistently renders results favorable to the most deserving litigants and unfavorable to the least deserving might, nevertheless, be deemed procedurally unfair. So, while it is not necessary here to take the hard line on whether civil justice is reducible only to access and reliability, these two criteria are plainly central and seem to go a long way to satisfy civil justice's demands. In any event, to frame all that follows, more must be said about each of these criteria, and in turn about the influence of litigation reform proposals that lack developed criteria for assessing the civil litigation system.

Access

Courts do not administer justice unilaterally. They do so when prompted by litigants advancing competing claims; courts need litigants to mobilize them. Thus civil justice is possible on the occasion when a wronged party seeks judicial redress. So if courts are inaccessible, legal wrongs cannot possibly be vindicated, which is to say civil justice cannot be realized. To be sure, "cases" threatened but never filed in any court can be settled between the would-be parties, who as a result of settlement need never access the civil litigation system. But such settlements presuppose the possibility of resorting to the litigation system in the absence of settlement, so again access remains central. It follows either way that the availability of the courts is one crucial condition of civil justice, a premise reflected in the many state constitutions that contain a general right to access to the courts.

This observation may appear obvious, and in a sense it is: surely one measure of the performance of any institution must be its very accessibility. The best hospital, library, university, or local government agency, for example, cannot be very efficacious if it is simply unreachable by those whom it is designed to serve. Accessibility is thus one criterion against which to evaluate most any open institution, including the court system. Still, access is such a minimal requirement that one may wonder why it warrants attention at all. Measuring the mere accessibility of an institution reveals very little about how well it operates for those who have access to it. The performance of an institution measured according to the substantive results it achieves might seem to be a better point of focus in its evaluation.

But mere access to the courts warrants emphasis precisely because it is often precarious. For one thing, it is inevitably costly (Barendrecht, Mulder, and Giesen 2006; Gramatikov 2009). As discussed in more detail below, one shortcoming of the civil litigation system is that would-be litigants often lack simple access given the costs. That is, many potential parties—plaintiffs and defendants alike—may be unable to cover the costs necessary to advance their genuine claims. For them, then, civil justice is elusive. Calls for greater access to justice are therefore commonplace, voiced frequently by legal aid foundations, pro bono organizations, bar associations, and groups advocating for those who cannot afford access.

Access has another facet as well. The civil litigation system is inaccessible *also* to those who could afford to litigate—in the sense that they could finance the costs of litigation, but for whom such costs would exceed the expected yield of their claim. For all practical purposes, they too are priced out of the civil litigation system. Put differently, the litigation system is inaccessibly costly for any potential party if either the costs of litigation are unaffordable in absolute terms, or the costs are prohibitively high relative to the expected benefits of the party's claim or defense such that advancing it would not be worth the costs. Access requires a meaningful opportunity to advance one's legal interests at a cost that does not overtake the expected benefits of doing so.

Yet access to the civil litigation system should not be costless, and this is where matters get complicated. Under certain circumstances, too much access may be undesirable, and from that perspective *some* level of costs may be welcome. First, too much access might potentially render the civil litigation system ineffectively crowded. Where courts are overwhelmed with too many cases, it becomes difficult for them to do their jobs well; the sheer volume of litigation may have adverse effects on the quality of decision-making, undermining the system's reliability. Second, and more importantly, where access is too easy, parties might use litigation not to vindicate legal wrongs, but rather to hassle other parties, extract payments for legally baseless claims, and generally waste resources, much as many critics of civil litigation allege. According to the common version of this critique, many plaintiffs initiate frivolous cases—that is, either cases brought by plaintiffs who know them to be utterly without merit (and thus brought in bad faith), or else cases filed by plaintiffs whose fundamental misunderstanding of the law and legal obligations leads them to bring patently meritless claims.

To see this possibility most clearly, imagine a civil litigation system that is absolutely accessible and for which access were entirely costless (or, likewise, a library with unlimited hours and from which users could borrow unlimited books with no late fees, or a hospital into which anyone could admit themselves for any reason, at no cost). In such a system, litigants could file cases and advance arguments at no expense. That would undoubtedly invite too much litigation, in the sense it would likely overwhelm the capacity of courts to adjudicate cases very well. Furthermore, because litigants would have incentives to bring even the most flimsy case—by hypothesis it would not cost them anything—such a system could also be overrun by cases with little or no merit. From this point of view, then, some limitation on access is not all bad (cf. Blasi 2004).

That said, it is necessary to be more specific about the kinds of claims that are undesirable and thus for which access to the civil litigation system should be controlled. In other words, what kinds of claims or litigants might threaten civil justice, were the system utterly accessible? For one, cases presenting very small stakes may not be worth the costs of traditional litigation, considering especially the costs of administering the justice system. Again, were the civil litigation system always accessible at very low or no cost, "de minimis litigants" might then overwhelm courts with very small cases. Fortunately, however, existing litigation costs seem high enough to price most de minimis litigants out of traditional litigation. Furthermore, common amount-in-controversy jurisdictional limitations—applicable in most states as well as the federal courts—in fact prevent small cases from clogging the courts. At the same time, and better still, small claims courts in most states provide a forum designed just for litigants with small claims. In other words, jurisdictional limits keep small-stakes litigants out of many general trial courts, while specialty small claims courts invite them in. Given that, cases too small to be worth the costs of burdening the civil litigation system do not likely pose a serious problem, and would not likely pose a problem were access to the courts further expanded. In fact, providing greater access for litigants bringing small cases, who are so often priced out of the general trial courts, would be desirable if this could be done cheaply, as proposed later in part 3.

"Nuisance claims" may constitute a more serious threat to the integrity of civil litigation. Nuisance suits are undesirable by definition—attempts by plaintiffs with knowingly weak claims to extort payment from defendants who might settle simply in order to avoid the higher litigation costs of prevailing. Although the defendant would expect to prevail upon litigating a nuisance suit, the costs of doing so might outweigh the costs of a small settlement. This is especially so for larger defendants who can employ attorneys who bill by the hour at high rates. Thus the blessing and the curse of defendants who can well afford to litigate because they can cover the cost of high hourly fees. On the one hand, they can pay whatever it takes to defend a suit, but on the other hand, that very ability may make them a nuisance target.

Such reasoning by plaintiffs or plaintiffs' lawyers motivates nuisance suits. Of course, if a defendant perceives that settling one nuisance suit will inspire other plaintiffs to bring them, a defendant might incur the high costs (relative to settlement) in order to discourage future suits. What approach any given defendant—or for that matter, plaintiff or potential plaintiff—will take in a given case is very context-specific, depending on facts concerning the likelihood an undeserving plaintiff might prevail, the number of potential plaintiffs, the likelihood of future litigation, the ability of the defendant to keep a settlement confidential, and so on. But the point remains that high litigation costs for defendants can, under certain circumstances, breed nuisance litigation by bad faith plaintiffs (Kozel and Rosenberg 2004; McMillian 2007), and that reasonable measures to limit access for such plaintiffs are therefore desirable.

The same goes for what could be called "nuisance defenses," the counterpart to nuisance suits, only advanced by defendants. Just as nuisance suits exploit litigation costs to secure settlement for undeserving plaintiffs against defendants for whom the costs of winning are too high, so nuisance defenses exploit litigation costs to force a low settlement on a deserving plaintiff for whom the costs of winning are too high. Wherever litigation costs are high, plaintiffs—not only defendants—with very strong cases may settle claims that they should not, or settle claims for amounts lower than they otherwise would. Cheap settlements are rational for plaintiffs whenever the costs of litigating through trial would exceed the expected net benefits of prevailing outright. Cheap settlements are also rational whenever a plaintiff simply cannot cover the costs of litigating further. Here again, ideally the civil litigation system would, to the extent feasible, limit the accessibility of nuisance defenses by making them more costly.

Claims brought by parties hoping to bank on the litigation system's mistakes constitute yet another species of litigation threatening the integrity of civil litigation and for which limitations on access to the courts may thus be warranted. Recognizing that the legal system sometime errs, some plaintiffs—"lottery plaintiffs"—hope to win by mistake. They willingly incur litigation costs as the price of their gamble. They realize their legal claims lack merit, which is what makes them bad faith litigants in the first place, but they litigate nonetheless believing they might reap the greater benefits of a favorable decision by a mistaken jury or court, or one they can fool. Here again, lottery plaintiffs are not the only gambling litigants. Defendants too may litigate hoping to benefit from the litigation's errors—"lottery defendants." These defendants advance very weak defenses, and incur litigation costs to do so. Knowing that their positions lack merit—positions that would fail in a civil litigation system that never erred—makes them bad-faith defendants. Just like lottery plaintiffs, lottery defendants seek to gain from the system's mistakes.

Yet the problem of lottery litigation seems easy to overestimate. After all, while litigation is a little bit like a lottery in that its outcome is uncertain, like any other type of lottery, gambling on a very weak case (or defense) is likely to be irrational. Thus, although some critics of the civil litigation system very often describe litigation in general as a "lottery," the analogy should not be taken too far; litigants (and their attorneys) have little economic incentive to incur large litigation costs to bet on a legally weak case. This is especially true for litigants whose attorneys are paid on the contingency that they prevail. In contrast to attorneys who bill by the hour, lawyers paid on contingency internalize the costs of bad gambles on weak claims.

On the other hand, where the costs of a gamble are extremely low (and the potential benefits very high), lottery litigation may indeed be a problem. Again, take the extreme hypothetical to see the point: in a system with no litigation costs, litigants might press cases that have no merit all at. Why not take a free shot at underserved victory? If the system makes a mistake, lottery litigants win something; and if the system makes no mistake, lottery litigants lose nothing, litigation being costless. In the absence of litigation costs, then, lottery litigation might be attractive. Similarly, where litigation costs are very low, the chance of undeserved victory might well justify—to a rational, bad-faith litigant—

those costs, particularly where the benefits of victory are high (such as high damages for undeserving plaintiffs and large damages avoided for undeserving defendants). Access to the courts should not extend to parties who would take very cheap bets on meritless claims or defenses. As explained in more detail below, however, litigation is not so cheap as to encourage a great deal of lottery litigation among plaintiffs. As for defendants who are already party to a case by virtue of having a claim made against them, however, they may be more likely to raise lottery defenses, where doing so is cheap—thus the "kitchen sink" defenses that are familiar to civil litigators. To that extent, making lottery defenses costly enough to deter them may be necessary.

Another form of undesirable litigation, a topic of extended focus later, is litigation that is undesirable *at the margin*. That is to say, whereas nuisance claims and lottery litigation are undesirable from the beginning—it would be better if such claims or defenses were never filed or raised at all in the first place—often cases filed or defenses raised in entirely good faith reveal themselves, over the course of the litigation process, to be weak or without merit. Again, the core purpose of the civil litigation process, costly though it may be, is to reveal the strength of opposing litigants' positions. The long pretrial stages of the litigation process, especially civil discovery, are designed to winnow the issues and prepare the case for a focused trial. Over the development of a case, then, it very often becomes clear that the positions of one or more parties taken in good faith at the initiation of a case cannot in good faith be maintained further. Yet parties who begin in good faith might nevertheless advance contentions that they discover through litigation to be untenable, which is to say that, from that point in the litigation forward, such parties over-litigate with respect to those specific positions.

Of course, the litigation process often reveals that certain aspects of a litigant's case is without merit even while other aspects remain tenable or even strong. To reiterate, distinguishing among strong claims and untenable claims is the purpose of the civil litigation process. As litigants commonly advance multiple claims or defenses within a single case, frequently a given litigant might continue to press certain positions in good faith even while recognizing that other positions can no longer be advanced in good faith. What is more, often the discovery process reveals that a given position is neither strong nor weak, but rather somewhere in between. Litigants, and especially their attorneys, who owe their clients an ethical duty to advance client interests aggressively, should not abandon a position just because it has been revealed to be weaker than expected.

That said, it is also true that litigants' positions are often revealed during the litigation process to be simply untenable in good faith. Indeed, it would be very surprising if that were not the case, given the rules and procedures governing civil litigation designed precisely to test the strength of competing contentions. Given that, parties should be discouraged from over-litigating exceedingly weak positions. The civil litigation system should not be accessible for advancing those positions further.

And in fact, litigants themselves frequently do abandon positions shown during the discovery process to be very weak or without merit. Plaintiffs often abandon claims stated in their initial complaints, focusing at the pretrial or trial stage on the subset of their initial claims, which the discovery process has shown to be stronger. Similarly, defendants often press only certain defenses among those stated early in a case. In such instances, the civil litigation process works well. But other times, parties press positions further than warranted. As explored at length in part 3, the civil litigation system should not be accommodating to bad-faith arguments made at the margins of a good-faith case. For parties who would make such arguments, the costs of access should be sufficiently high to discourage them.

Reliability

As the discussion up to this point implies, the civil litigation system's access and its reliability are linked in ways that warrant further exploration. For one thing, a lack of reliability makes access by bad-faith litigants more worrisome, because more are likely to succeed (and thus more are likely to be brought). But focus first on reliability. This demand of civil justice is satisfied to the extent that litigants who should prevail *do* prevail. If the civil justice system were perfectly reliable, courts and juries would make no legal or factual mistakes. Those with the strongest legal claims or defenses would always prevail, and those with weak positions would lose. Legal wrongs would be vindicated, and courts would not sanction those who committed no wrong. At the opposite extreme, if the system were not reliable at all, the outcomes of cases would not be at all correlated with their underlying merits. In an utterly unreliable system, random chance would determine litigation success and failure.

Because civil cases that do not settle ultimately produce winners and losers, whenever a party prevails who should not have, there is also a party who should have prevailed but did not. Reliability is thus violated on both sides of the "v." whenever the wrong side wins. In complex civil litigation involving multiple parties and multiple claims, which is common, matters become more complex practically, but not conceptually. There too reliability demands that those with stronger positions prevail over those with weaker claims.

Given that civil litigation is initiated by plaintiffs seeking remedies for alleged legal injury, civil litigation's false positives are made up of those cases in which a plaintiff should not prevail but does prevail. Here, the civil litigation system concludes that a legal right or duty requires vindication, and therefore provides some kind of remedy to the plaintiff based on the defendant's putative liability, though it should not have. An undeserving plaintiff prevails, and unless the relief provided is merely declaratory, a deserving defendant is required to satisfy some kind of judgment. That judgment is one that the defendant should not—and in a perfectly reliable system would not—have to satisfy. This unfortunate result reverberates, as similarly situated potential defendants now see themselves as subject to potential liability to which, if courts were infallible, they would not be subject.

Cases in which a plaintiff should prevail but does not, in contrast, constitute civil litigation's false negatives. Here, genuine legal harms go un-remedied. Meanwhile, the defendant avoids liability for legal wrongdoing. Because the defendant's legally wrongful conduct goes unsanctioned, that conduct may be repeated, by the same defendant or others, in the defendant's position. As with false positives, then, civil litigation's false negatives breed undesirable consequences extending beyond the immediate case.

Reliability has a second dimension as well. It requires not only that the most deserving party prevails, but also that where a plaintiff prevails the civil litigation system provides an appropriate remedy. More specifically, reliability requires that prevailing plaintiffs are neither under-compensated nor over-compensated, which is also to say that defendants correctly held liable do not avoid fully righting the legal wrong done, but neither are they made to provide a remedy beyond the amount of harm done. Here the most relevant form of civil remedy is monetary damage awards, which could be either inadequate or excessive. Injunctions or other forms of legal relief might potentially also be poorly calibrated to a prevailing plaintiff's injury, though the more common worry concerns the jury-awarded monetary damages. But the important point is that the civil litigation system's reliability depends not only on accurate determinations of liability, but also on remedies calibrated to be appropriately commensurate with proper determinations of liability.

The possibility of false positives and false negatives threatening reliability raises the question of how such outcomes might possibly be identified. A losing litigant on either side can always complain that the system erred, but that does not make it so. After all, the strength or weakness of a given case is often a matter of perspective. One measure of who *should* prevail looks to who *does* prevail? The difficulty, of course, is that such an approach assumes the civil litigation system's reliability. Only in a perfectly reliable civil justice system is it possible to identify who should have prevailed by observing who in fact prevailed. But this raises a problem: To the extent the system is unreliable, how is it determined which party *should* have prevailed in any given case? How can the civil litigation system's reliability be assessed?

Some external measures of reliability, or proxies for reliability, must be established, which is no easy task. For example, the civil litigation system's outcomes might be measured against sound science, the principles of economics, or irresistible common sense. Where litigation renders results at odds with uncontroversial scientific knowledge, for instance, the system is to that extent unreliable.

Alternatively, where there are no ready external criteria against which to measure the system's reliability, the soundness of its judgments might be measured against the quality and integrity of its internal processes. That is, if there are *independent* reasons to believe that the civil litigation's rules for resolving cases are themselves broken, those reasons may support the conclusion that the system was unreliable in general, though not necessarily in any given case. For example, if litigation's rules exclude evidence plainly relevant to its determinations of liability, or likewise include evidence clearly irrelevant to its determinations of liability, that would raise doubts about the system's reliability.

As will be seen later in part 2, one recurrent critique of civil litigation is best understood as a critique of the system's reliability. The notion here is that the civil litigation's decision-making process is broken, and for that reason plaintiffs win both too often and too much. Of course, one cannot argue that plaintiffs win (or lose) too often simply by pointing out how often plaintiffs win (lose). But if the system's decision-making mechanisms are flawed, demonstrably so, that demonstration would support that conclusion that the system is unreliable.

One cannot fairly argue, however, that the decision-making processes of the civil litigation system are flawed simply by observing how frequently (or infrequently) plaintiffs or defendants win. Only a showing that plaintiffs (or defendants) win too often as measured against external criteria—sound science, basic economics, and so on—would tend to demonstrate that the system's decision-making apparatus is somehow flawed. All of this is to say that while the civil litigation system cannot be perfectly reliable, conclusions about how and in which direction(s) it is unreliable require further analysis by which its unreliability is independently demonstrated. Unfortunately, however, most critiques of the civil litigation system's reliability are not accompanied by evaluative baselines.

In partial contrast to determinations of liability or non-liability, the reliability of monetary damage awards—or, for that matter, other civil remedies—lends itself to easier evaluation. Awards or even injunctions in one case might be compared to somewhat numerous awards or injunctions in similar cases, for example. And damages for economic losses in particular are readily measurable against relevant market metrics. So evaluating this dimension of reliability is simpler, making claims about the system's reliability with respect to the appropriateness of civil remedies easier to assess.

In all events, reliability is unambiguously desirable; the civil litigation system cannot be *too* reliable. The more that deserving parties and only deserving parties prevail and recover appropriately, the better. Not only are such results most faithful to the demands of the law, but they also avoid the undesirable reverberations of system error. So whereas the civil litigation system could be too accessible in certain circumstances—

inviting bad-faith or marginally undesirable litigation, for example—under no circumstances is it too reliable.

To say that reliability is unambiguously attractive is not to say, however, that greater reliability should always be pursued. Reliability is not free either. The civil litigation system might always be rendered more reliable through the adoption of additional processes designed to minimize the chances of error, but at some cost. Evidentiary standards and burdens of proof, for example, could always be made more exacting. But the higher costs of those additional processes would of course be borne by litigants, which would, therefore, reduce access. To that extent, there is some trade-off between greater reliability and greater access. For that matter, there is some trade-off between greater reliability and the cost of getting it, never mind the consequences for access. At some point, greater reliability is not worth the additional cost required to achieve it. Where the system's reliability can be promoted in ways that do not significantly increase the costs of litigation, however—for example, through rules conditioning expert testimony on knowledge in the relevant field of expertise—such steps should be taken. They improve reliability without increasing cost and, therefore, without threatening access.

The Central Relevance of Litigation Costs

As all of this suggests, litigation costs are integral to both access and reliability, and these criteria of a well-working civil litigation system cannot be considered independently from costs (accord Blasi 2004). Litigation costs impede access to the courts for potential parties who cannot afford to litigate, either in absolute terms or relative to the expected benefits they would realize from litigation. And in that sense, costs affect access for defendants and plaintiffs alike. Thus, promoting greater access requires lowering litigation costs. At the same time, however, the costs of litigation can usefully limit access in order to target unwanted claims, especially if those costs can be allocated or reallocated in a way to discourage bad-faith claims without also deterring good-faith litigants. For potential good-faith litigants, the lower the costs of litigation are, all else equal, the better—but not so for bad-faith litigants.

And with respect to reliability, reliability costs something. That is, many of the costs associated with litigation enhance the litigation system's reliability, even while other costs do not, and while still others—generated by unscrupulous litigants—may undermine unreliability by obfuscating relevant factual and legal issues and thus making it more (rather than less) difficult for a court or jury to render the right decisions. Litigation costs that enhance reliability might be justified on that basis, notwithstanding their adverse effects on access, at least if they are reasonable and proportional to the benefits that greater reliability brings. On the other hand, litigation costs that neither reasonably enhance the system's reliability nor manage access to it in a desirable way should be minimized as far as possible.

Later, chapter 6 will examine the extent to which litigation costs may be "high," which is to say the costs are either prohibitive for litigants relative to the expected benefits of litigation, or excessive in the sense they are greater than necessary to promote a reliable civil litigation system. Certainly the general proposition that litigation costs are often too high, especially for defendants, is a core component of the most common critique of civil litigation, as chapter 4 will explore. Yet more research on the costs of civil litigation—in both absolute and relative (to benefits) terms—is needed. Reda's excellent work (2012) calls the conventional critique—that litigation is too costly—into some question (see also Silver 2002). At the same time, it is clear that litigation often costs dozens of thousands of dollars, even for simple types of cases, and still more for other kinds of cases (Hannaford-Agor and Waters 2013), amounts that are prohibitive for many would-be litigants, as chapter 6 also explains. It seems clear also that attorneys believe that litigation is often unnecessarily costly (Lee and Willging 2010a). The immediate point, however, is that litigation costs are centrally relevant to considerations of both access and reliability, and thus to any analysis of the civil litigation system, as parts 2 and 3 will consider in depth.

Implications of an Imperfect System

In a completely accessible, perfectly reliable system, legally wronged parties enjoy easy access to the courts, and only they prevail. Because those with meritorious claims or defenses will prevail, they have incentives to pursue their cases. And because the system is accessible—because parties can afford to litigate—those with strong claims will pursue them.

Given that they do so, parties with weaker claims, recognizing that the system is reliable, are inclined not to pursue them. Thus, in an accessible, reliable civil litigation system, litigation tends to be pursued mostly by parties with strong legal positions.

This is not to say, however, that in such a system litigation is rare. For, again, some amount of litigation is necessary in order for parties to assess the strength and weaknesses of their positions. In other words, the strength of a potential litigant's position often cannot be determined very well before civil litigation is commenced. Sometimes that is possible, but often some amount of litigation is necessary to determine the applicability of various legal doctrines, to measure the strength of legal claims, and especially to clarify or test the facts of a case. Therefore, even a perfectly accessible and reliable civil litigation system will see litigation, although parties will tend to litigate all the way through trial only when both sides have roughly equally strong (or equally weak) positions, or else one side is mistaken about the matter.

Of course, no real civil litigation system is completely accessible or perfectly reliable. Matters become doubly bad where the costs of litigation are so high that many—plaintiffs and defendants alike—lack access because they cannot afford to litigate very far, and also where outcomes are so unreliable that, among those who can afford to litigate, parties with weaker claims often prevail over those with stronger claims.

On the other hand, to the extent the civil litigation is not very accessible, for whatever reason, that fact shrinks concerns about its unreliability even if it is unreliable. That is, the civil litigation system's mistakes matter only insofar as litigants have access to the system to begin with. So, to the extent plaintiffs in general have too little access, worries about false positives in particular recede. Likewise, to the extent defendants cannot afford to defend themselves, concerns about false negatives recede, as they will be less frequent. To capture further the relevance of access and reliability to civil justice, and to highlight their relationship to each other, table 3.1 contrasts exaggerated versions of the best and worst civil litigation systems, distinguished according to their extreme accessibility and reliability or lack of the same. In both of these exaggerated systems, there are few trials. Where the civil litigation system is extremely accessible and reliable, parties are not discouraged by litigation costs from pressing their claims, while they know that those with the stronger claims will prevail. Following

TABLE 3.1. Civil Litigation System Extreme Types

Type of Civil Litigation System:	Defining Conditions:	Parties' Incentives:	Expected Outcomes:
Ideal System: Fully Accessible, Perfectly Reliable Civil Litigation System	Easy access to the courts; Parties with strongest claims and defenses routinely prevail	Parties with strong claims and defenses inclined to litigate as necessary; Parties with weak claims and defenses not inclined to litigate further than necessary to assess their positions	Litigation to the extent necessary for parties to assess the merits of their claims; Frequent settlement and stipulated dismissals; Litigation through trial only of legally close cases, or where one side is misinformed; No bad-faith litigation; Well-calibrated remedies
Worst System: Highly Inaccessible, Highly Unreliable Civil Litigation System	Many lack access to the courts at all; Frequent false positives and false negatives for litigants who can afford access	Many parties discouraged or prohibited from litigating by high costs; Parties inclined to sue only when stakes are great enough to justify high litigation costs; Parties with weak claims or defenses may bring them anyway, if they can afford to do so and stakes are great enough	Litigation only of high-stakes cases by parties who can afford high costs; Undeserving parties often prevail; Considerable bad-faith litigation; Potentially inadequate or excessive remedies

pretrial litigation necessary for parties to assess the merits of their cases, they will tend to settle. So an accessible system, so long as it is reliable, might see many case filings, but few trials.

The inaccessible, unreliable system will also likely see few trials, but for very different reasons. Here, only few parties can afford to litigate. Only those with the resources to do so will litigate, and they will do so only if the benefits of litigation exceed the costs. Thus, an inaccessible system will see litigation mostly where the stakes are high—high enough to justify the high costs. Parties who can bear high litigation costs might litigate through trial, or they might not. Trial will be more of a gamble, given that the system is unreliable, which, relative to a reliable system, will more often encourage parties with weaker cases to go to trial but discourage those with stronger cases from doing so.

Of course, the actual civil litigation system falls somewhere between these stylized extremes; it is somewhat accessible and partially reliable.

And the implications of a mixed system are more complex. First, even if the real civil litigation system is not perfectly reliable—and surely it is not—to the extent the system's mistakes tend in the direction of false negatives, there is probably little reason to worry about plaintiffs bringing too many cases on the whole. In fact, to the extent the system's imperfect reliability owes mostly to false negatives, there are reasons to worry about too little access.

For prospective plaintiffs with strong claims might not bring them, knowing there is a chance they will lose even though they should prevail. More generally, to the extent the system produces false negatives, plaintiffs with strong claims will discount their likelihood of success by the extent to which the system produces false negatives, and thus will be under-inclined to bring litigation. Worries about too much access—too many cases—are especially well founded, then, only if the civil litigation system is imperfectly reliable such that it produces some false positives.

In addition, to the extent the real civil litigation system is unreliable in both directions—and to some extent surely it is—then it is just not clear whether too many or too few cases are likely to be filed. Given the possibility of false positives, some plaintiffs might bring suit who otherwise would not, encouraged by the possibility of an undeserved win. Meanwhile, given the possibility of false negatives, some plaintiffs also might not bring suit who should, discouraged by the prospect of an undeserved loss, while defendants may be inclined to litigate their weak defenses excessively. Thus, unless more is known about whether false positives outnumber false negatives on the whole, it is difficult to draw general conclusions about the direction in which imperfect reliability affects parties' incentives to litigate. On the other hand, once parties have filed claims, the system's lack of reliability might encourage parties to litigate farther than they otherwise would, in hopes of benefitting from the system's mistakes. In other words, undesirable litigation at the margins of a case seems most likely to plague an unreliable system, and to be a greater problem the more unreliable the civil litigation system is. Table 3.2 summarizes additional results, making alternative stylized assumptions about how a reliable system may be inaccessible. These observations focus on the likely consequences of a generally reliable litigation system that is plagued in one way or another by too little access. Likely general outcomes reflect how accessible the system is, and especially for whom.

TABLE 3.2. Reliable but Inaccessible Civil Litigation Systems

Type of Civil Litigation System:	Defining Conditions:	Parties' Incentives:	Expected Outcomes:
Reliable but Symmetrically Inaccessible System	Many lack access: Litigation too expensive for both plaintiffs and defendants; Few false positives or false negatives	Parties often cannot afford to litigate; Parties may use the costs of litigation opportunistically	Less overall litigation; Parties with stronger claims tend to prevail, if they can afford to litigate; Well-calibrated remedies
Reliable System That Is Inaccessible to Plaintiffs but Not Defendants	Litigation too expensive for many plaintiffs; Few false positives or false negatives	Defendants may use the costs of litigation opportunistically	Plaintiffs file fewer claims; Plaintiffs settle in the face of some bad-faith defenses; Parties with stronger claims tend to prevail, except plaintiffs forced to settle cheap
Reliable System That Is Inaccessible to Defendants but Not Plaintiffs	Litigation too expensive for many defendants; Few false positives or false negatives	Plaintiffs may use the costs of litigation opportunistically	Defendants settle some bad-faith claims; Parties with stronger claims tend to prevail, except defendants forced to settle bad-faith suits

As noted, however, the system's reliability could depend in part on the extent to which it is accessible. For instance, if the system were too accessible, in that it would be overrun with litigation, its reliability would likely be compromised. Courts may take procedural shortcuts to deal with an overwhelming volume of cases—reducing the costs the system dedicates to each case—with the result that the system is less reliable. For one example, judges overwhelmed by high case volumes may have less time for the details of parties' summary judgment motions, which might leave them prone to making more mistakes. For another example, judges with heavier dockets may feel pressure to limit the evidence parties may introduce at trial, again increasing the chances of error. At any rate, focusing now on violations of reliability, table 3.3 summarizes the consequences of a generally accessible but unreliable civil litigation system. To the extent such a system is accessible, its accessibility may discourage bad-faith litigation insofar as parties will not be discouraged by high costs to fight bad-faith claims. On the other hand, to the extent the system is not reliable, there will still be some bad-faith litigation—by

TABLE 3.3. Accessible but Unreliable Civil Litigation Systems

Type of Civil Litigation System:	Defining Conditions:	Parties' Incentives:	Expected Outcomes:
Accessible but Symmetrically Unreliable System	Easy access to the courts; Parties with strongest claims may or may not prevail—frequent false positives and false negatives	Parties with strong claims and defenses inclined to litigate, but also may settle given risk of losing; Parties with weak claims and defenses may litigate nonetheless, given possibility of prevailing	High litigation rates; Undeserving parties sometimes prevail, encouraging some bad-faith litigation, especially undesirable litigation at the margins of a case; Remedies may be inadequate or excessive
Accessible System in Which Plaintiffs Prevail Too Often	Easy access to the courts; Outcomes skewed towards false positives	Parties with strong claims and defenses not discouraged from litigating by high costs; Deserving defendants may settle, given risk that undeserving plaintiffs may prevail	No nuisance claims; Plaintiffs bring cases too often, and also tend to over-litigate cases, knowing they may prevail when they should not; Undeserving plaintiffs sometimes prevail; Plaintiffs receive excessive relief
Accessible System in Which Defendants Prevail Too Often	Easy access to the courts; Outcomes skewed towards false negatives	Parties with strong claims and defenses not discouraged from litigating by high costs; Deserving plaintiffs may not litigate given risk that undeserving defendants may prevail	Plaintiffs bring cases too infrequently; Defendants press weak defenses too far, knowing they may prevail when they should not; Undeserving defendants sometimes prevail; Plaintiffs sometimes receive inadequate relief

opportunistic parties seeking to capitalize on the system's mistakes. Furthermore, if the system's unreliability tends towards false positives, plaintiffs with weak claims will have a greater incentive to press them. If instead the system's unreliability tends towards false negatives, defendants with weak defenses will have a greater incentive to press those.

Needless to say, it is not clear which of these conceptual possibilities most characterizes the real civil litigation system. But they do help to sharpen that inquiry, and thus are useful to prepare the way for evaluating the actual system. Furthermore, it seems entirely possible that the above possibilities may correspond more or less to different specific types of civil litigation. For example, if the costs of litigation vary across different types of cases—for instance, simple slip-and-falls versus complex medical malpractice cases—which they do, the system may be less or more accessible to parties bringing different types of civil claims. Likewise, if courts can assess the quality of evidence more accurately in some kinds of cases than in others—for example, better in typical contracts cases than in complex patent cases—the system is likely to be more reliable for certain types of claims than for others.

Summary

Access and reliability provide two fundamental criteria for assessing the civil litigation system. Both promote civil justice; the absence of either undermines justice. Accordingly, the performance of the civil litigation system is properly gauged by the extent to which it is accessible to potential litigants, including defendants, which is to say accessible at a feasible cost. The system is properly gauged also by whether it produces reliable outcomes for those with access, in the sense that litigants with stronger legal positions tend to prevail over those with weaker positions, giving legally wronged parties their due, and also where remedies for prevailing plaintiffs are properly calibrated to the legal wrong done.

Further, access is desirable—the more access, the better—insofar as the litigation system remains reliable, and insofar as the courts are not overwhelmed by extremely small cases and especially by litigants bringing or pressing litigation in bad faith. To the extent the system is not reliable, its very unreliability may inspire parties with access to the courts to advance bad faith claims or defenses. Indeed, as will be seen shortly below, many criticisms of the civil litigation system are best understood as variations on the general theme that the system is routinely unreliable, and that it therefore breeds access for bad faith plaintiffs. In any event, access to the courts should be regulated, where necessary, to discourage bad faith litigation yet without discouraging good-faith litigation, including claims by good-faith litigants who happen ultimately to lose their cases. The allocation or reallocation of litigation costs may be an especially useful mechanism for controlling undesirable litigation. Otherwise, such costs should be reduced where possible.

Reliability too is desirable—the more the better—although reliability should not be purchased without regard to the increased costs and therefore adverse consequences greater reliability might have on access.

On the other hand, reliability requires some level of cost; the rules and procedures that make litigation costly often are what enhance its reliability. Wherever reliability can be improved without generating new costs reducing access, however, it should be. Changes in the way civil litigation is conducted that would promote both access and reliability at once, or either one without jeopardizing the other, are unambiguously desirable.

With this framework in mind, part 2 examines how the existing civil litigation system measures up, focusing first on its failures most commonly alleged.

PART II

Evaluations

Part 1 provided necessary background, the animating premise, and an evaluative framework to inform all that is to follow. It emphasized that civil litigation yields important social benefits, separate from the private benefits that motivate parties to litigate. Simply put, civil litigation instantiates the rule of law. Among other things, it promotes stable market transactions, discourages reckless behavior, and safeguards individual rights—not minor matters.

Part 1 also stressed that realizing the benefits of litigation requires, first, that courts are reachable. A well-working civil litigation system therefore must be accessible. To the extent the system is inaccessible, legal wrongs may find no vindication. Just as important, realizing the benefits of litigation also requires the civil litigation system to resolve matters reliably. Unless the system resolves matters reliably, the substantive law pursuant to which civil litigation is conducted is thwarted. Thus civil justice demands that accessible courts not reward undeserving litigants or disappoint deserving litigants. The myopic pursuit of either access or reliability, however, might jeopardize the other: ensuring greater reliability can bring higher costs that might impede access. And where the system is so overwhelmed with cases that it is accessible, especially with cases brought in bad faith, this could jeopardize its reliability.

With this framework in mind, the three chapters that follow turn to an assessment of the current litigation system. Chapter 4 presents a critical view of the civil litigation system notable for its continued influence. The core contention of that view is that civil litigation is too often socially harmful, a result of the civil litigation system's procedural and decision-making defects that render it unreliable. This view has motivated many litigation reforms at both the state and federal levels for decades.

Chapter 5 argues that this influential view has been merely pled, not proven. It trades too heavily on anecdotes that, upon scrutiny, do not support the critics' claims. Moreover, available data about how civil cases are resolved do not confirm the critical view's portrayal of civil litigation, though to be sure available data do not support *definitive* conclusions about how well the civil litigation system works more generally. That said, the data certainly do not, on their face, call into question the civil litigation system's reliability. Chapter 5 concludes, then, that if the civil litigation system is defective, it is not so exactly for the reasons influential critics have articulated.

Chapter 6 identifies two problems that seem more likely to threaten the civil litigation system. First, given substantial litigation costs, a problem the critics rightly if selectively emphasize with respect to defendants and not plaintiffs, there are reasons to worry that some would-be litigants enjoy little or no access to the courts at all, or at least not at a cost justified by their expected benefits of bringing a claim. Specifically, good-faith litigants with strong claims—but whose available remedies are likely to be modest—will tend to be priced out of the litigation system. That is regrettable from a social-benefits perspective. Second, the rules of civil litigation seem unlikely to go far enough to discourage litigating parties from making poor decisions to litigate at the margin of a case in progress, including in particular their decisions that require opposing parties to incur additional costs. To that extent, parties may litigate excessively, generating undesirable litigation costs that waste resources and impede access. Later, part 3 will propose several responses to these twin threats to a well-working civil justice system.

4

Influential Criticisms of Civil Litigation

Ask almost any average citizen—and certainly any taxi driver, small businessperson, or human-resources administrator—what is wrong with the litigation system, and the likely responses will be both consistent and surprisingly detailed. Critics of the civil litigation system, unlike its defenders, have provided a clear, consistent, and sustained message about what makes the system flawed. As a result, that message remains influential, especially among policymakers but also within the broader popular consciousness (prompting policymakers to respond). It therefore deserves attention and careful scrutiny. Accordingly, this chapter unpacks the critics' main allegations, and the following chapter evaluates them.

Alleged Failures

According to this critical view of civil litigation, the system is, firstly, simply too accessible for those who initiate litigation (e.g., Huber 1988; Crier 2003; Howard 2006, 2009). On this account, litigation has replaced more productive ways of resolving disputes, generating a "litigation society" (e.g., Percelay 2000; Howard 2002, 2009; Cassingham 2005). At the same time, the critics allege litigation is too costly—making it inaccessible to defendants. This accessibility asymmetry gives plaintiffs the upper hand. Worse, these critics allege that, because the system is unreliable in plaintiffs' favor, plaintiffs can bring bad-faith or otherwise flimsy cases, and defendants will have incentives to pay plaintiffs off to avoid the higher costs of litigating. The defective process through which civil litigation is conducted facilitates this result.

As formulated for example by the American Tort Reform Association's "Lawsuit Abuse Reform Coalition" in a report supporting federal litigation reform legislation:

It costs little more than a small filing fee and often takes little more time than generating a form complaint to begin a lawsuit. It costs much more for a small business to defend against it. The system is rigged to allow, in effect, legal extortion.[1]

Litigation is too often remunerative for those who bring it, while defendants too often face the prospect of paying either high sums to successful plaintiffs or the high litigation costs of a successful defense. Along the way, plaintiffs' lawyers profit as well, often excessively (e.g., Brickman 1989; Brickman, Horowitz, and O'Connell 1994; M. Horowitz 1995; Painter 1995, 2000; Brickman 2003a, 2003b, 2004, 2011; Taylor 2005), which fuels more litigation and perpetuates the "litigation society" (Olson 1992, 2003; Howard 2001, 2009; Crier 2003).

Plaintiffs and their attorneys stand to gain a lot from litigation in part because damage awards are often high. They are high in absolute terms, sufficient to outweigh the costs of litigation in many cases, and commonly high also relative to the actual injuries plaintiffs suffer. In other words, damage awards are often not only large enough to outweigh the costs of litigation, but also excessive. The civil litigation system does not reliably assess damages.

Specific categories of damages, in particular, are often excessive. First, juries are especially likely to award excess damages for "pain and suffering" and other non-economic losses (see generally Viscusi 1988; King 2004). Pain and suffering, unlike economic losses, is not objectively measurable. Accordingly, model jury instructions essentially ask juries to do what they think is right. Not constrained by market measures of such losses, juries often award large amounts. Given the open-ended nature of non-economic damages, it is difficult for even judges to tell a jury that the award of a given amount is wrong.

Punitive damages are even more problematic (e.g., Viscusi 2001; Gordon 2006). Here, juries are invited, explicitly, to punish the defendant. Many jurors perceive that punishment requires high damages. This is especially true for corporate defendants, which juries believe are less sensitive to punishment than are individual defendants, and thus for whom large punitive awards are necessary to alter their behavior—to "send a message." Not surprisingly, then, juries may award punitive damages in the tens or hundreds of millions of dollars (or in some cases even more).

Damages are not the primary problem, though, but a consequence of another. For excessive damage awards are not possible where juries resolve cases in favor of defendants. But juries too often find defendants liable when they should not (see Vidmar 1995; Hans 2007; Vidmar and Hans 2007; Vidmar and Holman 2010, all of which document the pervasiveness of this critique of juries). Again, the civil litigation system is not reliable, and its unreliability is skewed in the direction of false positives. This too is true for multiple reasons. Most of all, juries are not capable of making reliable decisions. They lack experience with complex legal, scientific, medical, and economic issues often relevant in civil litigation (e.g., Lyon et al. 2007; Saks 2007). The argument is not that jurors are hopelessly incapable. Rather, the problem is that the civil jury system often asks too much of them. Lacking the relevant background and experience, jurors are too easily influenced, and too prone to mistake (e.g., Viscusi 2002; Hersch and Viscusi 2004; Green and Smith 2005). Causal determinations and assessments of damages often require an understanding of material that is difficult for jurors to master in the course of a trial.

Jurors' judgments are therefore heavily informed by other considerations—their perceptions of the veracity of competing witnesses, the extent to which the parties appear sympathetic, the appeal or lack thereof of the lawyers, their raw instincts. In short, juries are biased in a cognitive sense; their judgments reflect considerations not centrally relevant to whether a defendant really committed a legal wrong, and, if so, whether the defendant's conduct really resulted in harm to the plaintiff. So, while civil plaintiffs bear the burden of proof, as noted in chapter 1, in fact jury biases favoring plaintiffs can often compensate for the scientific weaknesses of a plaintiff's case, which is one reason why the litigation system is often unreliable.

Unfortunately, jurors get help in this regard. Expert witnesses, for example, often provide a facade concealing the weaknesses of a plaintiff's claims. Not that all experts are blatantly dishonest, though some are. The problem, rather, is structural: experts vary in their beliefs and opinions, and also in their willingness to stretch the truth in the course of expressing those opinions. Plaintiffs' lawyers have incentives to select from one end of the distribution, enlisting experts most helpful to their cause. That incentive is not lost on experts themselves, who in turn have incentives to move towards that end of the distribution, realizing that otherwise their services will not be needed. This dynamic means that the experts in greatest demand to testify in support of plaintiffs' cases might be over-represented by those on one end of the distribution. As a result, juries do not hear from experts representing the median expert opinion on a given question, but rather from experts at the fringe, who influence juries with their "junk science" (e.g., Huber 1991).

Nor do civil litigation's rules of evidence and procedure go far enough to correct for such dynamics, according to the critics. While the Supreme Court has tightened evidentiary rules governing the use of experts in recent decades, plaintiffs' lawyers can still manage to rely on experts outside the mainstream.[2] By tradition, resolving disagreements among experts is what juries are for, and judges are reluctant to assume that role. Beyond that, though, parties may not know until shortly before trial whether a given expert will be allowed to testify at trial, which means that the parties can rely on whatever experts they want up until an expert's testimony is excluded. For example, a plaintiff might use an expert's testimony to support its motions and to oppose summary judgment during the pretrial stages of litigation. No matter how extreme an expert's opinions might be, they can be used in litigation up until the point—typically late in a case—when a judge rules that they cannot.

That is not all that is wrong, according to the critics. High litigation costs coupled with the system's unreliability put defendants in a precarious position. This combination means that defendants can, and often do, incur high litigation costs only to lose cases they should win—cases they would win if they were operating within a more reliable system. If the system were reliable, even if also expensive, defendants might pay a lot to litigate, but would at least have the satisfaction that those litigation costs would be well spent. In fact, however, defendants often incur high litigation costs yet lose cases they should win. This difficulty amplifies the problem of nuisance suits, as well as "strike suits" and other species of bad-faith litigation (e.g., Guthrie 2000; Schiller and Wertkin 2000). As explained in chapter 3, given high litigation costs, plaintiffs can file nuisance claims knowing that defendants will have an incentive—the incentive to avoid the costs of defending—to settle cases for amounts less than what a defendant would have to incur to prevail.

These problems do not exhaust the civil litigation system's alleged defects. For another example, procedural rules permitting class action litigation allows plaintiffs to bundle negligible individual harms into one large harm. Although harms of individual class members may be so small as to be unnoticed by them, class action plaintiffs' lawyers reap large awards from summing those losses across classes composed of thousands of plaintiffs, and then taking a contingency fee out of the total recovery. Class action litigation is thus often driven by plaintiffs' lawyers, not the nominal members of the class, many of whom may never even know that they were parties to a civil suit. Given its high potential for abuse, many critics allege, the class action mechanism is another serious problem with the civil litigation system (e.g., Scott 2001; Redish 2003; Garry et al. 2004; Hantler and Norton 2004). The civil litigation system is too accessible for attorneys bringing claims on behalf of merely nominal clients.

Class action litigation is but one species of the more general alleged problem of clientless litigation, however. Civil litigation is too often initiated by lawyers bringing "impact litigation" and purporting to represent the general public or other very broad interests. Thus environmentalists initiate expensive litigation against businesses. Advocates for welfare rights and other social services bring litigation against state and local governments. If litigation costs were low, that might not matter, but unfortunately here again the costs of defending weak cases brought by environmentalists, consumer advocates, and legal service organizations can impose large costs on defendants. In fact, such organizations might bring civil litigation that they know is likely to fail, in order to generate publicity about their larger cause. The criticism here is not that impact litigants representing the public always bring litigation without merit. The critique, instead, is that the civil litigation system has no mechanism to discourage them from doing so when that is their aim—another way in which the system is too accessible.

The critics often point to specific types of civil cases to highlight the alleged need for litigation reform. For example, they argue that false positives are especially problematic in torts cases. Juries responding to sympathetic plaintiffs decide in favor of legally undeserving plaintiffs too often, and award too much. The critics also argue that the tort system is especially unreliable in cases that pit individual plaintiffs against corporate defendants.

Particular types of tort litigation present acute cases of other problems with the civil litigation system. For example, experts outside the scientific mainstream are often highlighted as a problem especially in medical malpractice cases. Here, jury antipathy towards large, corporate defendants is not present. In many malpractice cases, individual doctors are the sole defendant. And even when plaintiffs sue hospitals as well, jurors do not view hospitals in the same negative light in which they view other corporations. But plaintiffs who succeed in finding an expert willing to testify that the treating defendant violated some medical standard of care are often able to recover against blameless doctors. Jury sympathy coupled with unscrupulous experts does the work, leading some reformers to call for specialized health courts to replace the traditional jury trial for medical malpractice cases.

Unscrupulous plaintiffs' experts are a problem in products liability litigation, where the merits of a case often depend on whether the defendant manufacturer's design of a product was defective. That determination requires expert testimony concerning the risks posed by the design in question, the benefits of that design, and alternative design choices available to the defendant. These issues raise complex questions, which typically involve technical engineering and economic considerations. Here again, when a plaintiff can enlist an expert willing to testify that the manufacturer's product caused the plaintiff's injuries, the plaintiff has a reasonable chance of prevailing no matter how soundly scientific consensus might reject the plaintiff's causal story. Given the civil litigation system's inability to police dubious expert testimony, products liability cases frequently create excessive liability.

But if tort cases constitute the paradigm of an unreliable and excessively costly civil litigation system (e.g., La Fetra 2003; see generally Hubbard 2006; Sebok 2007), again the critics point to many other types of civil litigation as emblematic of the need for reform. For one, the problem of nuisance litigation is often considered to be magnified in cases brought under federal securities law. In securities "strike suits," plaintiff stockholders seek quick nuisance settlements from corporations due to alleged violations of corporate managers' duties to protect the interests of shareholders. The problem is that the legal basis of such cases often is thin. In fact, some particularly aggressive securities lawyers file cases based on nothing more than a drop in share price. Although such claims might have no merit at all, corporations often settle such cases to avoid both the costs of defending such suits and a loss of share value from pending litigation (e.g., Alexander 1991).

Class action abuse, for another example, reveals itself in not only in securities litigation but also in myriad consumer cases as well. Cases brought under consumer protection statutes typically allege fraud or misrepresentation with respect to consumer products or services. When these suits succeed, prevailing class members often receive—almost always through settlement—some kind of coupon or discount redeemable from the defendant merchant or service provider, benefits of very little value if they are redeemed at all. Meanwhile, the lawyers representing the class reap large monetary fees based on the total face value of those coupons.

In litigation brought under the False Claims Act, which is supposed to protect the federal government by providing a cause of action and recoverable damages for whistleblowers who identify fraudulent claims against the government, extortionate litigants often target innocent health-care providers, seeking undeserved and costly settlements (Barber, Honig, and Cooper 2004).[3] In intellectual property cases, patent "trolls" bring expensive, undeserving suits to tax-productive business enterprises (e.g., Meurer 2003; Evenson 2004; Luxardo 2006; Jaffe 2008; McFeely 2008). Patent trolls are patent holders, or those who claim they hold patents, who never developed or sought to market the patented matter. Instead, they search for business whose socially productive activities arguably if very tenuously infringe on their undeveloped patent (e.g., Magliocca 2007; Fitzgerald 2008). The troll then sues the enterprise for infringement, halting the marketing of a useful product unless and until the troll is paid off.

Still other types of cases, including civil rights and welfare cases, also often exemplify the litigation system's excessive accessibility according to the critics. For example, various entities funded by the federal Legal Services Corporation (LSC), which is to say taxpayers, bring thousands of annual lawsuits, which its critics see as socially wasteful. According to some critics, LSC-funded litigation ultimately harms the poor, the very people it is ostensibly intended to benefit (e.g., Boehm 1997). LSC-funded lawyers are motivated by ideological considerations, and through litigation they impose the costs of their political agenda onto defendants and taxpayers.

Finally, just as certain types of cases capture the civil litigation system's flaws more dramatically than others, so too are those flaws magnified in certain jurisdictions. According to many critics, state courts and the behavior of state judges exacerbate the civil litigation system's unreliability. In certain jurisdictions, known as "judicial hellholes" (see generally Thornburg 2008), courts allow plaintiffs' lawyers to certify class actions that should not be certified. Judges also stretch jurisdictional rules to allow suits against out-of-state defendants, and then make evidentiary rulings that handicap those out-of-state defendants in favor of in-state plaintiffs. Juries also biased in favor of local plaintiffs, or in any event against out-of-town defendants, award exorbitant damages in cases that go to trial, which means that in such jurisdictions, defendants have strong incentives to settle cases at very high amounts to avoid trial. Thus, for the usual reasons but to a greater degree in these hellhole jurisdictions, an unreliable litigation system creates high costs for defendants and large but unjustified benefits for plaintiffs and their lawyers.

The Consequences of a Broken System

By themselves, the criticisms of the civil litigation system discussed so far do not address the question of why they are urgent. The litigation system may not be perfect, but perfect is a high standard. Moreover, the losses created for some by the system's imperfections presumably are offset by gains to others. Why is civil litigation reform so important as a matter of public policy?

The critics of civil litigation have a powerful response. They are focused not so much on injustices in particular cases, but rather on the larger social consequences that a broken system brings. In other words, too much litigation is regrettable not merely because it imposes burdens on defendants who have to answer too many lawsuits, but also and especially because of its effects on everybody else. Excessive litigiousness harms those who are never party to a lawsuit. Reforming civil litigation matters precisely because litigation's harmful effects are wide-ranging (e.g., Huber and Litan 1991; Viscusi 1991; Saxton 1996; W. Davis 1999; J. Baker 2004; Hantler, Behrens, and Lorber 2004).

As chapter 2 argued, the critics are in one important sense exactly right: civil litigation matters most of all because of its social consequences. How the civil litigation system resolves cases affects non-litigants by shaping the behavior of those similarly situated. If a given business is sued, others in the same business will react to the risk that they too could be sued. Product manufacturers will take precautions to minimize their potential liability. Sellers of securities will be more inclined to disclose information relevant to their value. Polluters who anticipate liability for their conduct will have incentives to reduce pollution. Where civil rights are enforced through litigation, those rights are more likely to be respected even by non-litigants, who would rather avoid being sued than violating rights.

These effects can be desirable or undesirable. On the one hand, the purpose of legal rules is precisely to influence the behavior of those beyond the immediate case. Again, just as criminal law seeks to influence the behavior of those other than criminal defendants, so too legal obligations enforced through civil litigation are supposed to affect the behavior of others. As explained, a primary purpose of tort law, for example, is to deter unreasonable behavior. Potential tortfeasors—manufacturers, drug companies, doctors, hospitals, automobile drivers—*should* react to tort rules by fashioning their behavior to comply with them. Likewise, the prospect of liability should inspire corporations to comply with the securities laws. Employers should consider the legal rights of employees. Polluters should consider the incentives that environmental liability creates. Local governments should be reluctant to violate civil rights laws. Yes, civil liability is supposed to influence behavior.

But this means that when the litigation system gets its wrong—when it in effect applies legal pressure where it does not belong, or fails to put legal pressure where it does belong—the law influences behavior in wrong directions. The consequences can be perverse, promoting wasteful rather than efficient behavior. And the problem with the existing system, according to many critics, is that it is routinely unreliable. In concrete terms, an unreliable civil litigation system discourages drug companies from introducing new drugs. Doctors and hospitals practice "defensive" medicine (e.g., Pate and Hunter 2006). Product manufacturers spend too much on safety. Firms invest less in research and development. Corporations are less willing to take risky but rational investment opportunities on behalf of their shareholders. In short, civil litigation has a chilling effect on many socially productive enterprises.

But there is an even bigger problem. Unfortunately, the effects that civil litigation has on non-litigants extend far beyond the excessive caution and missed opportunity by potential defendants. Their conduct too reverberates, which is to say that the consequences of a flawed civil litigation system spread beyond the boundaries of litigation, affecting far more than parties or even potential parties to a lawsuit. Those harmful consequences are impossible to contain.

If insurers do not underwrite insurance policies for city playgrounds, then cities will be forced to close their playgrounds, leaving the city's children to play in less safe environments. If the costs of medical malpractice insurance make rural medical practice difficult, then the supply of rural health care will be low, and people in those areas will be less healthy. If drug companies decide not to introduce new medicines, then patients miss the benefits of them, remaining ill or taking inferior medications. Lawyers who bring bogus consumer protection suits on behalf of victimless clients harm entire industries (e.g., Schwartz and Silverman 2005). When cities and local government have to devote resources defending excessive litigation, those scare resources cannot be spent elsewhere for the public's benefit. When manufacturers charge higher prices to cover the excessive costs of the higher liability risks they perceive, their consumers must pay higher prices. Excessive liability in securities fraud cases needlessly increases the cost of capital (e.g., Booth 2007; cf. Booth 2008, 2009). When undeserving plaintiffs prevail in civil rights cases against their employers, employers may become reluctant to hire minorities. Too much environmental litigation under citizen-suit provisions retards economic growth and competition (e.g., Barnett and Terrell 2001). Excessive sexual harassment litigation chills benign workplace dynamics (e.g., Henagen 1998; Bernstein 2004; Bass 2006; cf. Porter 2008). And so on. Put simply, a broken civil justice system does more than just enrich an undeserving few. It harms countless others.

Even civil cases that may not appear to affect those outside the boundaries of a case have substantial negative effects. For example, prisoner litigation requires the government, especially state governments, to spend scarce resources to defend those cases. As a result, states have fewer resources to dedicate to socially productive purposes. Meanwhile, the inundation of the federal courts in which most prisoner cases are brought means that parties with genuine legal needs must wait longer to have their disputes aired while courts spend time processing frivolous prisoner claims. Justice is delayed for everybody else. The harmful consequences of litigation reach far.

The Critics' Successful Reform Agenda

It is because civil litigation is allegedly socially costly, then, that the critics want to fix it. In other words, the critics are equally reformers as well. And as would be expected, their reform agenda tracks the problems the critics identify. To solve the problem of excessive damages, reformers propose damage caps. Because damages awards are highly variable, even within specific categories of cases, reformers sometimes propose damage schedules too. Given that pain-and-suffering awards in particular are often excessive, critics call for ceilings for non-economic injuries in particular. They call for punitive damages caps too, for the same reason.

Responding to junk-science experts and undisciplined evidentiary standards that lead to unreliable verdicts, the critics propose to make the civil litigation system more reliable by requiring judges to prevent evidence lacking scientific foundation from being introduced in a case. The critics thus propose, for example, that expert witnesses be subject to more exacting scrutiny to ensure that they are well qualified within their field and that their views are not outside of the acceptable range of opinion within their professional or scientific peer group.

To discourage bad-faith litigation, and nuisance suits and lottery litigation in particular, the critics would require unsuccessful litigants to pay some or all of their opponent's litigation costs, including attorneys' fees. If those initiating weak cases had to pay the costs of defeating them, defendants would be far less hesitant to pay to defeat them, knowing that in the event they prevail, they will shift the costs onto the bad-faith plaintiff. Some go so far as to propose the "English Rule," the strongest version of "loser pays," according to which the non-prevailing party must pay the prevailing party's attorney's fees.

Concerns about the undesirable accessibility that contingency fees create lead reformers to propose changes to the rules that govern attorneys' fees. Such proposals include the possibility of placing caps on attorneys' fees for plaintiffs. These caps could be calculated by the number of imputed hours spent on a case; based on new contingency percentage ceilings for different kinds of cases; or estimated as different percentage caps depending on when a case ended (for example, early in discovery or following trial). Related proposals would tax attorneys' fees—sometimes at proposed rates of over 100%—that exceeded certain amounts or amounts per hour.

Reformers also propose more vigorous application of Rule 11 of the Federal Rule of Civil Procedure, which authorizes courts to sanctions parties for bad-faith claims, as a response to bad-faith litigation. As courts' willingness to employ Rule 11 to deter nuisance claims and lottery litigation has varied over time, the critics propose more strict enforcement of it, particularly for nuisance and lottery litigation. Reformers have further proposed that state courts similarly make greater use of state rules of procedure analogous to the federal Rule 11, as well as state rules aimed specifically at frivolous and vexatious cases by frequent litigants. Some have proposed that Rule 11 itself be made available in any state litigation affecting interstate commerce (see Hoffman 2006).

The critics also advocate for reforms tailored to specific types of civil cases they view as especially problematic in one way or another. For example, in addition to limitations on pain and suffering and punitive damages generally, reformers call for caps on both kinds of damages in medical malpractice suits in particular. With respect to class actions, reformers call to make the litigation system less accessible for class actions or at least for class actions brought in state court, and also propose requiring unsuccessful class plaintiffs to pay more of the costs of defending class cases. With respect to securities class actions in particular, reformers favor stricter pleading standards. For legal services litigation, reformers have called for limiting the types of cases, especially impact cases, that legal service organizations can bring at all. In patent cases, reformers call for a reduced role for lay jurors, who lack the competence to evaluate highly technical infringement cases and side with plaintiffs too often. The critics of civil litigation thus complement their general civil litigation reforms with targeted measures applicable to certain types of litigation. They propose reform on the federal as well as the state level (e.g., Moncrieff 2009).[4]

The critics' reform agenda is no wish list. To the contrary, over recent decades, they have realized much of what they proposed, even while calls for litigation reform continue up to the present. Since the 1980s, reformers have seen a series of litigation reform successes throughout the states (see generally Allen 2006; Avraham 2006a, 2006b; see also H. Cohen 2005). Many states capped damages for pain and suffering, some for medical malpractice only, some for civil cases across the board. The legislated damage caps in many states have two tiers, applicable according to the severity of the injury in question. But no matter how serious the injury, damage awards for pain and suffering, emotional distress, and other types of non-economic injuries are, collectively, often limited. Limits range from $250,000 to $750,000. In addition, some states capped total compensatory damages—pain and suffering and economic damages combined—in medical malpractice cases, as medical malpractice reform was enacted as part of a larger wave of tort reform (e.g., Avraham 2006a; Avraham and Schanzenbach 2010).

Many states also adopted limits on punitive damages. These states imposed either specified caps on punitive damages, or limited punitive awards to some multiple of compensatory awards, or (in six or seven states) eliminated punitive damages altogether. Some states also, or alternatively, expressly conditioned the availability of punitive damages on cases where the defendant plainly showed some level of "willful and wanton" conduct, of which plaintiffs must now show specific evidence. Relatedly, some states also bi-furcated trials, such that plaintiffs have to prove in a separate, punitive proceeding that the defendant should pay punitive damages. Criticisms of punitive damages—concerning both excessive levels and their variability—also led to the Supreme Court's holding in *State Farm v. Campbell* that constitutional due process itself caps the amount of punitive damages that can be imposed against civil defendants.[5] While the Court did not set a specific limit for all cases, it held that punitive-to-compensatory ratios greater than 9 to 1 would be constitutionally suspect and exceptional.

Reforms of punitive damages took an additional form as well. Some states also now require that some percentage of all punitive damages be paid into a state fund. According to "split-recovery" statutes, as much as 75%, and in some cases between 20 and 50%, of punitive damage awards are allocated either to state treasury funds or state trust funds. In a couple of states, punitive damages are allocated to funds dedicated to health care or legal services.

Concerns about indulgent expert testimony and unreliable verdicts also led to reform accomplished in the U.S. Supreme Court. In *Daubert v. Merrell Dow Pharmaceuticals*, the Supreme Court held that experts must be qualified before they are allowed to give trial testimony.[6] Specifically, they must have demonstrated credentials and experience appropriate to provide relevant and reliable testimony, and their testimony must be measured against a proposed expert witness's use of the scientific method in generating testimony. The *Daubert* case, as refined by the Supreme Court in subsequent cases, thus requires lower courts to do more to ensure that plaintiffs' evidence reflect sound science. In 2000, the Federal Rules of Evidence governing the admissibility of expert testimony were amended accordingly.[7]

Several state legislatures went farther. For example, some states now require medical malpractice complaints to be accompanied by an "affidavit" or "certificate of merit" swearing that the claim has merit. That is, any plaintiff suing for medical malpractice must enlist a doctor with relevant expertise and qualifications to review the medical record and to affirm in a sworn affidavit that the plaintiff's case has genuine merit. These certificates must be filed in court and served on the defendant contemporaneously with the filing and service of the civil complaint. In practice, this means that a plaintiff must assemble the case enough in advance for a reviewing doctor to be able to affirm that the case has merit before the plaintiff has had the benefit of discovery. This is no easy task, and it reduces the accessibility of the litigation system for medical malpractice cases. This new procedural requirement was imposed to reduce bad-faith medical malpractice cases. According to its proponents, if a plaintiff cannot find a doctor willing to vouch for the case from the beginning, the plaintiff should not be allowed to bring a case.

To address bad-faith litigation more generally, several states enacted "frivolous litigation statutes." These acts allow courts to reallocate both costs and attorneys' fees when courts deem a case to have been filed frivolously. The standards to be applied vary somewhat in their precision, from greater judicial discretion in states like Michigan, to jurisdictions requiring finding a complete absence of a justiciable issue, law, or fact, such as Florida. But whatever the particulars, frivolous litigation statutes discourage bad-faith claims by reallocating costs to those who bring them.

Responding to perceived abuses associated with contingency fee litigation, some states now require judicial approval of contingency fees. Other states legislated caps on contingency fees, or amended existing caps to provide for lower maximum percentages. For example, in California and Delaware, the legislature limited contingency fees dramatically in medical malpractice cases, capping them at 10% of any amounts plaintiffs receive in excess of $200,000, while in Florida contingency fees are limited to 10% of amounts over $250,000. Several states require judicial review of contingency fee awards in all civil cases under a "reasonableness" standard. In most cases, these changes were accomplished by legislation overriding state legal ethics rules.

Litigation reformers have succeeded on the federal level as well, especially but not only in the mid-1990s. For example, in addition to the passage of several specific federal tort reforms (Apelbaum and Ryder 1998), the Prison Litigation Reform Act (PLRA) of 1996 imposed new requirements for prisoner litigation that expressly sought to make federal courts much less accessible for civil rights claims brought by prisoners.[8] The purpose of the act was to reduce frivolous prisoner litigation, and the PLRA seeks to do so by adding procedural requirements to suits that render many prisoner complaints procedurally defective (Ostrom, Hanson, and Cheesman 2003). As a result, many prisoner cases are now dismissed for their failure to exhaust administrative remedies as required by that statute. At the state level, several states amended their procedural rules to allow for summary dismissal of prisoner claims, without litigation by the defendant, if they appear frivolous to the court.[9]

For another example, changes to the Legal Services Corporation Act also in 1996 forbids LSC-funded organizations from filing certain types of impact suits thought to be often baseless or socially unproductive, including but not limited to class actions.[10] Thus LSC-funded entities may not file welfare, housing, or any other type of class action whatsoever. Reform legislation also barred LSC-funded organizations from representing illegal immigrants, for example, or plaintiffs in cases involving reproductive rights, or cases involving prisoners. These restrictions have limited litigation of civil rights cases by legal services organizations, which in many areas of the country are the only organizations bringing such litigation.

In the securities law context, the Private Securities Litigation Reform Act (PSLRA), passed in 1995, altered litigation brought under the securities statutes in a number of ways (Choi 2004).[11] Most generally, the PSLRA eliminated "notice pleading"—which requires a civil complaint to provide only enough information about the legal wrong alleged to put the defendant on notice of the nature of the wrong alleged—in securities litigation. Under the PSLRA, a plaintiff must specify which statement by the defendant misled the plaintiff concerning the value of a security, and how it was misleading. In addition, the plaintiff must allege that the defendant knowingly made the misleading statement. As interpreted by the Supreme Court since the PSLRA's passage, the act requires plaintiffs to allege facts establishing a strong inference that the defendant's misleading statement intended to deceive the shareholder plaintiff. The act also requires plaintiffs to go farther than previously necessary in providing evidence that their loss was caused by the defendant's misleading statement. Follow-on legislation (the Securities Litigation Uniform Standards Act of 1998)—passed to address plaintiffs' attempts to avoid the PSLRA by filing in state court—requires most securities suits to be brought in federal court.[12]

Reformers accomplished subsequent victories as well. The Class Action Fairness Act of 2005 (CAFA), another major federal reform, expanded federal diversity jurisdiction over all class actions, not just securities cases, involving amounts in controversy of $5 million or more (for background, see Erichson 2007; Clermont and Eisenberg 2007).[13] Before the CAFA, class action plaintiffs might file in state rather than federal court wherever at least one party on each side of the case was from the same state, thereby defeating "complete diversity" and thus ensuring that defendants could not move the case to federal court. The CAFA now allows defendants to remove class actions filed in state court to federal court whenever at least one plaintiff and one defendant are from different states—"minimal diversity"—unless most plaintiffs and the main defendant(s) are from the same state. In practical terms, the CAFA has allowed many defendants to move class actions cases to federal court. In addition, the act also instructs courts to scrutinize class action settlements before approving them, especially "coupon settlements" where class members receive a non-monetary settlement.

The Supreme Court has also curbed class action litigation (Gilles and Friedman 2012); and concerns about excessive litigation more generally also led the Supreme Court to tighten pleading standards for civil litigants, making dismissals of cases early in the litigation process easier (see generally, A. Miller 2003, 2010, 2013).[14] In *Bell Atlantic v. Twombly* (2007), for example, the Supreme Court required civil complaints—in order to avoid an initial motion to dismiss—to provide plausible allegations with enough "heft" to give the court a reasonable expectation that the discovery phase of litigation would likely show the plaintiff was entitled to relief. The Court explained that "naked" assertions without factual enhancement are not sufficient for a plaintiff to proceed. In so holding, the Court specifically noted the substantial costs associated with civil discovery, in particular in the area of antitrust which was the basis of the plaintiff's claim in that case. Shortly thereafter, the Supreme Court in *Ashcroft v. Iqbal* (2009) reiterated that surviving a motion to dismiss in any civil case, not limited to antitrust law, requires the plaintiff to state allegations plausible on their face, which need not be detailed but on the other hand cannot be merely conceivable or conclusory.

Notwithstanding reformers' considerable accomplishments, though, civil litigation reform remains very much alive (e.g., Hubbard 2006, which explains tort reform as a movement not an initiative). At the state level, reformers seek to accomplish in additional states what they have realized elsewhere. Civil litigation reform regularly occupies the federal agenda as well. But whether the kinds of reforms the critics continue to call for are desirable depends on whether the critics' basic picture of the civil litigation system is compelling. It may be that the civil litigation system is far from perfect, yet not in the ways its most influential critics have alleged. Chapters 5 and 6 pursue these issues.

Summary

According to the most influential view on the subject, the civil litigation system works rather poorly. The system's failures are, on the whole, the result of defects in the very processes by which civil litigation is conducted—defects that render the system often unreliable across many different types of civil litigation. It is often too accessible to those with weak claims, who are encouraged to file cases given the system's unreliability, another defect. And this defective civil litigation system brings adverse social consequences, in most general terms by creating undesirable incentives due to the perversion of the law's substantive obligations. Thus, continued reform is necessary. While the civil litigation reform movement has seen substantial successes over recent decades, litigation reform remains on the policy agenda.

The following chapter assesses the strength of this view of civil litigation.

5

The Unsubstantiated Case for Litigation Reform

The previous chapter recounted the most familiar and influential critique of civil litigation, and the considerable reform agenda associated with it. The question arises whether the critics are right. This chapter shows that the critics' picture of the civil litigation system is not compelling. The available evidence about how civil cases are resolved does not tend to suggest the civil litigation system is systematically unreliable in plaintiffs' favor, much less that it should be made less accessible to those initiating cases. The system might well be far from perfect—and it is, as the next chapter will suggest—but its imperfections are not those most frequently and successfully ascribed to it.

Unconvincing Anecdotal Evidence

It is fair to say that the most ardent proponents of civil litigation reform are not dispassionate policy analysts. Rather, the interests that stand to gain most from reducing access to the courts often are its biggest champions. Business and insurance interests in particular are well represented among proponents of reform, as are certain professional associations. (It is also fair to say that those who oppose litigation reform most adamantly—trial lawyers especially—are those who have the most to lose as well.) For example, the Institute for Legal Reform (ILR), funded by the U.S. Chamber of Commerce, issues presses releases and "Lawsuit Abuse Impact" analyses advocating for civil litigation reform.[1] It also commissions studies from business insurance consulting firms like Tillinghast-Towers and Perrin that supply the ILR with provocative figures to demonstrate the adverse social consequences of an excessively costly civil litigation system. For instance, the ILR once reported that "America's civil justice system is the world's most expensive, with a direct cost in 2005 of $261 billion, or 2.09% of GDP." It further claims that "the average American family of four paid a 'litigation tax' of more than

$3,500 [per year] due to increased costs from lawsuits and other liability expenses that force businesses to raise the price of products and services," and that such an amount "is equivalent to nearly an 8% tax on wages." The Pacific Research Institute, which also advocates for civil justice reform, provided a higher estimate: $9,827 per family of four.[2] These are staggering figures indeed.

The American Tort Reform Foundation (ATRA) is another leading proponent of litigation reform.[3] Comprised of manufacturing firms, insurance companies, and medical associations, ATRA publishes numerous reports and white papers concerning the need for civil litigation reform. ATRA also advocates for civil litigation reform and monitors legislative developments in all fifty states. ATRA offers voluminous resources to advance the cause of litigation reform, and maintains a list of "judicial hellholes" mentioned in the previous chapter.

Like the U.S. Chamber of Commerce's ILR, the National Association of Manufacturers launched its own American Justice Partnership (AJP) in 2005.[4] Similarly, the AJP's core mission is to advocate for "legal reform," particularly at the state level. Its supporters include major corporations, think tanks, and trade associations. Also like the ILR, the AJP issues press releases and publishes editorials. It solicits stories from "lawsuit abuse victims" to help make its case for legal reform. It also identifies policymakers and candidates for office who are "legal reform champions," and provides resources for those who advocate for reform. Its website features a "Lawsuit Counter," which apparently counts and tracks every kind of civil filing.

The American Medical Association (AMA) also promotes civil litigation reform, targeting "America's medical liability crisis."[5] It too solicits studies and issues materials making the case for federal and state medical malpractice reform, and supports reform proposals that extend beyond medical malpractice cases. The AMA actively lobbies for legislative reform in particular, and promotes legislative candidates in state and federal elections who favor civil litigation reform. Doctors for Medical Liability Reform, an interest group of 230,000 practicing medical specialists, similarly advocates for federal legislation, and does so on the grounds that an unreliable litigation system makes health care unaffordable or even unavailable.[6]

Several influential think tanks also publish materials advancing the case for civil litigation reform. For example, the American Enterprise Institute publishes white papers and other materials on the ills of litigation and the need for reform.[7] Similarly, the Cato Institute maintains *Overlawyered.com*, a blog chronicling "the high cost" of the civil litigation system and advocating for reform. The Manhattan Institute houses a Center for Legal Policy that focuses on reform of the civil litigation system—with the mission to "communicate thoughtful ideas on civil justice reform to real decision-makers."[8] It also publishes reports, entitled "Trial Lawyers, Inc.," that describe how trial lawyers use unscrupulous tactics to the detriment of the U.S. economy as a whole.[9]

These examples are by no means exhaustive. And, importantly, the fact that such groups have a clear point of view of course does not mean they are wrong. The real question asks about the nature of their case—that is, does the civil litigation system warrant the kinds of reforms for which these organizations advocate? Perhaps not. As Haltom and Mc-Cann (2004) have demonstrated compellingly, and as many others have shown as well, leading litigation reformers tend to rely rather heavily on anecdotes and under-supported "facts" rather than empirical evidence to make their case (e.g., Zalesne 1999; McCann, Haltom, and Bloom 2001; Baker and Silver 2002; Robbennolt and Studebaker 2003; A. Miller 2003; Rhode 2004b; T. Baker 2005; Eisenberg and Wells 2006; Nockleby 2007; Eisenberg 2009). Most of all, these reformers point to well-publicized cases of undeserving plaintiffs who prevail against legally blameless defendants, and of blameless defendants who spend exorbitant amounts to defeat patently meritless cases, in order to show that the civil litigation system is unreliable and too costly for defendants (see also Reda 2012).

In fact, often these cases receive publicity in large part *because* civil litigation reformers rely on them to advance their cause; reformers' web sites, press statements, and white papers feature them. For example, the Center for Individual Freedom's website maintains a "Jester's Courtroom" documenting "ridiculous and sometimes funny lawsuits plaguing our courts." Similarly, the American Justice Partnership maintains a list of "Looney Lawsuits." The website *FacesofLawsuitAbuse.org*, a project of the ILR, asks visitors to "vote for last month's most ridiculous lawsuit" from among a list of cases.[10]

Resulting media coverage of such cases, in turn, provides opportunities for reformers to advance arguments and offer statistics, the latter often of unclear derivation, about the adverse social consequences of a civil litigation system that is both too friendly to plaintiffs and too costly to defendants. The McDonald's coffee case is the classic example, the most well-known tort case of a generation (see McCann, Haltom, and Bloom 2001). Seventy-nine-year-old Stella Lieback purchased hot coffee at a McDonald's drive-through window in Albuquerque, New Mexico. Shortly after her purchase, she took the plastic lid off her coffee to add cream and sugar. In so doing, she spilled the coffee on her lap and the sweat pants she was wearing. For her self-inflicted injury from a cup of coffee, the civil justice system rewarded her with $2.9 million. Something—the reform argument goes—must be wrong. And the case echoes to the present: The more recent (2014) widely reported case concerning a supposed $1.5 million lawsuit against McDonald's by a customer who received too few napkins (as reported in the *Orlando Sentinel* and *Business Insider*, among other places) is not only evocative of the McDonald's coffee case, but likely receives press attention in part for that reason as well.[11]

The "missing pants" case is another widely famous example.[12] In 2005, Roy Pearson, a customer of Custom Cleaners dry cleaners in Washington, D.C., sued its owners, Jin and Soo Chung and their son, for allegedly losing a pair of his suit pants. He filed his case under a consumer protection statute. Mr. Pearson originally sought $1,150 in damages, his estimated cost for a replacement suit. But in the course of unsuccessful negotiations, he raised his demand, even after the Chungs offered him $12,000, far above the value of his lost suit. Instead, he sued them for $67 million, an amount he later reduced to $54 million. At the end of what reformers characterized as a "massive civil lawsuit" lasting over two years, the Chungs prevailed, but at a purported cost of over $100,000 in legal fees and an emotional and financial strain that caused the Chungs, Korean immigrants, to close two of their three dry cleaning shops.

The "flying shrimp case" provides another example highlighting the need for litigation reform.[13] Jerry Colaitis died from a severe infection following two spinal operations in late November 2001. His estate sued the Benihana restaurant chain, alleging that Mr. Colaitis injured his neck during a family visit to a Benihana restaurant some eleven months earlier, when he ducked to avoid a piece of flying shrimp tossed by a chef (mimicking a scene from a Jackie Chan movie). The plaintiffs claimed that Mr. Colaitis's neck injury eventually led to his surgery, although he had significant other health problems. They sued Benihana, on their flying shrimp theory, for $16 million.

The flying shrimp case competes with the infamous "peanut butter case," in which a prisoner filed suit because he wanted creamy instead of chunky peanut butter. Other well-publicized prisoner cases include a case brought by a prisoner seeking towels of a different color, and a prisoner who filed suit because he did not like a salad bar. Indeed, prisoner litigation provided many high-profile examples of purported bad-faith litigation, leading congressional supporters of prison litigation reform to maintain a list of "top ten" frivolous prisoner cases, all of which were read in to the *Congressional Record* as part of the legislative history of the Prison Litigation Reform Act mentioned in the previous chapter.

The above cases, and others like them, became causes célèbres for advocates of civil litigation reform. Again, references to them punctuate innumerable websites, interest-group white papers and press releases, and other advocacy materials. Indeed, for several years following her case, Stella Lieback herself personified an unreliable civil litigation system. In one march upon Capitol Hill by proponents of tort reform, representatives of the U.S. Chamber of Commerce carried a large banner that read simply "She Spilled It On Herself"; so salient was the McDonald's coffee case that the banner's meaning was lost on no one.

The Chamber of Commerce also publicized the "missing pants" case, in part by organizing a fundraiser for the Chungs to cover their legal defense costs. That fundraiser was co-sponsored by the American Tort Reform Association, which "condemned" the suit and whose president sent a letter to its membership about the case, taking it as representative of what is wrong with the civil litigation system.[14] The Chungs' legal defense fund eventually collected over $100,000. The Center for Individual Freedom featured the case on its website documenting frivolous cases. The *Wall Street Journal* featured the case on one of its blogs. The case was covered extensively by talk radio and even by the international press, especially in Korea.

The *Wall Street Journal* kept a blog about the flying shrimp case too, which Fox News also covered extensively. The *Insurance Journal* also provided extensive coverage of the shrimp case, documenting it as an example of frivolous litigation.[15] The Association of State Attorneys General and the Attorney General of New York published separate letters in the *New York Times* about the prisoner peanut butter case and other prisoner suits, including the case brought by a prisoner who sued because his prison towels were white instead of beige, as he preferred (Newman 1996a, 1996b). Their letters argued that prisoner cases concerning peanut butter and the color of towels showed why litigation reform was necessary. And these are only some examples of the use of high-profile cases to advance the cause of litigation reform.

Such cases—hot coffee, flying shrimp, missing pants, prison peanut butter—have become major symbols of litigation reform, and indeed part of the public consciousness. *Lieback v. McDonald's* inspired the annual "Stella Awards" competitions. Contestants nominate outlandish lawsuits by reporting them to contest organizers, who post the top ten "worst" cases and an overall "Stella Award Winner" for each year on websites dedicated to the project. The Stella Awards, reported on the web, and provided material for the book, *The True Stella Awards* (Cassingham 2005).

But reformers' anecdotal advocacy is not limited to torts cases, consumer suits, and prisoner litigation. Reformers also highlight, for example, litigation brought by legal services organizations as well. Borrowing from the Stella Awards, the National Legal and Policy Center runs a "Legal Services Monitor" that documents alleged abuses by Legal Services Corporation (LSC) and collects examples of purportedly outrageous cases brought by entities funded by the LSC.[16] These examples too are designed to show how legal services litigation on behalf of the poor is abusive and socially wasteful, and furthermore how it often makes the poor worse off. The parallels to the Stella Awards and other litigation horror stories are close.

In the consumer class action context, reformers feature the Blockbuster, Cheerios, and Crayola cases, in which class plaintiffs received very modest or in-kind compensation for their alleged injuries (e.g., Hantler and Norton 2004). Coupon settlements in general make favorite examples for the critics, who object to class action attorneys who settle cases generating large monetary fees for themselves while class members receive coupons that they may or may not ever redeem. The critics of the coupon class action cases often argue that contingency fees should be calculated based on the redemption rate of small coupons, rather than their face value. In any event, the Blockbuster, Cheerios, and Crayola cases, in which class members received one dollar off of their next movie rental, one free box of cereal, and a 75-cent coupon towards a box of crayons, while their lawyers were paid hundreds of thousands of dollars or more, are well-known examples of the excesses of consumer class actions.

To reiterate, the observation that the critics trade on anecdotes and broad generalizations to make their case for reform is not new. But the extent to which this is so warrants emphasis. That is, the critics' favorite cases do not serve merely to *illustrate* findings revealed through systematic empirical study of the civil litigation system. Instead, they frequently substitute for such study; outlandish cases are offered to *demonstrate* that the civil litigation system is too accessible to bad-faith plaintiffs, excessively costly for defendants, and unreliable in the direction of false positives. The implicit argument is that a civil litigation system that generates cases like these simply must be deeply flawed, and because the existing system generates cases like these, it requires serious reform (Robbennolt and Studebaker 2003).

But given the argumentative weight that highly publicized cases carry in making the critics' case, a lot hinges on the accurate portrayal of them. Yet the facts of high-profile cases often are more complicated than commonly presented, as others have shown (e.g., Rustad 1992; McCann, Haltom, and Bloom 2001; Baker and Silver 2002; Haltom and McCann 2004; Bogus 2004; Nockleby 2007; Thornburg 2008). In truth, Stella Lieback suffered third degree burns on over 6% of her body, requiring skin grafts and debridement over her thighs, buttocks, and genitalia. She spent eight days in the hospital, and was treated over the course of months. Her family (self-described Republicans and proponents of tort reform) sought to settle the case for $20,000, representing in part Ms. Lieback's daughter's lost work in caring for her mother.

The jury, members of whom later said in interviews that they were initially skeptical of Ms. Lieback's claims, awarded her $2.7 million in punitive damages, representing two days of McDonald's coffee sales, following testimony that McDonald's served its coffee at dangerously high temperatures notwithstanding repeated complaints from the Shriners

Burn Institute. But the jury also found Ms. Lieback partially at fault for the spill, for which her damages were reduced by 20%. More importantly, the trial judge reduced the punitive award still further to three times her reduced compensatory award of $160,000, even though the judge found McDonald's conduct in this case to be reckless, callous, and willful. Ultimately, the parties settled on appeal, for a confidential amount almost certainly less than the judicially reduced award of $640,000. If anything, the McDonald's coffee case may exemplify how the litigation system proved reliable: A skeptical jury was convinced by credible evidence that the defendant's conduct was wanton; it awarded damages to the plaintiff but reduced them because it found her to be at fault as well; the jury's punitive award, though high, was not arbitrary, and yet the judge, though agreeing with the jury that the defendant's conduct was wanton, reduced it by about 80%. Nor does the civil litigation system appear to be too accessible to bad-faith coffee litigants; such cases have been both rare and unsuccessful since the Lieback settlement.

The full stories behind many well-known cases of prisoner litigation are likewise more complex than presented in the popular press or the legislative history of the Prison Litigation Reform Act (Newman 1996b; Puplava 1997; Brill 2008). For example, the infamous prisoner who reportedly sued over the wrong kind of peanut butter in fact sued to correct a mistaken debit to his prison account after he returned peanut butter brought to him by mistake. He had been transferred to another prison, but his account remained erroneously debited. Likewise, the prisoner who reportedly sued over the color of his towels did no such thing. Instead, he sued for the return of towels and a jacket mailed to him by his family that were confiscated by the prison authorities as "contraband" because, in the case of the towels, they were not prison-issued. He requested their return so he could send them back home. Prisoners do bring some bad-faith litigation, as discussed at length in later in part 3. But they also initiate some meritorious litigation, and the critics of prisoner litigation have made some very weak arguments about prisoner litigation that fail to distinguish the two. Thus proponents of the PLRA offered in support of their view that the act was necessary to curb frivolous litigation the fact that "only a scant 3.1%" of prisoner cases reach trial (see generally Puplava 1997). That argument appears to forget that only about 3% of *all* civil cases of all types reach trial.

The missing-pants case further illustrates the critics' indulgent use of marquee cases. It is no surprise that Mr. Pearson, the plaintiff in that case, *lost* his case against the Chungs—but reformers provided real-time coverage of the case as if he might prevail (otherwise, why would the story be considered newsworthy?).[17] Moreover, the judge that ruled against Mr. Pearson ordered him to pay the defendants' costs of the suit, including their attorney's fees, properly allocating the costs of litigation to a plaintiff who needlessly generated litigation costs for the opposing party. Given that the plaintiff lost, and that he was liable for the defendant's attorney's fees, it is not at all clear why the case proves any need for litigation reform: a plaintiff (widely reported to have personal and emotional challenges) filed a suit on his own behalf—not represented by a contingency-fee lawyer—seeking obviously excessive damages for a minor loss—and not only lost the case but was chastised by the judge along the way.[18] Nor apparently has any plaintiff anywhere successfully sued a dry cleaner for millions of dollars resulting from lost clothes. Like the McDonald's coffee case, if anything the dry-cleaner case shows that the civil litigation system reliably resolved that case, properly allocated the costs of the litigation, and all without breeding undesirable access to the courts by follow-on bad-faith litigants.

Some may nevertheless argue, however, that the case shows how much the defendant Chungs had to pay, or might have had to pay, in order to prevail against an outrageous lawsuit—$100,000 and the loss of their two businesses. But this response seems very difficult to credit. First, although reformers' coverage of the case emphasized that the Chungs had to close two of their dry cleaning shops, why they did so is not at all clear. If their shops were profitable, and they did not have to sell them to raise funds for their defense, the costs of which were covered through contributions collected by the Institute of Legal Reform and the American Tort Reform Association, it is not apparent why the lawsuit forced them to sell their businesses. Indeed, this aspect of the story makes no sense at all: when all of the dust settled, the Chungs' out-of-pocket expenses that arise from Mr. Pearson's lawsuit seem to have been zero.

More importantly, the proposition that defending against Mr. Pearson's outlandish case could have cost the Chungs "over $100,000" strains plausibility for anyone who has litigated civil cases. The missing-pants case involved no medical or scientific testimony, no battle between experts, indeed no expert testimony of any kind as the plaintiff alleged no personal injury. Nor did the case involve extensive paper discovery, or any electronic discovery. It did not require market analyses, accident stimulation, document review, extensive depositions, or any other costly aspects of the civil discovery process. In fact, the judge supervising the discovery phase in the case refused to allow Mr. Pearson to engage in excessive discovery. Nor did the case involve extensive civil motion practice. The missing-pants case was, instead, a very simple civil case presenting few issues. How the litigation costs associated with it could have reached $100,000 is therefore not clear at all. The missing-pants case is not a great case for litigation reformers, though it was turned into one.

The plaintiffs in the flying-shrimp case also lost.[19] Here too, then, it is unclear how the case shows that the litigation system is unreliable. To be sure, the plaintiffs' claims were far-fetched, likely brought in bad faith, and probably in order to generate a nuisance settlement. But the civil litigation system—in a case tried by a jury and pitting a family against a deep-pocket corporation—proved reliable. Here again, though, critics might respond that the case illustrates the burden simply of defending against bad-faith claims, and thus that the case at least demonstrates how the civil litigation system is too accessible to bad-faith claims.

But here too, those burdens are easily exaggerated, as they seem to have been in this case as well. For example, the *Insurance Journal's* coverage of the flying-shrimp trial described it as a "month-long trial." But a month-long trial to resolve the causal question whether flying shrimp led to blood poisoning seems most far-fetched. In fact, less than 1% of all civil trials in the United States last a month, and those that do represent the most complex, multi-party cases.[20] The flying-shrimp case could not plausibly have been one of them. The *Insurance Journal's* reference likely counts the time from jury selection to jury verdict. But the case, tried in New York state court, was but one of dozens on the court's docket during that month, and the court did not convene a month-long trial over a piece of shrimp. Once again, on closer investigation, one of critics' favorite cases proves far less helpful in demonstrating the civil litigation reform than it first appears.

That reformers emphasize stylized versions of high-profile cases does not establish that they lack other types of evidence, however. The real question is not whether reformers' celebrated cases accurately show that civil litigation reform is necessary, but rather whether available evidence supports that conclusion. Yet it is difficult to identify systematic studies providing clear factual support for the influential critics' reform agenda, even while many careful analyses call the critics' claims and corresponding proposals for reform into question, as the following section will show.

To be sure, scholars who generally support civil litigation reform have undertaken some serious studies (see Rubin and Shepherd 2007). But such work provides neither systematic nor consistent support for the reform agenda outlined in the previous chapter. For one example, Kip Viscusi's (2004) analysis of punitive damage awards by judges and juries concludes that juries award higher punitive awards than judges do, but argues that this is so largely because of a low number of outlier jury awards. Moreover, Viscusi aims to explore whether judges or juries render higher awards, and his analysis provides no grounds for concluding that most jury awards are too high or otherwise problematic. White (2003) provides another welcome example of systematic analysis in her study of the consequences of plaintiffs' lawyers' choice of forum in asbestos litigation, in which she unsurprisingly concludes that tactical efforts to bring cases in certain courts increased the expected value of claims.

For another example, an excellent book published by the Independent Institute, *Judge and Jury*—written by Helland and Tabarrok (2006), who repeatedly describe themselves as "critical of modern tort litigation"—provides careful examination of whether juries or judges make larger damage awards, and whether contingency fees create desirable litigation incentives. With respect to the former, the authors conclude that the most of the differences between damages awards by judges and juries is the result of the types of cases that the two decide. They furthermore conclude that low-income jurors give high awards more often, but they do not conclude that jury awards are "too high." Concerning contingency fees, Helland and Tabarrok conclude that there is little evidence that contingency fees lead to bad-faith litigation, and in fact, the evidence suggests that the contrary is true: restricting contingency fees leads to more bad-faith litigation as attorneys take weaker cases and bill them by the hour.

The Doubtful Empirical Basis for Reform

High-profile cases aside, if the critics' central claims that (1) the civil litigation system is too accessible, especially for bad-faith plaintiffs, because (2) it is unreliable in favor of plaintiffs are correct, several predictions follow. Generally speaking, the road for plaintiffs from filing a complaint to receiving a sizeable damage award should be short and smooth. A little more specifically, plaintiffs would be predicted to prevail over defendants very often, and should regularly receive substantial damage awards, especially for cases tried by juries as opposed to judges, and likewise for cases resolved in state courts, which are more responsive to parochial interests at the expense of non-local defendants than are federal courts. Applying the framework developed in chapter 3, table 5.1 summarizes the general predictions that flow from the critics' basic description of the civil litigation system. The question becomes whether these expectations might find support from available evidence about how civil litigation is resolved.

The short answer is that they do not. First of all, as noted in chapter 1, most plaintiffs never see a jury or, therefore, any damage award. The overwhelming majority of civil cases are abandoned, dismissed, or settled short of trial. This observation does not provide much support for the critical view of civil litigation. If civil cases are so rare, then going to

TABLE 5.1. The Civil Litigation System According to the Influential Critique

Type of Civil Litigation System:	Defining Conditions:	Parties' Incentives:	Expected Outcomes:
Asymmetrically Accessible for Plaintiffs; Unreliable with Excessive False Positives	Plaintiffs can bring claims too easily; Defending against claims is costly; Courts and juries err most often in plaintiffs' favor	Plaintiffs and plaintiffs' lawyers have incentives to bring many claims, including bad-faith claims such as nuisance suits; Defendants have incentives to settle even bad-faith claims	Excessive litigation by plaintiffs, who file too many claims and over-litigate claims filed as well; Undeserving plaintiffs often prevail or secure undeserved settlements rationally informed by unreliable litigation outcomes; Trial verdicts are skewed in plaintiffs' favor; Damage awards or other remedies are excessive

trial must be a small threat to defendants. To be sure, if the trial process is broken, then it should be fixed because, among other reasons, an unreliable trial process will likely skew the terms of settlement. But even so, the critics' frequent focus on trial outcomes reveals little about the civil litigation system as a whole given the small percentage of cases that are tried, and given that so much happens in pretrial litigation. Trials and the outcome of trials probably receive so much attention for the simple reason they are easily observable. But even focusing on cases tried to verdict, the available evidence does not appear to vindicate most critics' predictions; plaintiffs often lose, and when they do prevail, they often recover modest compensation. Given the widespread perception that the plaintiffs routinely see large damage awards, a bird's-eye view of how civil cases are resolved is illuminating.

Consider the following. Among cases that proceed through trial, and taking all general civil cases together, plaintiffs win at trial just over half of the time. According to the Civil Justice Survey of State Courts (collected by the U.S. Department of Justice's Bureau of Justice Statistics) for 1992, 1996, and 2001—data spanning the period during which many civil litigation reforms were adopted—each of which examine the resolution of civil trials in the seventy-five largest counties in the nation, civil plaintiffs prevailed at trial 52% of the time for 1991 and 1996, and 55% of the time for 2001.[21]

In torts cases specifically, plaintiffs prevail about half of the time. According to the BJS surveys of tort trials, tort plaintiffs prevail at trial very nearly 50% of the time.[22] Taking all types of torts cases together, this is a general success rate that has proven constant over recent decades. In contracts cases taken as a whole, plaintiffs prevail more often, 62 to 65% of the time.[23] In contrast, the BJS surveys find that plaintiffs in real property cases prevail only 32 to 38% of the time.[24] Civil rights plaintiffs also usually lose at trial, prevailing between 29 and 35% of the time.[25]

Within these broad categories of cases, however, plaintiffs' success rates vary based on the specific type of claim. Among torts cases, plaintiffs prevail in only about one-quarter of medical malpractice cases, for instance—even though the large majority of medical malpractice cases involve death or permanent injury—and about one-third of the time in products liability cases (other than asbestos), another type of litigation often emphasized by the critics of litigation. Tort plaintiffs do better in automobile cases and intentional torts cases, prevailing over 60% of the time at trial in the former and more than half of the time in the latter. Here again, these rates at which civil plaintiffs prevail are quite consistent over time.[26]

In contracts cases too, plaintiff success rates at trial vary by the nature of the suit, in ways relatively stable over time. Sellers of goods and services prevail as plaintiffs more often than buyer-plaintiffs do. In addition, plaintiffs in mortgage foreclosure cases—banks and other lending institutions—prevail much more often than, for example, plaintiffs in employment cases. In fact, plaintiffs in employment cases are the only subcategory of contracts plaintiffs that consistently prevail less half of the time.[27]

In civil rights cases too, plaintiffs' success at trial depends in small part on the nature of the action, though overall plaintiffs prevail only one-third of the time. In the largest category of civil rights claims, the employment discrimination case, plaintiffs prevailed about 37% of the time from 2000 to 2006.[28] Schwab and Clermont (2008) analyze data from the Administrative Office of U.S. Courts and conclude that employment discrimination plaintiffs prevail less frequently relative to other types of civil plaintiffs (accord Selmi 2001), while Schneider (2010) argues that civil rights plaintiffs generally fare more poorly than other litigants due the changing nature of civil pretrial practice in the wake of civil litigation reform. Across several important categories of civil cases, then, plaintiffs' trial success rates seem at odds with the expectation that the civil justice system too often rewards undeserving plaintiffs, or in particular that juries are unreliable in favor of plaintiffs.

To be sure, the trial process could be heavily biased in plaintiffs' favor, and still trial success rates for plaintiffs could be low, or at least hover around 50%. Parties will tend to settle where they have overlapping estimations of the trial outcome, and will tend not to settle where their estimations differ. It is not impossible, then, that trials are unreliable and severely biased against defendants, that both plaintiffs and defendants understand that fact, and that still parties choose to go to trial when they have different estimations of the probability of success having *already* adjusted for the trial bias—all possible. But while trial success rates do not finally prove anything one way or another, they are suggestive. If the civil litigation system is as unreliable in plaintiffs' favor as the critics suggest, one might reasonably expect plaintiffs to do better at trial than the findings here show.

Available data about damage awards do not seem to vindicate the critics' expectations about unreliable litigation outcomes either. According to the Bureau of Justice Statistics, which collects extensive data on damage awards across many types of civil cases, the median damage awards among all prevailing torts plaintiffs was only $24,000 for 2005.[29] This low amount reflects the fact that the overwhelming majority of torts suits are, even in the age of no-fault auto insurance, ordinary automobile cases. The median award in auto cases was around $15,000 for 2005, while the median award for slip-and-fall cases was approximately $98,000. Damage awards for asbestos cases are at the other end of this spectrum, with the median amount exceeding $680,000. The next two highest median awards were for products liability ($500,000) and medical malpractice ($400,000) cases.[30]

Over recent decades, between one-quarter and one-third of prevailing medical malpractice plaintiffs receive over $1 million. But whether medical malpractice awards are "high" is not at all clear given that one-third of medical malpractice trials involve cases of death, and almost 60% are brought by plaintiffs who are permanently injured.[31] Leading studies of medical malpractice litigation conclude that medical malpractice plaintiffs are *not* overcompensated (e.g., Vidmar 1995; T. Baker 2005; Sloan and Chepke 2010; Hyman and Silver 2006, 2013) and that damages caps in medical malpractice cases result in under-compensation for those most seriously injured (e.g., Mello 2006; Nelson, Morrisey, and Kilgore 2007). And according to data analyzed by the National Center for State Courts' Court Statistics Project (Lee and LaFountain 2011), the median damage award for medical malpractice resulting in death is 50% of the median damage award for other types of wrongful death cases. Punitive damages in medical malpractice cases are rare even relative to other types of tort litigation, ranging over recent decades from 1 to 4% of cases in which plaintiffs prevail.

The median award for contract cases is higher than for tort cases, but the variance across types of cases is somewhat smaller. Moreover, the median damage award in contracts cases is not very high; for example, in 2005 it was $35,000.[32] In addition, among tried contracts cases, business plaintiffs are almost as common individual plaintiffs, and damage awards in contract cases are generally higher for business plaintiffs, in part likely because the alleged injuries are greater. Thus the median damages award for cases alleging tortious interference with contract ($169,000 in 2005) and for partnership disputes ($120,000) typically exceeds the median award among all contracts cases, as do mortgage foreclosure cases ($78,000). Contracts cases alleging employment discrimination ($175,000) also exceed the overall median award. But overall, damage awards in contracts cases, although higher than in routine tort cases, do not on their face seem high enough to support an argument in favor of civil litigation reform.

The same is true for civil rights litigation. Monetary damage awards are available in some types of civil rights cases as well, such as employment cases, though more infrequently in others, like voting rights cases. But median damage awards are not exorbitant. In federal court, where a civil rights plaintiff receives any monetary award—though, as noted, plaintiffs prevail in civil rights trials only about one-third of the time—the median awards for most cases concluded between 2000 and 2006 range from the low to middle $100,000s, depending on the specific type of case.[33]

None of the above damages figures, which vary some from year to year but not by orders of magnitude, seem to support the view that the civil litigation system over-compensates civil plaintiffs. To be sure, hard conclusions cannot be drawn from these data alone. For one thing, determining whether juries over-compensate plaintiffs would require baseline information about the "correct" level of compensation, or in other words the true size of plaintiffs' harm—information not easily available, to say the least. But on the face of the above figures, they do not seem excessive. Furthermore, scholarly studies of jury awards consistently conclude that reformers' view of civil juries as too generous to plaintiffs does not square well with the evidence (e.g., Eisenberg and Henderson 1992; Daniels and Martin 1986, 1995; Eisenberg 2009; Merritt and Barry 1999). Thus, for example, Seabury, Pace, and Reville (2004) conclude—based on the longest time series on jury verdicts collected— that "real average awards have grown by less than real income over the forty years in our sample," and that all of this growth is explained by case characteristics and claimed economic losses, and "the growth (or decline) does not appear substantial enough to support claims of radically changing jury behavior over the past forty years."

Nor is the case for punitive damages reform apparent from available data about the frequency and size of such awards, as studies consistently show (e.g., Eisenberg et al. 1997; Rustad 1998, 2005; Eisenberg et al. 2005; Vidmar and Holman 2010), notwithstanding the attention punitive damages receive among litigation reformers and specifically reformers' argument that the availability of punitive awards leads to nuisance or lottery litigation. According to the BJS state court data, prevailing plaintiffs receive punitive damages only about 5 to 6% of the time, a stable rate over many years.[34] In other words, plaintiffs receive a punitive damages award roughly 6% of the time out of the 52% of torts cases in which plaintiffs prevailed at trial, from among the approximately 4% of torts cases that proceed through trial. Here once again, the very low overall incidence of punitive awards does not lend obvious support to the claims that the civil litigation system is unreliable in plaintiffs' favor.

Moreover, it is not the case that punitive damages are especially problematic in the types of cases litigation reformers emphasize most. The median punitive damages award in civil cases in state court—where the amount of punitive damages awarded per year varies in the middle tens of thousands of dollars—is lower in torts cases than in contracts cases.[35] Thus, it is not the case that personal injury cases, where the plaintiff's injuries might be assumed to motive high punitive awards from biased or unduly sympathetic juries, drive most high punitive awards. In fact, among tort cases, punitive damages are most common in defamation and other intentional tort cases, not personal injury cases including medical malpractice and products liability.[36]

To illustrate with one specific year: in 1992, a year during one of the peak early periods of civil litigation reform, among all products liability trials sampled from the country's seventy-five most populous counties, of which there were 360, only three of the 142 prevailing plaintiffs received punitive damages (for 2% of prevailing products liability plaintiffs or less than 1% of all products liability plaintiffs). The same year, the country's seventy-five most populous counties held a total of 287 toxic tort trials, in which only thirteen of the 202 prevailing plaintiffs received a punitive award (6% of prevailing toxic tort plaintiffs and 4.5% of all toxic tort plaintiffs). Of the 403 medical malpractice cases in which plaintiffs prevailed, out of 1,370 jury trials, punitive damages were awarded in thirteen cases (3% of prevailing medical malpractice plaintiffs and less than 1% of all medical malpractice plaintiffs).[37] Punitive damages, particularly but not only in products liability, toxic tort, and medical malpractice cases in which the critics have suggested most require punitive damages reform, are just not very common.

These BJS data comport with other studies of the frequency of punitive damage awards. Studies of punitive damage awards before the first large wave of punitive damages reform may be especially instructive. According to a RAND study of some twenty-four thousand jury verdicts in California's Cook County and San Francisco County from 1960 to 1984, punitive damages were awarded in a total of six products liability cases (Peterson, Sarma, and Shanley 1987). Other researchers (Daniels and Martin 1990) reviewed a similar sample size of twenty-five thousand jury verdicts from forty-seven jurisdictions from 1981 to 1985, again the period covering the so-called liability crisis leading up to wide reform. They found that of the 967 products liability cases from that period, thirty-four plaintiffs received punitive damages. Likewise, a study attempting to collect all punitive damage awards in products liability from 1965 to 1990 identified a total of 355 cases in which plaintiffs received punitive damages, ninety-five of which were asbestos cases (Koenig and Rustad 1993). Across all of these studies, punitive damage awards were uncommon.

Likewise, Vidmar and Holman's (2010) more recent study—based on data from the 2005 Civil Justice Survey of state courts together with a comprehensive database constructed from 2005 reported cases—shows that punitive damage awards are both infrequent and very rarely constitute a high ratio to compensatory damages, and even then, it is almost always in cases involving egregious conduct by a defendant. That finding comports with other leading studies (e.g., Eisenberg et al. 1997; Eisenberg, Hans, and Wells 2006; Eisenberg et al. 2010; Eisenberg, Heise, and Wells 2010). Given that punitive damages are legally available only where the defendant's behavior was willful and wanton, it is not surprising that punitive damages would be unavailable in the majority of cases, including personal injury cases involving severe injury. For the same reason, it is to be expected that, among torts cases, punitive damages are awarded most frequently in cases involving intentional torts or other intentionally wrongful behavior (e.g., Vidmar and Holman 2010; Eisenberg, Heise, and Wells 2010; BJS 2011).

To be sure, there are much-discussed cases in which juries have imposed extremely large punitive awards—the "blockbuster" punitive damages cases (Viscusi 2004; Del Rossi and Viscusi 2010)—and these cases are often mentioned as justifications for punitive damages reform. The problem, however, is that such cases constitute real outliers, and for that reason do not provide a basis for general reform. First of all, outlier punitive awards can be, and have been, modified by trial courts through judicial doctrines such as remittitur or similar mechanisms. Second, outlier punitive awards can be, and have been, reversed or reduced on appeal (as was done in the McDonald's coffee case). For that reason too, the case for punitive damages reform is not made by observations that *juries* have awarded record-breaking punitive awards in only a handful of case (Viscusi 2004). If the concern is that neither trial judges nor appellate courts are able or willing to guard against excessive—as opposed to high—punitive damage awards, then juries have been an improper focus of damages reform.

Moreover, if blockbuster cases are really a problem even after corrections by trial and appellate courts, which has not been demonstrated, that problem can be eliminated with caps applicable specifically to blockbuster awards. Although outlier awards are infrequent (by definition), they do happen, and reforms targeting the blockbuster cases may make some sense. The problem, however, is that most punitive damages caps are not targeted to blockbuster cases. For example, punitive caps of $250,000 are justified only if punitive awards of, for instance, $300,000 were commonly unjustified. But there is a long distance between legislated cap amounts, on the one hand, and the awards infamously given in the blockbuster cases, on the other. But because legislated caps are now triggered in non-blockbuster cases, they limit awards in a set of cases never shown to be problematic (e.g., Eisenberg and Wells 2006).

Available data also provide no confirmation for the arguments that juries or that state courts render the civil litigation system unreliable in favor of plaintiffs (Vidmar 1995; Vidmar and Rose 2001; Eisenberg et al. 2002; Eisenberg and Heise 2009; Eisenberg, Heise, and Wells 2010; Eisenberg et al. 2010). First, it is not the case that plaintiffs prevail before juries more often than in cases tried before judges. To the contrary, available data show that plaintiffs generally prevail in bench trials more often than in jury trials, and furthermore that tort plaintiffs in particular win more often before judges than they do before civil juries, and across every type of tort case over recent decades.[38] In federal court too, tort plaintiffs prevail more often in bench trials than they do in jury trials (54 to 46%).[39] Finally, according to a statistical analysis done by the National Center for State Courts, local and commercial "verdict reporters" that serve as a source for media reports of trends in jury verdicts and the size of awards systematically overstate the frequency with which civil plaintiffs prevail and the size of compensatory and punitive damage awards given by juries.[40]

Again, descriptive results like these do not *prove* anything decisively about the civil litigation system's reliability. Juries might be biased in favor of plaintiffs, and still find in favor of plaintiffs less often than judges do. The difficulty with comparing the results of jury trials with those of bench trials is that such comparisons assume everything else is equal. But of course everything else is not equal. Whether a case is tried by jury or by judge is not random, but rather depends upon both sides' preferences, reflecting their expectations about the relative advantages of each. Given that civil jury trial rights generally extend to defendants and plaintiffs alike, whenever a case is tried by jury, that is because one side or the other perceived a jury to be somehow advantageous to it.

On the other hand, if juries were *highly* biased in favor of plaintiffs, presumably plaintiffs would virtually always, rather than sometimes, exercise their jury trial rights, and would be expected to fare far better before juries. But rather than identify data supporting the view that juries are systematically unreliable, the critics instead rely on exceptional cases. Given such a claim, one would reasonably expect that plaintiffs win with juries both more often than they do, and more often than they do in bench trials. The fact that courts find in favor of plaintiffs more than juries do does not prove that the critics are wrong that the litigation system is unreliable, but it certainly casts some doubt on one way in which they might be right.

Nor do available data concerning damage awards rendered by juries and judges plainly support the claim that juries are unreliable in favor of plaintiffs. First, to generalize across categories of cases, the median damage award by juries is usually higher than the median bench award, but not by a great deal. And for some categories of torts cases, median awards given by judges are higher than median jury awards. In 2005, for example, median awards for medical malpractice in bench trials was $631,000 as compared with $400,000 for jury trials in which plaintiffs prevailed.[41] In addition, judges are about as likely, or for some types of cases more likely, to award punitive damages. On the other hand, punitive awards by courts instead of juries are usually for smaller amounts, especially at the upper end of the distribution.

On the whole, such results do not demonstrate jury bias (or judicial bias). Most of all, the differences just are not very great. Moreover, demonstrating jury bias requires analyzing the data inferentially, and controlling for other independent variables—including case types, venue, and types of litigants. Two teams of scholars have done so, but they reach different conclusions. Eisenberg et al. (2002) analyze the data to conclude that there is no significant difference between judges and juries with respect to punitive awards. Relying on the exact same data set, Hersch and Viscusi (2004) argue that juries are more likely to award punitive damages, and to award higher punitive damages as well. These different analyses reflect the authors' alternative approaches to categorizing and testing the data (see Eisenberg and Wells 2006, which provides a critique of the Hersch and Viscusi methodology). But as noted, Helland and Tabarrok's (2006) similar analysis concluded that differences between the damage awards made by judges and those made by juries are modest, and higher awards are not associated with juries so much as with low-income jurors. Thus, whether juries award higher punitive damages, holding everything else equal, is not perfectly clear, but again any differences do not appear to be great.

Other explorations of jury bias, beyond comparing jury results with the results in bench trials, also conclude that juries are not biased in favor of individual plaintiffs. For example, T. Baker's (2005) analysis of medical malpractice litigation, which surveys the research on jury bias utilizing various methodologies, concludes that, if anything, juries favor defendants in medical malpractice cases (see also Vidmar, MacKillop, and Lee 2006; Robertson and Yokum 2012). For another example, Hans's (2000) tests for anti-business bias in civil litigation generally—which considers especially cases by individual plaintiffs against business defendants—concludes that many jurors are, rather than especially sympathetic to individual plaintiffs, skeptical towards individual plaintiffs. Hans also concludes that juries only occasionally show any anti-business prejudice, and that the "deep pockets" hypothesis (according to which juries are inclined to assess high damages against defendants able to pay high awards) finds no evidence to support it. Vidmar's (1993, 1995) analyses of the deep-pockets hypothesis in medical malpractice specifically also rejects it. Those findings make unsurprising that, according to BJS data on contract cases, business plaintiffs prevail in cases against individual defendants more often than individual plaintiffs prevail in cases against business defendants.[42] Again, this finding does not itself disprove the critics' claim that juries are biased in favor of individuals and against businesses, but it certainly does not support the claim either.

Finally, the critics' suggestion that state courts are especially unreliable relative to federal courts also finds little empirical support. Available data show that it is not generally the case that tort plaintiffs fare better in state court than in federal court. Rather, plaintiffs are about as likely to win or lose in state court as in federal court. With respect to damages, median awards are comparable or higher for most every category of common law case, though this is almost certainly because cases brought in federal court tend to be larger, not because federal courts are friendlier to plaintiffs.[43]

As explained in chapter 1, in federal torts cases where jurisdiction is based on diversity, federal courts apply state tort law. So, the substantive law applied in both jurisdictions is the same, and makes the comparison between state and federal courts at least somewhat meaningful, although here again it is difficult to hold all else equal. But one practical difference between state and federal courts is the geography and size of jury pools; federal courts select jurors who reside in federal districts, which span many state counties, in contrast to state courts, which draw from counties or subdivisions of counties. Interestingly, however, expanding the size of jury pools does not appear to shrink the size of damage awards, given that damage awards in federal court are as large or larger than in state courts. While not too much should be made of this observation (among other reasons, given amount-in-controversy jurisdictional requirements in federal court), it is at odds with reformers' suggestion that more localized and insulated juries necessarily render higher damage awards because they are biased in favor of local plaintiffs.

Nor is it clear that federal judges themselves are more inclined to combat perceived flaws in the civil litigation system, or indeed that they believe the civil litigation is flawed in the ways the critics allege. According to a survey of federal district judges by the Federal Judicial Center (Rauma and Willging 2005), the overwhelming majority of judges do not believe that frivolous litigation is a problem. Seventy percent of responding judges called groundless litigation a "small" or "very small problem," while 15% said it was no problem at all. Three percent called it a "large" or "very large problem."

For several reasons, then, available data do not suggest that state courts or state juries are, on the whole, biased in favor of plaintiffs. None of this is to rule out the possibility that some states or specific state courts are friendlier to plaintiffs than others. But as a general proposition, states do not seem advantageous to plaintiffs. Moreover, the fact that plaintiffs will do better in certain state courts than in others proves very little by itself. Inevitably, there will be some jurisdictions where plaintiffs do the best. By the same token, there will be jurisdictions where plaintiffs will do the worst even holding the underlying substantive law the same. Of course, state substantive law, including the law governing remedies, varies from state to state, so for substantive reasons—as opposed to biases or other flaws in the civil litigation process—plaintiffs may prevail more often or receive higher damage awards across different jurisdictions. But all of this is the consequence of a large legal system with multiple jurisdictions. While the civil litigation process might be flawed in certain jurisdictions, the conclusion that the civil litigation system as a whole is unreliable requires evidence beyond the observation that plaintiffs may do better in some jurisdictions than in others.

Summary

The case for litigation reform that enjoys the most influence finds surprisingly little factual support. The critics often depend on high-profile cases to show how the civil litigation system is routinely unreliable, too friendly to plaintiffs, and too costly for defendants. But that dependence seems misplaced. On close inspection, those very cases usually provide poor illustrations of the critics' claims about what is wrong with civil litigation. Nor do available data about how civil cases are resolved support predictions generated by the critics' basic account of civil litigation. Plaintiffs do not routinely prevail, nor do they routinely see high damage awards or better treatment from juries as opposed to judges or from state courts as opposed to federal courts. To be sure, it is difficult to draw hard conclusions solely from descriptive statistics about how civil cases are resolved—absent both techniques for holding independent variables equal, and also some normative baseline for evaluating how often plaintiffs should win or lose or how much prevailing plaintiffs should receive; facts require some benchmark for their interpretation. But then the critics supply no such benchmarks, nor do they otherwise enlist systematic evidence to support their claims. While the civil litigation system might reward underserving plaintiffs in ways difficult to detect (and not persuasively articulated by the critics), the available facts do not seem to support such a contention.

The following chapter considers the extent to which the litigation system is more likely characterized not by excessive access and inadequate reliability, but instead by inadequate accessibility—for reasons many critics should recognize—and whether it is inaccessible especially for potential litigants who have suffered genuine but moderate legal injury.

6

Real Threats to Civil Justice

Chapter 5 showed that a familiar and influential critique of the civil litigation system does not find supportive evidence in proportion to its influence. Yet even so, the system may be far from perfect. This chapter suggests that a serious threat to civil justice is not the litigation system's excessive accessibility, but, rather, its frequent inaccessibility. That is, there are good reasons to suppose that the civil litigation system is often undesirably inaccessible.

And the civil litigation system seems likely to be inaccessible for reasons the critics emphasize. Litigation is costly. The critics are in one important sense right that the costs of litigation often can exceed its expected yield. One deep tension in the critics' argument, however—one never resolved—is found in the twin premises that litigation is inexpensive for plaintiffs (who are therefore able bring so many meritless cases) *and* expensive for defendants (who therefore are forced to spend too much litigating or else to settle cases brought in bad faith). But because plaintiffs and defendants litigate according to the same rules and procedures, it is not clear why high litigation costs would be problematic primarily for, or especially for, defendants.

For whenever litigation costs are high, good-faith potential plaintiffs, with claims that would likely be meritorious, might be priced out of civil litigation—unable to secure legal representation at all perhaps, or unable to mount a complete case or to litigate fully against nuisance defenses, for example. One corollary of this observation is that small potential litigants—those with moderate expected compensatory damages—seem most likely to be priced out of access to the courts. And while high litigation costs no doubt affect the extent to which the civil litigation system is accessible both for plaintiffs and defendants alike, such costs may be a greater problem for plaintiffs, who must cover certain costs in order to commence a case at all and, relatedly, who bear certain procedural and evidentiary burdens in order to advance a case.

But this is just to say again that the critics' partial focus on litigation costs is, if uneven, well placed. Moreover, even for those who can afford to litigate—including of course defendants defending against modest claims—litigation costs should be reduced wherever doing so is practicable and does not unreasonably jeopardize the litigation system's reliability. In other words, litigation reformers need not choose between promoting greater access, on the one hand, and controlling high litigation costs, on the other hand. Those projects are reinforcing. Nor is there any contradiction between making the litigation system more accessible for small claimants *and* less costly for large defendants. As this chapter will show, there are strong reasons to think that many deserving parties lack access to the courts, *and* that litigation costs—both costs generated in bad faith and costs that are simply wasteful—could be better controlled for all litigants. Later, part 3 will propose a number of reforms responsive to both issues.

Litigation Costs and Access to the Courts

As explained in chapter 1, a potential plaintiff able to satisfy the burden of persuasion on a legally cognizable claim by demonstrating harm with admissible evidence may have a legally viable case. Given that litigation is not costless, however, the crucial question becomes whether that case is *economically* viable; legally cognizable injuries must be demonstrable at a cost that does not exceed the expected benefits. Thus, the costs of litigation constrain a potential claimant's ability to initiate a case. Because litigation is seldom cheap, potential litigants with shallow pockets in particular may find it very difficult to advance their potential claims.

Among litigation costs, legal representation is often the greatest (e.g., Kritzer et al. 1984). Preparing and litigating a civil case can take many hours—from dozens of hours in the simplest cases and hundreds of hours in factually and legally complicated cases. An attorney's hourly rate might range widely, from $50 an hour to well over several hundred dollars an hour, depending on the legal subject matter and the relevant legal market. That means significant costs for each stage of a civil case, from the work leading to the filing of a complaint, through motion practice, discovery, pretrial, and possibly trial.

Attorneys typically require clients to enter into a contractual retainer agreement, and to pay an initial lump-sum fee when an attorney agrees to represent a client, who is then billed periodically during the course of representation. Clients are expected to pay for representation during the course of a case, which not surprisingly means the longer a case proceeds, the more expensive it becomes. Civil discovery is expensive in large part because it is time-consuming for attorneys, who among other things must prepare for and conduct or defend depositions, each one of which can easily consume dozens of hours of time. Thus, attorneys' fees can quickly total thousands of dollars for each stage of a civil case. In complex cases involving sophisticated parties, the cost of legal representation can easily exceed tens or hundreds of thousands of dollars. Potential parties unable to bear such costs will be unlikely to secure legal representation.

Contingency-based attorneys' fees provide some potential claimants with an alternative to paying for legal representation by the hour (see generally Kritzer 1998, 2004). According to a typical contingency-fee arrangement, the lawyer receives one third of whatever the plaintiff recovers, and only if the plaintiff recovers (e.g., Hyman, Black, and Silver 2014 (collecting sources)). Contingency contracts thus allow plaintiffs to finance a substantial source of the costs of litigating against the expected return on litigation. These contracts are regulated by state legal ethics codes that prohibit lawyers from entering into contingency-fee contracts for compensation above some maximum percentage of the client's recovery. State ethics boards only cap contingency-fee percentages, however; they do not impose specific percentages. At the bottom end, contingency-fee percentages are limited by what lawyers are willing to accept in exchange for their services. Sometimes, contingency-fee contracts will provide for two different percentages, a lower one—such as 20 or 25%—for cases that are resolved early because, for example, they settle out of court quickly before most of the preparation for a trial has been done, and a larger percentage—usually 33%—for cases that proceed far into the discovery process or to trial.

As chapter 4 observed, contingency fees are a favorite object of litigation reform. According to the critics, plaintiffs' lawyers may take meritless cases in bad faith hoping, in effect, to win a lottery. Not one of those cases is likely to make much profit for the lawyer, but as long as the lawyer recovers handsomely once in a while, that is enough to encourage lottery litigation. Thus, the argument goes, the contingency-fee arrangement fuels too much accessibility, and by the wrong kinds of plaintiffs.

But that argument does not find factual support (Eisenberg and Miller 2004, 2005), and it ignores an important feature of the contingency-fee arrangement, which is that somebody—in particular, the contingency-fee attorney—must incur the costs (including the opportunity costs) of litigating unsuccessful cases. This observation shows the illogic of the claim that contingency fees promote lottery litigation (accord Inselbuch 2001). As explained in chapter 4, although contingency-fee cases are often analogized to lotteries, contingency-fee lawyers are unlike lottery players in important ways. Unlike lottery purchasers, contingency-fee litigators do not gamble for entertainment, nor do they systematically misunderstand their chances of prevailing in a case. Indeed, they are severely punished economically for miscalculating their chances of success. They take economic risks, yes, but the risks they take are calculated risks with positive net expected returns. Contingency-fee gamblers, and those who calculate risks poorly, do not survive over time.

Consequently, contingency-fee plaintiffs' lawyers agree to represent only a very small percentage of prospective clients who come through their doors. They accept a tiny percentage of prospective clients in part because most individuals who solicit their services have, economically speaking, bad cases. Even if their harm is one that the law recognizes, still a legally injured person will generally be unable to find legal representation unless the size of his legal injury is substantial (e.g., R. Abel 2006). This follows from the high costs of litigation.

To illustrate, there are few competent plaintiffs' lawyers who would take a contestable but strong medical malpractice case where the potential damages totaled much less than $200,000. At first blush, $200,000 may seem like a lot. For the injured party, that amount could represent several years of lost employment, or considerable pain and suffering, or some combination thereof. But against the prospect of recovering such an amount, a lawyer who considers representing such a person must weigh the costs of bringing a successful case. Of course, the $200,000 is not assured in a contestable case; the plaintiff might lose even a very strong case given that the civil litigation system is not perfectly reliable. Thus, the costs of litigation must be balanced against the expected benefits of recovery—$200,000 discounted by the chance that the plaintiff will ultimately prevail. Assume, for example, that there is a 65% chance that a given medical malpractice plaintiff with $200,000 of easily demonstrable damages will prevail at trial, 65% because the case is quite strong. The expected award from trial—to be divided between client and lawyer—is thus $130,000, an amount that constitutes the expected benefit from litigating ($200,000 multiplied by a 65% chance of prevailing).

One difficulty is that the costs of litigating the case could easily consume much of the expected benefit. If the suit were ultimately successful, the lawyer would stand to receive $66,000 ($200,000 award multiplied by the 33% contingency fee, assuming it comes out of the total award), and thus the attorney's expected benefit from the case is $42,900 ($66,000 in fees multiplied by a 65% chance of prevailing). The potential client's expected benefit given a successful suit is $87,100 (that is, the $200,000 award minus $66,000 in fees, multiplied by 65%). Thus, for the plaintiff to receive any benefit from the litigation, the plaintiff's out-of-pocket litigation costs must not exceed $87,000—that is, before discounting for the prospective plaintiff's risk-aversion to paying out-of-pocket litigation expenses (win or lose) against the chance of recovering $87,000. If the attorney bears those out-of-pocket expenses instead off the top, they would have to total less than $43,000 just for the attorney to break even before adjusting further for the attorney's lost time dedicated to the case.

And the costs of such a case are likely to be significant, and can easily run in the dozens of thousands of dollars. Medical malpractice cases require a plaintiff to show that the defendant violated a standard of medical care. This, in turn, requires the plaintiff first to establish what the applicable standard of medical care was, and then to show how the defendant deviated from it. In addition, the plaintiff must demonstrate his damages. Carrying this burden of proof typically requires expert medical testimony; such matters are beyond the ordinary knowledge of judges and jurors. Consequently, medical malpractice litigation typically requires retaining and paying medical experts, often more than one, who provide expert reports and serve as deposition and trial witnesses. As their hourly fees typically run several hundred dollars, expert witness fees can thus quickly total dozens of thousands of dollars. Taken together with the other, routine costs of civil litigation, litigation costs can quickly approach the size of the expected damage award.

Thus the recent report "Estimating the Cost of Civil Litigation," from the Court Statistics Project at the National Center for State Courts (NCSC), concludes based on survey data that the median costs for a medical malpractice case—counting *only* the attorney's time (typical hours expended multiplied by average hourly rate) plus expert witness fees—is $122,000, to which out-of-pocket expenses must be added as well (Hannaford-Agor and Waters 2013). For this reason, many plaintiffs' attorneys will not take medical malpractice cases unless the prospective plaintiff suffered some permanent, debilitating injury. Litigating to recover for permanent but minor injuries, or likewise for major but temporary injuries, often is simply not economically feasible. This explains why, as noted in chapter 5, nearly all litigated medical malpractice cases involve death or permanent injury. Contingency fees—as a mechanism for financing the costs of legal representation in cases where litigation is ultimately cost-justified—do not alter the underlying rationality of pursuing a case or not, nor are contingency contracts very useful for small potential plaintiffs. If the expected benefits of litigation are low relative to the total costs, plaintiffs' attorneys will not be inclined to take such a case on contingency.

Attorneys' fees aside, the out-of-pocket costs associated with civil litigation can be prohibitive as well. As noted earlier, those expenses include, among others, court-filing fees, and the costs associated with investigating a case, interviewing witnesses, taking depositions of parties and witnesses, producing and reviewing documents, and enlisting the testimony of experts. Such costs too can quickly exceed the expected return on litigation, even for strong claims brought in good faith. According to the NCSC study, discovery constitutes the second most costly stage of a case that goes through trial, and the most costly stage of a case not litigated through trial (Hannaford-Agor and Waters 2013).

For example, as noted, expert witnesses, like attorneys, require hourly compensation, both for the preparation of any report or testimony and for testimony in a deposition, hearing, or trial (and expert witnesses, for ethical reasons, may not be paid on contingency). Depositions require payment for court reporter services, as well as prepared transcripts following a deposition. Document production requires a document management system, and civil litigation thus typically requires the services of paralegal professionals, whose services further add to the costs of litigation. And so on. In short, civil litigation commonly requires parties to incur a number of out-of-pocket costs, in addition to the costs of legal representation, in order to advance a case. While the costs of litigation are susceptible to exaggeration, as noted in chapter 5 and as demonstrated in Reda's (2012) excellent work, litigation in all but routine cases is commonly costly, and its costs can exceed its expected benefits (see generally Black et al. 2008; Willging and Lee 2010; Lee and Willging 2010a, 2010b; Hannaford-Agor and Waters 2013).

Contingency-fee contracts may provide that a lawyer accepting a case on contingency will also bear the risk of out-of-pocket expenses, though in practice, this varies. That is, depending on the specific arrangement, an attorney might bill the client for all out-of-pocket expenses as the case progresses, or instead recoup them if and only if the client ultimately collects a favorable judgment. But in either case, the higher these overhead litigation costs are, the fewer potential plaintiffs will be able to initiate cases—either because they will be unable to pay them (when the client has to absorb them), or because their attorneys will be unwilling to take smaller cases (when the lawyer agrees to absorb them instead, thus reducing the expected net benefit of a case for the lawyer).

Thus for rather straightforward economic reasons, the cost of litigation necessarily limits access to the civil litigation system. The higher the minimum litigation costs required to initiate a claim or defense, the higher the expected (private) benefits of a case must be in order to justify them. Or put differently, the lower the expected benefits of litigation, the sooner litigation costs will overtake those benefits such that potential parties will effectively be priced out of the civil litigation system. For a given level of *minimum* costs necessary to mount a claim at all, then, a corresponding level of expected benefits is necessary for litigation to be cost-justified.

This observation raises empirical questions about when minimum litigation costs in fact exceed the benefits of litigation, and for which types of claims. In other words, across different types of civil cases, at what thresholds do actual minimum litigation costs overtake the average expected benefits of litigating, such that strong claims are never brought? While in general, and with some variation across types of cases, the costs of litigation appear to exceed what most ordinary individuals can finance themselves (American Bar Association 1984, 2009; Hannaford-Agor and Waters 2013), more empirical work (like Black et al. 2008; Silver and Hyman 2009; and updates to Trubek et al. 1983; and Kakalik and Pace 1986) is necessary to determine at what point, and in which types of cases, litigation becomes unaffordable relative to its expected benefits.

The Likely Distribution of Access

Given the significant costs of litigation, one would expect some legal harms to go un-remedied. This would seem likely not only for the impecunious, but for many others as well; many may lack access to any legal representation whatsoever, no matter how deserving their legal claims might be. One might likewise expect that much of the high-stakes litigation is generally conducted by parties who can afford to pay litigation's substantial costs.

There is some evidence supporting these expectations. For example, the legal needs of poor individuals—defined as those earning less than 125% of the income level that constitutes poverty—go mostly unmet. According to a well-known American Bar Association (ABA) study (1994, 1995, 1996), and surveys by the Legal Services Corporation (2005, 2009) and state bar organizations, the poor routinely have genuine legal needs yet lack legal representation. This finding is confirmed by many others (e.g., Brodoff 2008; Houseman 1998, 2009; Houseman and Perle 2007; Rhode 2004a, 2004c, 2009; Sandefur and Smyth 2011). Here "legal needs" include issues that give rise to legal interests and potential legal claims even if they may well not require filing a case. For example, problems with creditors, insurance companies, landlords, and utility companies commonly constitute legal needs. In addition, real estate transactions, employment problems, and tax difficulties also create legal needs.

When the poor do find legal assistance, they often do so through organizations that receive funds from the federally chartered Legal Services Corporation. LSC is the largest single source of funds for low-income representation, contributing approximately 30% of all funds to entities providing legal aid, distributed geographically according to census results. States also provide between 20 and 25% of total funding for legal assistance, most of which is financed through court fees and fines. In addition, IOLTA funds—interest on lawyer trust accounts, in which attorneys are required to pool funds they hold on behalf of their clients—comprise another some 17% of legal assistance funds, though the amount has decreased in recent years given recent interest rates. Private donations, including financial contributions from lawyers, comprise some 10% or so of funding for legal assistance. State-specific access-to-justice initiatives provide modest but significant support for representation as well.

Federal funding for the Legal Services Corporation has totaled between $300 and $400 million dollars a year, with considerable fluctuation over the years and a substantial decline in recent years. This amount represents approximately half of the inflation-adjustment amount of LSC funding in 1980 (Houseman 2009). In very rough dollar terms, spending on civil legal assistance for low-income persons from all sources totals approximately $600 million per year, which leaves many legal needs unmet. In addition, as noted in chapter 4, by statute LSC funds cannot be used for certain types of cases at all, including class action cases, prisoner claims, claims by illegal and certain legal aliens, and civil rights cases involving abortion or legislative redistricting cases—restrictions that apply to all LSC-funded organizations.

Responding to this lack of access, the American Bar Association strongly encourages its members to undertake some amount of pro bono representation, and state bar organizations encourage or require their members to devote a certain amount of time to pro bono representation as well. In part as a consequence, there are programs that provide unpaid representation to those who cannot afford it that do not draw from legal aid funding sources. There are dozens of programs providing legal assistance to the poor affiliated with private charities as well.

Still, there is little doubt that all of these, taken together, provide representation for only a small fraction of low-income persons with legitimate legal needs. For example, LSC-funded organizations report that for every client they accept, they reject another with a legally worthwhile claim (Legal Services Corporation 2005, 2009). Given LSC's finite resources, this amounts to approximately 1 million cases in each category, against a backdrop of over 20 million low-income households in the U.S. and some 60 million persons eligible for LSC-funded assistance, many of whom never seek it in the first place. As another measure of access to legal representation among low-income persons, there is one attorney employed by any legal aid organization for every 6,900 persons below the poverty line, against a background of one attorney for every 525 people in the United States. Even where legal aid organizations undertake representation, limited resources often require them to advocate on behalf of a client informally, without filing a case in court. Representation for the poor, where it is provided, often does not translate into full access to the courts.

This state of affairs is undesirable, given the potential social benefits associated with legal representation for the poor, as noted in chapter 2. While proponents of legal aid have historically based the argument in favor of greater commitment to legal representation for the impecunious instead on the grounds that, for some category of cases, the poor should be entitled to representation, the argument here does not depend on any notion of entitlement. Nor are legal services best understood as a matter of charity or goodwill. Instead, good-faith civil litigation on behalf of the poor is desirable because it creates social benefits, such as reducing homelessness and domestic violence. Quantifying such benefits may be difficult (L. Abel 2010; Prescott 2010; Greiner and Pattanayak 2012), but their existence seems clear (Murphy 2002; Farmer and Tiefenthaler 2003; Elwart et al. 2006; Boyle and Chiu 2007; L. Abel 2009, 2010; Abel and Vignola 2010; Sandefur 2010; see also Worcel, Finigan, and Allen 2009; Finigan et al. 2010 (collecting sources)).

The problem of unmet legal needs is not at all limited to the poor, however. According to the original 1994 ABA study, roughly half of all U.S. households have one legal need per year, while another quarter have two or more per year. According to the surveys of the sixteen states included in LSC's 2007 and 2009 studies, legal needs per household ranged from 1.1 to 3.5 per year, and there is little difference between low- and moderate-income households with respect to their legal needs. The ABA study concluded that only 20% of all household legal needs are handled by an attorney or legal aid employee; 80% are not, a finding reinforced by subsequent analyses (Cantril 1996) and follow-on state surveys (e.g., State Bar of Wisconsin 2007).

Individuals with moderate levels of income thus are not much better represented than those with low income, and often worse. In fact, given that those above modest income levels are not eligible for assistance by legal aid organizations—LSC funds come with maximum income eligibility requirements, as do other sources of legal-assistance funding— middle-class individuals in particular often lack legal representation. As a result, like many low-income citizens, they rely on self-help and self-representation to address their needs, though there is some evidence that moderate-income persons seek legal representation or advice more often than do low-income persons, albeit sometimes from non-lawyers (American Bar Association 1994, 2006). For such individuals, the availability of legal representation depends on contingency-fee arrangements or the possibility of recoverable attorneys' fees. When litigation costs are too great—relative to the size of expected benefits of a case—to make contingency-fee representation impractical, and recoverable fees are not available, prospective litigants are most unlikely to find legal representation. They will therefore lack access to the courts.

In concrete terms, this means that many non-poor individuals with small contracts cases, torts cases, consumer cases, civil rights cases, or other types of good-faith civil claims—that is, those with strong potential claims on the merits but for whom expected monetary recovery would be modest—likely enjoy little access (e.g., Rhode 2004a, 2009; Hadfield 2000, 2010). Although they might be expected to prevail in a reliable civil litigation system, the problem is that the expected benefit of their cases might total only thousands, or in the very low tens of thousands, of dollars. The modest expected values of their claims mean that the costs of traditional civil litigation are likely to exceed the benefits of litigating. Nor do contingency fees help, as plaintiffs' lawyers too will calculate that a case worth only a few thousand dollars or so, even if strong on the merits, is not justified against the required investment (e.g., Silver and Hyman 2009). Such would-be plaintiffs cannot advance their claims in small claims courts either, because the jurisdictional limits of small claims court are usually too low.

While again it is difficult to quantify the number of would-be plaintiffs in this category, no doubt there is a significant gap between cases small enough to satisfy jurisdictional limitations of small claims court, on the one hand, and cases large enough to be worth the costs of traditional civil litigation, on the other hand. Those with potential claims within that gap are likely to lack access to the civil litigation system. Or, given that the cost of representation usually constitutes the highest cost for potential plaintiffs, many pursing a claim may have to rely on self-representation. And indeed, in both state and federal court, pro se cases are very common. For one example, of the some 285,000 civil cases filed in federal court in 2013, over 77,000 were pro se cases (the overwhelming majority of which were not prisoner cases).[1]

Given the benefits of litigation—including the social benefits—this state of affairs is undesirable. Thus experts on civil litigation who have emphasized insufficient access to justice (e.g., Rhode 2004a, 2009; A. Miller 2010, 2013) are on target. In fact, one might generalize that a lack of meaningful access to court for small would-be plaintiffs means that modest legal injuries often are not remedied at all (notwithstanding Greiner and Pattanayak's (2012) important cautions), a consequence not likely lost on parties whose behavior or activities may lead to only small legal harms.

Then there are those who can afford legal representation. Some potential litigants can secure representation through contingency-fee contracts, because plaintiffs' attorneys calculate that the expected benefits of a claim are high enough to warrant the overhead litigation costs and the costs of the attorney's time. Another set of potential litigants pay for legal representation by the hour, which they find cost-justified against the expected benefits of their claims. These parties include wealthy individuals, who may retain lawyers to protect their financial interests or to settle property disputes. Much more often, though, it is business entities that can afford hourly representation to advance their legal interests.

As chapter 1 observed, contract cases—rather than tort cases, employment cases, class actions, environmental cases, and so on—constitute the majority of all general civil cases, although calls for litigation reform oddly do not focus on this most common kind of general civil litigation at all (accord Nockleby 2007). Setting aside very small claims, many contract cases involve business entities as parties. For example, approximately one-third of all contracts cases in federal court are insurance cases. These are disputes that often concern how the costs of insured risks are allocated between or among insurance companies. For another example, the single largest category of a contracts case that proceeds to trial in state courts involves a plaintiff who was the seller of some good or service which gave rise to a suit, typically a business enterprise.[2] Individual parties commonly litigate small contracts disputes as well, but contracts cases worth litigating fully very frequently involve business enterprises.

Beyond contracts cases, businesses are frequent litigators more generally. This observation is not surprising, but it warrants emphasis. Not only are the costs of litigation often prohibitive for individual litigants (e.g., Hadfield 2000; Rhode 2009), those costs are more economically born by litigation's repeat players, and businesses are far more often repeat litigators (Hadfield 2005). As a result, typically only business entities can afford to litigate where those costs are substantial, and accordingly business firms populate large civil cases (Blasi 2004). Moreover, areas of the law that have seen a growth in litigation in recent years, that growth owes in part to increased litigation initiated by business entities (Dunworth and Rogers 1996). Indeed, substantial evidence shows that, over recent years, business entities have consumed an increasing share of the universe of legal services, whether measured by the proportion of attorneys whose work serves corporate clients or by total expenditures on legal services (Galanter 2006; extending Galanter 1974)). Business litigators also often succeed, prevailing against individual litigants far more often than the other way around, with the largest corporations doing especially well (Eisenberg and Farber 1997; Dunworth and Rogers 1996).

Even civil cases that nominally involve individual parties often are litigated only because individuals have an insurance policy—for their health, automobile, or property—and the cost of litigating is economically justified for their insurance carriers or creditors, not the individual policyholders themselves. In other words, data about the frequency with which individuals appear as named as parties in a civil case filing overstate the extent to which individuals themselves litigate or exclusively stand to gain as a result of the outcome of a case. Such nominally individual litigation often is undertaken because it is cost-justified to the insurance companies whose policies are implicated.

To be very clear, business litigation is not only a legitimate but also a socially valuable mechanism for resolving disputes. Contract litigation serves many important and beneficial purposes, as chapter 2 argued. Fundamentally, it is how contract terms are specified and standardized, and makes contracting possible by giving contracting parties confidence that their rights will be respected. The same is true for commercial litigation generally. Commercial litigation provides a means for allocating legal risks, and its very availability facilitates the enterprise of business, an invaluable social function.

But the immediate point is that, among those with legal needs, large business entities and other large parties are over-represented in the civil litigation system, and not surprisingly. They more often have the wherewithal, relative to most individuals and small enterprises, to secure legal representation—and the size of their claims, especially given their susceptibility to large economic harms owing to their size, justifies the costs of advancing them. While the civil litigation system is formally open to all, as a practical matter it is not equally accessible to all, a gap that some worry has grown greater in recent years (A. Miller 2010, 2013). Reforms that would render the system more accessible, not less—and in particular more accessible to parties with modest claims—and most especially reforms that would promote greater accessibility without undermining the system's reliability, would seem to be in order.

Excessive Litigation Revisited

A central element of the critics' account of the civil litigation system—its excessive costs—warrants still more exploration. The fact that many lack access to the courts does not mean that the costs of litigation could not be better contained for those who enjoy access. And, the litigation system, even if often reliable, still might resolve cases at a cost that is too great, or that could at least be minimized. Again, sound reform need not choose between promoting greater access to justice, on the one hand, and containing litigation costs, on the other hand; these two can be harmonious. The case for curbing litigation costs applies with special force, moreover, to litigation expenditures that do not promote the civil litigation system's reliability.

That is, among litigation costs, some enhance the system's reliability—by clarifying relevant factual or legal issues and thereby fostering the correct resolution of those issues. For example, the costs expended on a legal brief may purchase the articulation of a party's legal position, and therefore promote assessment of the legal strength of that party's case. For another example, the costs expended on expert testimony may purchase clarification of the scientific, medical, or economic strength of a litigant's position, and thus illuminates the strength of that party's factual arguments. Similarly, the costs of depositions may purchase a better understanding of evidence potentially relevant to a case, including the strength of an opposing litigant's case. After all, this is largely why litigants incur such costs—to advance their case by demonstrating the strength of their position and exposing the weaknesses of opposing positions. So while litigation may be expensive, and while reformers are right to highlight the problem of excessive litigation costs, litigation expenditures very often buy something of significant value, advancing the system's reliability. Provided that those costs are commensurate with the stakes of contested issues, reliability-enhancing litigation costs may be altogether desirable, as necessary to vindicate deserving legal claims.

Imagine instead a civil litigation system without motions, briefs, discovery, and most other trappings of the litigation process. Such a system would be very inexpensive. But without the rigors associated with ordinary civil litigation, such a system would likely also be less reliable. A civil litigation system where the outcomes of cases were determined simply by a coin toss would be very cheap indeed, but utterly unreliable and therefore unattractive. Insofar as the common features of civil litigation, though costly, allow litigants useful opportunities to demonstrate the merits of their cases, again the costs associated with them come with important offsetting benefits on which the litigation system's reliability depends. From this point of view, promoting more exacting evidentiary standards in civil litigation, such as ensuring the scientific rigor of expert witness testimony, may be desirable towards promoting more reliable results. Again, so long as those costs are commensurate with the issues at stake—that is, so long as they do not swamp the stakes of the issues involved—litigation costs might bring offsetting benefits large enough to be justified.

Sometimes, however, litigation expenditures do not clarify the issues at stake in a case at all. Indeed, sometimes litigation costs are expended in order to obfuscate the issues at stake, potentially compromising the civil litigation system's reliability. Litigation costs also are sometimes imposed on opposing parties to discourage them from litigating, or from litigating further. Examples are familiar. Unscrupulous experts can mislead courts and juries with dubious testimony that requires costly rebuttal from credible experts. Document dumps during civil discovery can needlessly run up litigation costs for an opposing party by requiring the opposition to spend many hours sifting through irrelevant documents and by effectively hiding relevant documents through voluminous disclosures. Excessive motion practice can both confound courts and raise opposing parties' litigation costs unnecessarily. And so on.

Litigation costs can be excessive in another way as well. Apart from costs generated in bad faith in order to discourage an opposing party from litigating further or to obfuscate relevant issues, some litigation costs may be wasteful. That is, sometimes they may be poor investments even for the party generating them. Furthermore, because litigation decisions by one side to a case typically require the other side to incur costs as well—for example, requests for documents require the other side to produce the documents, and likewise depositions held by one side require the other side to prepare for and attend them—parties lack adequate incentives to make the right marginal decisions about when litigation costs are justified and when they are not. In short, litigants not only sometimes make poor decisions about when to incur litigation costs, but they also can impose on each other part of the costs of wasteful litigation, compounding the problem. That litigants commonly do not internalize fully the costs of their decisions implies a tendency to generate wasteful litigation expenditures. Figure 6.1 specifies these possibilities.

The most fundamental distinction here is between litigation expenditures that enhance the civil litigation system's reliability, and those that do not. Reliability-enhancing expenditures are preferable to those that do not enhance reliability, for obvious reasons. Among reliability-enhancing costs, those commensurate with the stakes of a given issue constitute well-justified litigation costs. Those not commensurate with the stakes of an issue may be poorly spent—that is, not cost-justified— though they may be still useful in that they promote reliable outcomes. Expenditures that are not reliability-enhancing are undesirable. Among them, those generated to obscure relevant legal or factual issues are the most undesirable. Those that do not enhance reliability, though unintentionally so, constitute wasteful but not malicious costs.

To be sure, the hard part is distinguishing, within any given case, reliability-enhancing litigation costs, on the one hand, from reliability-undermining and simply wasteful litigation costs, on the other hand.

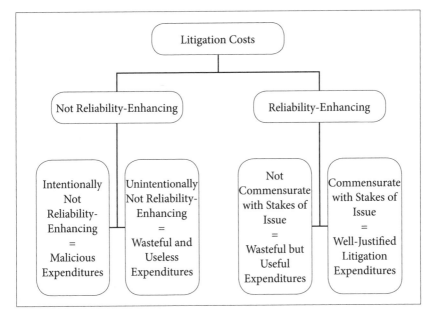

Figure 6.1. Typology of Litigation Costs

Still more difficult may be further distinguishing the subspecies of these, though at times it will be clear (at least retrospectively) that a litigant generated costs that intentionally did not enhance the system's reliability. The challenge is that litigants can always argue that their actions are necessary or at least reasonable to advance their case aggressively, even if they appear to be overkill. As there is no sure way to distinguish litigation costs generated in good faith from those generated in bad faith, discouraging reliability-compromising litigation costs can be difficult in practice.

But as part 3 will explore in more detail, litigation costs might be allocated, or more precisely reallocated, in ways designed to reduce undesirable litigation, both the initiation of bad-faith claims or defenses in the first place, and undesirable marginal litigation as well. One way to discourage litigants from generating litigation costs that are not reliability-enhancing, and likewise costs that needlessly require opposing litigants to incur higher costs, is to require litigants to internalize more of the wasteful litigation costs they generate, especially but not only maliciously. In short, litigation costs can be reallocated to reduce undesirable litigation decisions. Parties forced to internalize wasteful costs will be deterred from generating them in the first place, including costs generated at the margins of cases filed or defended in good faith.

To anticipate that analysis very briefly, parties can be made to internalize poor decisions to generate wasteful litigation costs by being made to cover more of such costs on an ex-post basis. That is to say, a losing party, by virtue of having lost, may be required to bear some of the costs otherwise incurred by the prevailing party. To the extent a litigant anticipates that losing will bring higher costs, that party will be less inclined to generate litigation costs to advance what prove to be losing positions. The current litigation system already imposes some pay-to-lose costs. But as chapters 9 and 10 will argue, further discouraging litigants from generating excess litigation costs—through retrospective and carefully administered reallocation of them—would be desirable. What is more, there is room within the rules governing the civil litigation process to address excessive litigation costs.

Summary

So which is it? Is the existing civil litigation system plagued by too little litigation, given the barriers to access for certain would-be litigants and the beneficial externalities associated with litigation? Or is there too much litigation, given that litigants have inadequate incentives to make sound decisions about litigation expenditures, especially considering that they externalize some costs on their opponents? The answer is both. There are reasons to conclude that the civil litigation system is not sufficiently accessible to certain parties—those for whom the costs of litigation exceed its benefits—whose legal harms therefore go unremedied, and that the social benefits that would flow from more complete enforcement of the law's obligations thus remain unrealized. At the same time, litigants who enjoy access to the courts seem likely to over-litigate, at least whenever they have insufficient incentives to avoid wasteful and potentially malicious litigation costs, some of which are born by their opponents. Thus the civil litigation system can be characterized at once both by too little and by too much litigation; some desirable cases will not be brought at all, and some cases will be litigated farther than is desirable. These worries are compatible. Part 3 addresses both.

PART III

Reform

To recount recent steps, part 2 argued that the most common and influential criticisms of the civil litigation system seem overstated and do not easily comport with what is known about who litigates or how most civil cases end. Even so, critics' concerns about the costs of litigation seem well placed, and these concerns will be addressed in the next two chapters, even if the critics' observation that high costs are problematic for defendants tells only half of the story. High litigation costs are relevant for plaintiffs and would-be plaintiffs too, especially those with valid legal claims but not high expected damages who, for that reason, will have difficulty securing legal representation and finding access to the courts. Indeed, because plaintiffs are by definition the first movers in litigation, it is reasonable to expect that high litigation costs are especially problematic for them, recognizing as well that once a case is initiated, high litigation costs burden defendants too. Meanwhile, parties who enjoy access to the courts may lack adequate incentives to discourage them from generating litigation costs that are wasteful, or from externalizing litigation costs on their opponents in undesirable ways. The civil litigation system is not at all beyond improvement, then, especially if there are achievable ways to promote greater access to the courts *and* to lower litigation costs for those who have it.

If these general points are more right than wrong—and they are— they raise the following questions: What could be done to discourage all forms of bad-faith litigation as well as over-litigation? And what steps could be taken to provide greater access to the courts for those currently priced out of the civil litigation system?

The balance of this book proposes a variety of reforms to reduce litigation costs and increase access, and thereby advance the aspirations of civil justice. To foreshadow core prescriptive themes, the pages that follow call for: (1) expanded procedural tools to filter undesirable cases from the litigation system altogether; (2) the reallocation of litigation costs on those who make poor decisions to litigate, in particular poor marginal decisions to litigate cases already underway; (3) the development of more types of civil proceedings that are commensurate with varying size and stakes, including among others the creation of a new "court of medium claims"; and (4) greater support for access to the courts in the form of cross-subsidies across classes of litigants.

Chapters 7 and 8 take up litigation costs. Such costs might be reduced in three basic ways. One is simply to avoid litigation outright, to discourage the filing of cases in the first place; claims never aired do not cost anything. But given the private and social benefits generated from litigation, litigation should be avoided altogether only for litigants bringing nuisance claims, lottery claims, or other categorical forms of bad-faith claims or defenses. Because civil justice is not served by those who litigate in bad faith, discouraging such litigation altogether is desirable. Accordingly, chapter 7 proposes a number of ways to do so, including subjecting claims to greater initial scrutiny, in part through mechanisms that some critics of civil litigation favor.

For all other litigants—those who advance claims or defenses in good faith—litigation costs might be reduced either by lowering the more or less "fixed costs" of traditional litigation—costs that litigants must incur in order to advance a claim at all—or by encouraging litigants to litigate less extensively by lowering the more or less "variable costs" of litigation over which they have some control. Put differently, litigation costs can be reduced by lowering not just its "price" but also its "quantity consumed." Chapter 8 proposes ways to discourage parties from "consuming" too much litigation—that is to say, from making poor decisions to generate litigation costs for themselves and their opponents at the margin of a case already underway. By requiring parties to internalize more of the *marginal* costs of their decisions to litigate, parties are likely to litigate less extensively, and thus will lower the costs of litigation for their opponents as well. Chapter 8 proposes qualified versions of "pay to lose"—or what might be more accurately called "pay to impose"—in order to incentivize parties to make better litigation decisions at the margin of a case.

Turning to accessibility, two general approaches would render the civil litigation system within reach for more potential litigants. One is simply to make litigation cheaper. To the extent litigation is less expensive on the "supply side," more potential parties could afford access. In that sense, any reform rendering litigation less expensive will promote access. Another approach, on the "demand" or "finance" side, is to provide more resources for litigants or potential litigants. In other words, even holding the costs of litigation constant, greater access can be promoted by providing would-be litigants with more support to cover those costs.

Chapters 9 and 10 recommend both approaches. Chapter 9 proposes increased use of litigation procedures substantially less costly than traditional civil litigation. Most importantly, chapter 9 proposes the establishment of new "medium claims" courts, partially analogous to small claims courts but tailored to cases too large for small claims yet not large enough to justify the costs associated with traditional litigation. In the same vein, chapter 9 also proposes expanded use of small claims courts and experimentation with "small claims juries," greater adoption of new forms of "summary" or "expedited" trial procedures, and more generally the use, in all cases, of procedures tailored to the stakes of a given individual case—all in the interest of increasing access by providing less costly modes of litigation. Turning to the finance side of access, chapter 10 proposes several forms of greater support to potential litigants, including certain cross-subsidies among classes of civil litigants and their attorneys, a justified proposal given the social benefits of litigation.

Fortunately—and this point warrants emphasis—the reforms proposed in the four chapters that follow are achievable as a practical matter, and for that reason should be attractive to judges, court administrators, legislators, and policymakers generally. Some consist of modifications to well-established litigation practices or more rigorous application of existing procedural rules. Some embrace variations of reforms proposed elsewhere or indeed already adopted or partially adopted in some jurisdictions (which underscores their feasibility), though justified by and calibrated specifically in light of the analysis provided here. But as explained below, even the most ambitious reforms proposed here—including the establishment of whole new litigation procedures for cases of moderate size—can be accomplished within existing institutions and without burdensome investment by state or local judicial systems or, thus, taxpayers. Meaningful reform of the civil litigation system is within reach.

7

Reducing Undesirable Cases

The problem of frivolous litigation is susceptible to exaggeration, as chapter 5 demonstrated. Often, the significant costs of litigation discourage the filing of frivolous claims, at least knowingly frivolous claims. That said, however, some parties, especially pro se litigants, may bring frivolous cases. And to be sure, sometimes even represented parties might file frivolous claims notwithstanding the costs. Still others may in bad faith bring very weak cases, hoping to benefit from the civil litigation system's imperfect reliability. To the extent frivolous litigation—or litigation brought in bad faith, including nuisance cases and lottery litigation—is common there is every reason to discourage it. Frivolous and bad-faith litigation undermines the integrity of the civil litigation system. They threaten civil justice.

Fortunately, discouraging undesirable cases does not require establishing conclusively just how many or few of them there are. Corrective mechanisms can be put in place to discourage undesirable cases, including but not limited to sanctions for those who bring them. Then, the greater or smaller the problem really is, the more or less those mechanisms can do whatever prophylactic work may be necessary. Accordingly, fully accepting the critics' premise that the civil litigation system is plagued by some undesirable litigation—however much—this chapter proposes ways to prevent or discourage potential litigants from initiating claims that should not enter the civil litigation system at all. Because it addresses the initiation of litigation, the recommendations proposed here apply mostly to plaintiffs, designed for the benefit of potential defendants. At the same time, though, defendants sometimes advance undesirable positions as well, such as frivolous defenses or counter-claims that lack merit, and therefore some of the proposals below would apply to defendants too, for the benefit of plaintiffs. In any event, the target of the discussion below is legal claims (broadly understood) that should not be advanced in the first place—any form of frivolous or bad faith litigation—as opposed to the over-litigation of claims initially brought in good faith, to be addressed in the chapter that follows.

Rules of Practice and Procedure

Certain rules of civil procedure and practice, if properly applied and expanded, provide potential mechanisms to discourage undesirable claims.

A More Muscular Rule 11

To begin with one familiar potential tool, Rule 11 of the Federal Rules of Civil Procedure—"Signing Pleadings, Motions, and Other Papers; Representations to the Court; Sanctions"—requires litigants to certify to the court (by giving their signature on every pleading and motion) that their pleadings and motions are not being brought for improper purposes, and that they are warranted by law, and further that they are supportable by facts. State courts have closely analogous rules. The language of the federal version states that attorneys and unrepresented parties must certify that their pleadings and motions are not "presented for any improper purpose, such as to harass, cause unnecessary delay, or *needlessly increase the cost of litigation*" (emphasis added).[1] Rule 11 also requires attorneys to certify specifically that their "claims, defenses, and other legal contentions" are "non-frivolous."

Rule 11 should not be considered mere exhortation, even though it could be argued that courts usually treat it that way. When a court determines Rule 11 was violated, the rule provides that the court can impose sanctions sufficient "to deter repetition of the conduct or comparable conduct by others similarly situated." Such sanctions can include "non-monetary directives," an order "to pay a penalty into court," and an order to pay the opposing side, including "part or all of the reasonable attorneys' fees and other expenses" of the opposing side.[2] The Rule also authorizes a judge to dismiss a case altogether, and even to refer an attorney in violation of the rule to professional disciplining authorities. Thus courts enjoy considerable discretion to sanction those who violate Rule 11's prohibition against unwarranted litigation. Further, Rule 11 is applicable not only when opposing litigants request sanctions, but also on a court's own initiative. And while the imposition of monetary sanctions at a court's own initiative requires the court to give the potentially offending attorney or party an opportunity to respond, courts can impose monetary as well as non-monetary sanctions under the rule without request by the opposing party. Rule 11 therefore could be used as a powerful tool to discourage claims not worthy of the civil litigation system.

Yet judicial reliance on Rule 11 is too selective. Courts typically invoke Rule 11 only in extreme circumstances, which may reflect several understandable concerns. For one, the line between creative lawyering and bad-faith lawyering is sometimes blurry. Yet creative lawyering is often necessary—to test new legal theories, to resolve ambiguity in the law, and indeed at times to move the law forward by showing how old legal rules do not fit new factual or social circumstances. Thus, judges may be hesitant to discourage creative lawyering. On top of that, lawyers have an ethical duty to represent their clients zealously, and that duty requires them to press their claims aggressively (more on that topic shortly). Attorneys also have a duty to take common-sense steps to ensure that, for example, what their clients tell them is not false, as well as a duty not to mislead a court. But to establish particular facts is what litigation and its discovery processes are for. Judges may thus be reluctant to punish zealous advocacy as well. They may also be reluctant to sanction parties for resorting to the civil justice system more generally, implicitly recognizing the importance of access to the courts.

There is another explanation for Rule 11's infrequent use, however. Rule 11 was last amended in 1993. At the time, it was a matter of controversy, following a widespread perception that courts had used the rule to sanction attorneys too often (see generally Joy 2003). For most of its earlier history, in contrast, Rule 11 saw virtually no use. From 1938, when the Federal Rules were first adopted, until 1983, there were only nineteen reported cases in which parties filed Rule 11 motions, and courts found violations in only eleven of those and issued sanctions in only three. (Courts at that time too could issue sanctions under the rule on their own, without a motion, but that practice too was rare.) In practice, then, Rule 11 meant very little. As a result, in 1983 the rule was revised to encourage judges to issue sanctions more often. Judges took the cue, and the decade between 1983 and 1993 produced seven thousand opinions involving the rule. That extensive use and the controversy it engendered prompted the Rules Advisory Committee to amend Rule 11 again in 1993, in an effort to "scale back [its] more draconian aspects" (Vairo 1998).

As a result, judges now seem to have now over-corrected, invoking Rule 11 infrequently and sanctioning litigants under it even more rarely. Whatever the explanation, certainly there is room for the pendulum to swing back part way. Rule 11, and its many state counterparts, should be used more often to sanction parties who bring bad-faith claims. The rule provides a useful tool to discourage the filing of litigation that seeks to exploit the civil litigation system's mistakes, and greater use of it would require nothing more than increased judicial resolve. Rule 11's explicit focus on the costs of litigation and on the possibility of harassment litigation and frivolous litigation is noteworthy; its express purpose is to discourage the wasteful costs associated with undesirable cases. It should be employed to do so.

To be sure, the line between aggressive advocacy and frivolous advocacy sometimes blurs. But at the same time, some cases can only be understood, from any angle, as brought in bad faith. Claims that are arguably frivolous should not be sanctioned, nor should boundary-pushing civil litigation be chilled. But, when a party or especially an attorney has unambiguously crossed the line by certifying falsely that their claims are warranted by non-frivolous legal arguments, or that factual allegations have evidentiary support when they clearly will have none, judges should respond. More frequent sanctions under Rule 11 and its state counterparts would give those who file frivolous or patently bad-faith cases more pause, promoting better quality control for the civil litigation system.

While greater application of Rule 11 risks discouraging good-faith litigation by parties who may fear undeserved sanctions, that risk can be managed with judicious application of the rule, and judges are moreover well positioned to know when applying the rule is appropriate. Courts should err on the side of caution—saving sanctions for clear cases and avoiding derivative litigation over whether Rule 11 violation has occurred. But the critics' suggestion that the civil litigation system is plagued by frivolous litigation assumes that such litigation is, at least at times, easy to identify. If that is right, judges too should be capable of identifying it, and apply Rule 11 in those clear-cut cases, as some critics have proposed.

Furthermore, although questions about Rule 11's applicability tend to be raised in immediate response to the filing of a pleading or motion, courts also should keep the applicability of Rule 11 and its state counterparts in mind over the life of a case. That is to say, when litigation of a given case shows that a party's original filings were frivolous when made, courts should provide sanctions for the original filings. For example, in cases where discovery shows that certain factual allegations in a complaint were entirely baseless and have to have been made in bad faith—for example, because during discovery the plaintiff could provide no support at all for those allegations, while the fruits of discovery show that the plaintiff must have known the allegations could not be true—courts should provide sanctions for the unjustified allegations in the original complaint. More generally, because whether a party has any support for claims often cannot be determined until later in the case, courts should rely on Rule 11 as litigation unfolds, and litigants should consider filing Rule 11 motions not only in immediate response to an opponent's initial pleading, but also at appropriate times throughout a case.

Rule 11's application, like that of its state analogues, is not limited to plaintiffs, however, nor should it be. Defendants too can make frivolous legal arguments and allege facts without any evidentiary basis, and bad-faith pleading by defendants also raises the cost of litigation and undermines the litigation system's integrity. And, as chapter 3 explained, nuisance defenses in particular can discourage plaintiffs from pursuing deserving claims simply by raising the cost of defeating such defenses. But while courts have used Rule 11 against defendants, that practice is also rare. Courts should use Rule 11 more often against defendants as well as plaintiffs, again in the interest of discouraging wasteful litigation. The civil litigation system has a ready tool to address cases or defenses filed in bad faith. In clear cases, it should be employed.

An Anti-Frivolous Rule of Civil Procedure

As explained in chapter 1, the rules of civil procedure provide various grounds for a defendant to move to dismiss a plaintiff's case very early in litigation, immediately upon the filing of the plaintiff's complaint. These grounds include, among others, lack of personal jurisdiction, lack of subject-matter jurisdiction, and failure to state a cognizable legal claim. In federal court, this initial motion is made under Rule 12(b), which also has counterparts in state rules of civil procedure that provide similar grounds for dismissing a case in state court.[3] As chapter 1 also observed, it is not uncommon for cases to be resolved by initial motion.

A strong case could be made for amending these initial-motion rules of procedure to give defendants an additional explicit reason for moving to dismiss a case—dismissal for frivolousness. An expanded federal Rule "12(b)(8)" (the current Rule 12(b) has seven sub-parts), for example, would allow a defendant to protest that the plaintiff's claim is, on its face, not worthy of the legal system—providing for dismissal for "plainly frivolous pleading" or "abuse of the civil process."

As with the other Rule 12(b) motions, the court would rule on the motion early, before either side has devoted meaningful resources to the case. Similar to the existing Rule 12(b)(6) motion—which permits a motion to dismiss for "failure to state a claim"—a Rule 12(b)(8) motion would ask a court to dismiss because the claim is not worthy of the legal system, even if the complaint satisfies the purely technical requirements of a claim. If the court agreed, the court would dismiss the case resolving it in favor of the defendant. Or, just as defendants currently often motion to dismiss part of a case under Rule 12(b)(6)—certain claims but not all of them—so too could the court dismiss certain claims under a new Rule12(b)(8), leaving the plaintiff to litigate remaining non-frivolous claims.

To some extent, Rule 12(b)(6) already provides some grounds for a defendant to move to dismiss a frivolous suit. As explained in chapter 1, a motion to dismiss for failure to state a claim essentially protests that the plaintiff's alleged wrong is not recognized by the legal system. So where a frivolous claim is frivolous because it is not legally cognizant, Rule 12(b)(6) provides a mechanism for its dismissal. But some claims may be frivolous not because the legal system does not recognize them at all, but rather because the causal connection between the alleged legal injury and the defendant's conduct is facially implausible, for example, or because while the injury would be recognized, the plaintiff clearly has not suffered it, or because the plaintiff could not possibly have incurred the extent of damages the plaintiff seeks to recover. These types of frivolousness are not captured by the routine 12(b)(6) motion to dismiss for failure to state a claim, even under the Supreme Court's decisions to apply Rule 12(b)(6) somewhat more expansively in recent years.

In fact, most any competent plaintiff's lawyer should be able to avoid dismissal for failure to state a claim, simply by being careful to state legally sufficient pleadings. To a large extent, a failure to state a claim for the purposes of Rule 12(b)(6) results either from pleading error or from a mistaken understanding of the law. So while the existing Rule 12(b)(6) motion can filter out some frivolous claims, it cannot capture technically sufficient but nevertheless facially frivolous claims.

Crucially, such a new motion would have to satisfy a high threshold to succeed, reserved by judges selectively for plainly frivolous cases. Rule 12(b)(6) motions and their state counterparts are already extremely common, and defendants may be inclined to use any new basis for dismissing a claims far too often, as every case might become, in the eyes of the defendant, an arguably frivolous case. If an expanded new rule merely added to the costs of litigation by providing litigation about its applicability routinely, that result would be counterproductive.

But a new rule could be explicitly reserved for plainly frivolous cases, and judges could thus use it appropriately. To ensure that the rule would be applied only in cases that undermine the civil litigation system's integrity, courts would have to be prepared to sanction defendants for its overuse. For example, defendants who move under a new Rule 12(b)(8) and lose might be forced to pay the plaintiff's attorney's fees as well as any costs incurred responding to the motion. Alternatively, defendants who move unsuccessfully under a new rule could be presumed liable for the plaintiff's attorney's fees incurred to respond, where that presumption could be overcome if the court determines that the defendant's motion was reasonable, because the question was close, though unsuccessful. One way or another, however, defendants could be discouraged from abusing the availability of that motion, saving it for patently frivolous cases.

But even used sparingly, a new rule of procedure focused specifically and explicitly on frivolous cases would likely have beneficial deterrence effects. For one, plaintiffs would be less likely to file nuisance cases when seeking a settlement from defendants who might be inclined to settle even a meritless case for some small amount rather than incur the greater costs of prevailing. That is, plaintiffs would now realize that defendants, and judges, have a ready mechanism to end such suits. A new Rule 12(b)(8) and state equivalents could also trigger allocating costs and attorneys' fees to defendants who prevailed on such a motion. For where a court concludes that the plaintiff's complaint was frivolous, that could justify the availability of costs and fees under Rule 11. Plaintiffs should bear the costs of cases dismissed on the grounds that they were frivolous, a risk that would further discourage frivolous cases. To the extent frivolous litigation is a problem, a new rule of procedure providing a ready mechanism to filter undesirable cases from the civil litigation system would be beneficial.

Frivolous and Vexatious Litigation Statutes

Many states have, through legislation, created the rough equivalent of the new rule of civil procedure proposed here. State statutes on frivolous litigation, as noted in chapter 4, allow courts to dismiss cases early on the grounds that they were filed frivolously. These statutes amend or supplement state courts' rules of procedure, in response to concerns about meritless litigation. Properly calibrated and properly applied, they too provide a useful tool for combating undesirable litigation.

For example, New Jersey's Frivolous Litigation Statute provides that a prevailing plaintiff or defendant can recover all reasonable costs as well as attorneys' fees "if the judge finds at any time during the proceedings or upon judgment that a complaint, counterclaim, cross-claim, or defense of the non-prevailing person was frivolous."[4] This statutory provision supplements New Jersey's court Rule 1:4–8, the state's equivalent to federal Rule 11, which authorizes the reallocation of costs and fees for conduct by attorneys that a court considers unwarranted. In fact, several states' frivolous litigation statutes were intended expressly to align state civil procedure with the federal Rule 11, as in the case of Wisconsin.[5] Others are more expansive. For example, South Carolina's frivolous litigation statute allows a court upon motion to consider, following trial, directed verdict, or summary judgment, whether a claim or defense was frivolous, and to impose a variety of possible sanctions or fines, including attorneys' fees.[6]

South Carolina's version, to take one example, provides a very useful tool for courts to assess, at the end of a case, whether a claim or defense was frivolously litigated. At that point, courts have the substantial benefit of retrospective review of the parties' litigation decisions.

South Carolina's provision also contains one draconian provision, however, that may make courts rightly reluctant to make full use of that tool: the statute requires that courts, in determining a claim was frivolous, to make a report to the state's Commission on Lawyer Conduct and to the South Carolina Supreme Court.[7] That goes too far. And although this is likely intended to provide a substantial deterrent to frivolous litigation, such provisions may ironically make judges hesitant to conclude a party's position was frivolous, given the serious adverse professional consequences for the attorneys in question. While professional disapprobation and sanctions can be warranted for attorneys who repeatedly bring frivolous litigation, as will be proposed shortly, those adverse professional consequences should be reserved for truly extreme cases and repeat offenders. Otherwise, judges should have ready vehicles for reallocating the costs associated with frivolous litigation liberally, thereby discouraging it, without being required to raise the stakes so high by initiating professional discipline for attorneys in isolated cases. In short, a tool used more frequently seems more desirable than a harsh rule that courts are understandably reluctant to use.

Several states also have "vexatious litigation" statutes, which have common law roots (and some states, such as Connecticut, recognize common law claims against vexatious litigants,[8] providing yet another mechanism for reducing undesirable cases, with many targeting pro se litigants specifically.[9] Some of these prohibit litigants, once they are deemed to be "vexatious," from filing a case at all without prior leave of a court, a prohibition enforceable through contempt of court; in other words, litigants judged to be vexatious thus no longer enjoy unauthorized access to the courts. Some of these statutes define a vexatious litigant as one who has filed multiple cases, often within a specified period, as in the case of California, Florida, and Hawaii for example.[10] In other jurisdictions, vexatious litigation is defined simply as litigation initiated with malice and without legal cause in order to harass the opposing party, even if not brought repeatedly.[11]

A vexatious filing need not be exactly frivolous, however, because often what makes a litigant or a case vexatious is repetition, even of a claim that in the first instance was not frivolous at all. Likewise, most frivolous litigation is not vexatious in that it is neither repetitively brought nor necessarily brought with malice, and state frivolous litigation statutes are more common than vexatious litigation laws. Moreover, vexatious litigation, almost by definition, is brought by plaintiffs, whereas defendants might raise frivolous defenses or frivolous counterclaims under many states' frivolous litigation statutes. That said, certainly there is some overlap between frivolous litigation and vexatious litigation, or there can be. And some states, such as Ohio, combine frivolous and vexatious litigation by treating them the same and under the same court rule.[12] Like frivolous litigation statutes and state equivalents to federal Rule 11, vexatious litigation statutes empower courts to discourage, if not prevent, that form of undesirable litigation as well.

Vexatious litigants may have to post a bond in order to advance their cases, in some states by motion of the defendant.[13] The bond is payable to the defendant in the event that a court determines a new case to constitute continued unwarranted litigation. In Texas, for example, a defendant can file a motion alleging vexatious litigation in lieu of answering a civil complaint, and the plaintiff is then required to post "security" to be paid to the defendant if the plaintiff's complaint is determined to be vexatious.[14] California's vexatious litigation statute similarly requires a vexatious litigant to post security.[15] In general, such provisions are designed to ensure that vexatious pro se litigants are able to cover the opposing party's costs and possibly attorneys' fees if their new cases are found to be without merit. In Connecticut, vexatious litigants may have to pay double damages to those they have sued without any justified cause, or treble damages if they sued without any justified cause and with malice.[16]

Requiring vexatious litigants to absorb the costs of their litigation, just as requiring those bringing clearly frivolous litigation to bear those costs, is justified in the interest of curbing undesirable litigation. Here again, courts should make full use of these statutory tools in appropriate cases. And again, the utility of this tool—as with greater use of Rule 11 and a new grounds to dismiss a case on the pleadings—does not depend on resolving any dispute about just how common frivolous, vexations, or other types of categorically undesirable litigation might be. Whether the civil litigation system's critics who allege that the system is fraught with such litigation are right or wrong, any amount of that litigation is too much. Therefore, inexpensive tools to reduce it should be available to be used with whatever frequency may be necessary.

Ad Damnum Clauses

Better use of Rule 11 and its state counterparts, and likewise of new rules and statutory vehicles to dismiss cases as frivolous, vexatious, or otherwise facially meritless, all would be facilitated by eliminating or reforming "ad damnum" clauses in civil complaints—the part of a complaint stating the amount of damages the plaintiff seeks for the harm alleged. Because harm is an essential element of a civil claim, a plaintiff's complaint must include allegations of harm and the damages the plaintiff seeks as compensation for that harm. Furthermore, as chapter 1 explained, many courts, as well as federal courts exercising diversity jurisdiction, have amount-in-controversy requirements which effectively require a plaintiff to state a damages claim for an amount above some dollar threshold in order to satisfy a court's jurisdiction.

But ad damnum clauses are largely formalities, and may to some extent encourage frivolous damages claims as well as make good-faith filings appear to be frivolous. Beyond satisfying a necessary element of a claim as well as possible jurisdictional requirements, ad damnum clauses otherwise mean little in most jurisdictions. Importantly, they have no necessary connection to how much a prevailing plaintiff might recover in a case, because recoverable damages will depend not on the face of a plaintiff's complaint, but rather on evidence introduced during the case substantiating the plaintiff's claim of legal injury (and as tested against contrary evidence provided by the defendant). Nor do ad damnum clauses define the range of settlement negotiations, or serve any other real purpose in many jurisdictions.

In some jurisdictions, however, the amount specified in an ad damnum clause does carry certain consequences. First, in some jurisdictions a plaintiff may not seek or recover more than the amount demanded in the complaint. In such jurisdictions, the ad damnum clause effectively imposes a ceiling on the amount a plaintiff can recover, which encourages plaintiffs' attorneys to include very high figures in them. This is not the case in federal court or most state courts today, though, as plaintiffs are allowed to introduce evidence supporting recovery greater than that specified in their ad damnum clauses. Second, in some jurisdictions, ad damnum clauses purport to establish the amount the plaintiff may seek in a default judgment, in the event the defendant never responds to the lawsuit at all—another reason why plaintiffs' lawyers commonly include very large numbers in their clauses. Here again, though, in default proceedings in most courts, plaintiffs are still required to support their claimed damages with evidence and cannot simply rely on the amount stated in their complaint.

In short, ad damnum clauses have little continued legal significance, though they still have some. The continued use of ad damnum clauses that state high amounts is largely and simply a longstanding convention of civil pleading. In fact, it is probably safe to say that many attorneys include high ad damnum clauses in their complaints without a great deal of deliberation. So long as a plaintiff seeks an amount high enough to satisfy jurisdictional requirements, it does not matter whether a complaint seeks a whole lot more. High ad damnum clauses will not affect how a case is litigated or what the ultimate damages award will be. The limited significance of ad damnum clauses is well understood among litigators and judges.

But again, on the surface, ad damnum clauses might make good-faith claims appear frivolous, and these clauses may make distinguishing good-faith from bad-faith cases difficult. This is true because such clauses can make it hard to discern how large of an injury a plaintiff truly intends to allege or how much the plaintiff reasonably expects to recover. In short, ad damnum clauses can make many cases appear to be large cases, wherever the plaintiff's lawyer habitually includes a large figure in the clause, even if that is not the plaintiff's expectation. As a result of this dated pleading convention, then, critics of civil litigation—and with them, the media—frequently emphasize the amounts plaintiffs seek in their complaints as evidence that the civil litigation system is plagued by cases seeking exorbitant damages for minor injuries.

Indeed, for many of litigation reformers' marquee cases, it is the size of the damages stated in a complaint that constitutes much of the story. For one example, had Mr. Pearson—the missing-pants plaintiff discussed in chapter 4—sued the Chungs for the replacement costs of his suit, seeking only reasonable compensatory damages, that case likely would never have generated the enormous media coverage it did. Many casual consumers of such celebrated cases make the assumption that a plaintiff has asked for exorbitant damages based on some genuine hope or expectation of receiving them. To be sure, in some cases, including cases filed in bad faith, plaintiffs may genuinely seek exorbitant awards. But many other times they do not, and the point is that ad damnum clauses may not fairly indicate what the plaintiff seeks to recover.

Any residual legal incentives for plaintiffs to include high damages claims in their complaints should be eliminated. To the extent that high ad damnum clauses are simply the product of unchecked convention, plaintiffs' lawyers should reconsider that convention and exercise greater deliberation with respect to the amount of damages alleged in a complaint. In those jurisdictions that do not allow damages to exceed those stated in ad damnum clauses, courts should change that rule. Recoverable damages should be based instead only on the evidence presented in a case, no more and no less, and not subject to outdated pleading conventions. By the same reasoning, in the few jurisdictions where a plaintiff would be presumptively entitled to the amount specified in the ad damnum clause in the event of a default judgment, that practice too should be changed. Plaintiffs winning a default judgment should always be required to provide evidence of their injury, and not automatically collect the amount stated in their ad damnum clauses.

Changes to practices surrounding ad damnum clauses may appear to constitute rather minor reform, to be sure. At the same time, however, changing this aspect of civil practice would significantly alter the way civil litigation is *understood*; often cases pled as multi-million dollar cases are not truly multi-million dollar cases, not even in the eyes of the plaintiff. No less, such reform would also facilitate the administration of the reforms proposed here to discourage bad-faith cases through more robust use of Rule 11 and its state counterparts together with expanded rules to dismiss frivolous cases and the use of frivolous litigation statutes. That is, once plaintiffs' lawyers no longer state claims seeking exorbitant damages simply as the result of pleading conventions, the amounts stated in civil complaints then could be taken more seriously at face value. Plaintiffs and their attorneys then can fairly be held accountable for the amount of damages they claim; they would be less inclined to state claims for many millions in damages unless they meant it. In cases where plaintiffs do intend to seek damage amounts so high as to render their cases frivolous, courts would be better positioned to treat their cases accordingly.

Institutional Filters

Judicially administered rules of procedure applicable in individual cases are not the only way to discourage undesirable litigation, though their greater use would be very helpful to that end. More could be done also at an institutional level to discourage and sanction the filing of frivolous and bad-faith claims.

Frivolous Litigation Panels

First, the organized bar could do more to self-regulate in this area, especially given the harm that bad-faith litigation does to the profession's image and to the reputation of the litigation system as a whole. For example, to address frivolous litigation, attorney discipline boards should establish their own "frivolous litigation panels," or "frivolous litigation subcommittees." This proposal focuses on the bad-faith lawyer rather than the bad-faith claim, just as the civil litigation system's critics focus not only on frivolous cases but also on the lawyers who, they argue, too often bring them. To the extent that they are common, cases brought entirely in bad faith are probably filed by a relatively small number of attorneys for whom existing disincentives are, for whatever reason, not sufficient. Thus, reform measures targeting those most willing to abuse the civil litigation process seem in order.

Such a measure would require only minor modification of existing practices. State bars and state supreme courts already have attorney conduct boards, and attorneys who habitually bring frivolous cases can already be referred to such boards in many states. Opposing counsel on the other end of repeated frivolous lawsuits might grieve an attorney filing such claims. Judges who see repeated frivolous claims by the same attorney also might refer the attorney to a grievance committee. New "frivolous litigation panels," created out of existing disciplinary bodies, would require no new personnel or expenditures. Such entities should focus only on attorneys shown to have brought bad-faith cases repeatedly, not wholly unlike some states' treatment of vexatious litigants as mentioned in the previous chapter—though this effort would focus on targeting attorneys rather than parties.

Making frivolous litigation explicit grounds for possible attorney discipline could bring substantial benefits. The very formation of a frivolous claims committee would make clear that the bar (and the courts) will not tolerate such litigation. What is more, with such a body officially in place, lawyers and judges may be more inclined to report frivolous litigation to such a committee. Finally, to the extent some attorneys repeatedly bring claims in bad faith because they face little real risk of disciplinary action, a newly established panel focusing on such cases would likely deter some bad-faith filers.

Defense counsel as well as plaintiffs' lawyers should be subject to such a body, although a frivolous litigation panel is likely to see more referrals concerning plaintiffs' counsel given that frivolous complaints are more apparent on the face of pleadings that initiate a civil case, whereas frivolous defenses are harder to detect. But like on the plaintiff side, some defense lawyers are less scrupulous than others. They too should be targeted for increased professional scrutiny; defense counsel who repeatedly state nuisance defenses, or take other measures in bad faith to make litigation unnecessarily expensive, should be subject to a frivolous review panel as well. Defense attorneys who consistently fail to comply with discovery, or who aid in concealing or destroying evidence relevant to a plaintiff's claims, also should be subject to greater professional review. But again, a frivolous review panel should be engaged selectively, only to address demonstrable and repeat abusers of the civil litigation system.

Like existing attorney discipline boards, the membership of a frivolous litigation subcommittee must be drawn from experienced attorneys, held in esteem by their professional peers, who volunteer their time. They must be balanced in appearance and in fact: committee members must represent both the plaintiff and the defense side of the practice, and in states with professional review boards with partisan affiliations, they must be bi-partisan so that they are not perceived to reflect any interest over another. Existing professional review panels provide a ready model. Again, creating committees focused on frivolous litigation, or charging existing disciplinary committees explicitly to address recurrent bad-faith litigation, would require only minor changes to existing practices, and would provide another useful (even if in part prophylactic) mechanism to discourage bad-faith litigation.

Designated Prison Counsels

As chapter 4 explained, litigation by pro se prisoner-plaintiffs is frequently mentioned by advocates of civil litigation reform as an example of litigation that proves the civil litigation system is defective—even following the passage of the Prison Litigation Reform Act (PLRA) and changes in some states' rules of civil procedure allowing for summary dismissal of prisoner cases. Prisoner cases have been a favorite example of litigation reformers because they have been voluminous, and because they very often lack merit. As chapter 5 explained, however, the critics' reliance on prisoner litigation as proof that the civil litigation system is defective is misplaced. For unlike most litigants, prisoner plaintiffs are typically unrepresented, so they lack the important check on the merits of their cases that attorneys provide. Lacking legal representation, prisoners file claims that represented parties would never file. In addition, the costs of litigating for prisoners are unusually low. So prisoners frequently litigate. The volume of prisoner litigation—representing, by some estimates, one-fifth of all annual federal civil filings in some years—coupled especially with perceptions of its frivolousness (often exaggerated perceptions, as chapter 5 pointed out) led to the PLRA's passage.

Yet the problem of prisoner litigation seems somewhat oversold. For one thing, the percentage of prisoner cases among all cases filed in federal court provides a misleading picture of the problem: because many cases are dismissed quickly and without extended litigation, mere case filings overstate the resources committed to the adjudication of prisoner claims. Moreover, many studies demonstrate that even if some reform of prisoner litigation was necessary in the mid-1990s to aid overburdened courts, the PLRA went too far (Roosevelt 2003; Schlanger 2003; Chen 2004: Brill 2008; Schlanger and Shay 2008). For some prisoners have valid legal claims, and yet the PLRA provides no mechanism for distinguishing legitimate from frivolous claims. As a result, prisoners with valid claims are now often procedurally barred under the statute from bringing them (e.g., Winslow 2001; Roots 2002).

Critics nevertheless continue to identify prisoner litigation as illustrative of the need for litigation reform. One reason they do so is that prisoners continue to file cases. Although most prisoner claims are now bound to lose under the PLRA due to procedural defaults that pro se prisoner litigants would seldom foresee, prisoners are not typically aware of that fact. In other words, a prisoner will often not learn that a case is barred by the reform statute until they bring a case forward. So the implementation of the PLRA meant that more prisoners would lose cases, but it could not and did not stop all prisoner cases from being filed in the first place. Eventually prisoners learned that the statute imposed strict exhaustion requirements, so the number of prisoner cases eventually dropped somewhat after the passage of the act. Even so, to the extent prisoners are inclined to bring cases without merit—the premise underlying the PLRA—then it is no surprise that a statute rendering their claims meritless would not completely solve that problem.

To better address the problem of frivolous prisoner litigation, courts—in jurisdictions where prison litigation is taken to be the greatest problem—could appoint "prison counsel" or "prison advocates" (cf. Feierman 2006). These counsels or advocates would be capable of reviewing high volumes of draft complaints or inquiries from prospective prisoner litigants in a short amount of time. Prison counsel could help to filter prisoner litigation, to discourage prisoners without any valid claim from filing a case at all, and to assist prisoners with potentially valid claims to prepare those properly. That is, appointed prison counselors could review draft prisoner complaints and prisoner inquiries about potential cases to determine whether their claims have any merit. By weeding out meritless cases before they are filed, prison advocates could save courts, judicial staff, and also defendants (i.e., the state and local governments and officials named as defendants in prisoner litigation) considerable resources.

Prison advocates would provide legal assistance to prisoner plaintiffs only for civil claims, not for litigation relating to any criminal matters. Young lawyers might be enlisted by courts to serve as prison advocates, or court law clerks could be assigned to review prisoner filings to suggest that they be withdrawn or amended to cure defects, or that they be withdrawn altogether as without merit. Prison counsel could receive training about the nature of prisoner claims, the procedural and substantive requirements for stating valid claims, and how to distinguish quickly between legitimate and frivolous prisoner cases. Alternatively, courts could instead solicit bids from public interest law firms or other organizations already active in this area (such as the American Friends

Service Committee) willing to sponsor prison advocates for some number of cases or some duration of time. Either way, prison counsel could provide streamlined review of potential prisoner cases. Courts' civil cover sheets, already required to accompany a civil complaint, could be amended to allow for an indication whether a prison advocate has reviewed a prisoner's case and recommended filing the suit or recommended against it, providing judges and their staff useful information about the likely merits of the case. Under a number of possible and cost-justified arrangements, prison advocates could help to discourage frivolous litigation while preserving meritorious claims.

To anticipate an objection, some will argue that, among all potential civil litigants, prisoners deserve legal assistance the least. This objection fails to consider, however, that prisoner cases already consume scarce judicial resources. Courts already often designate clerks to review prisoner cases, some courts have staff attorneys for the same purpose, and magistrates also devote significant resources to handling prisoner litigation. In various ways, then, judicial and administrative resources are already committed to managing prisoner litigation. On top of that, the defendant officials named in prisoner suits, again, are typically represented by government lawyers, who must also spend time and other resources responding to cases (ultimately at taxpayers' expense, even if they will be dismissed without extensive litigation). So prisoner litigation already consumes resources. Given that cases, once filed, require some kind of response and review, the question becomes how to handle prisoner cases most efficiently. Designated staff to review prisoner filings may make sense especially in states such as Florida, South Carolina, and Wisconsin that provide for expedited dismissal of prisoner claims, to ensure both that viable claims are properly framed and that unworthy claims can be dismissed quickly.

In short, existing resources committed to prisoner suits are probably not allocated as efficiently as possible. Reviewing prisoner cases and potential cases before, rather than after, they are filed would likely consume fewer total resources. With an attorney providing legal advice to prisoners before they file pro se cases, some cases currently filed would never be filed; prisoners would not have to file a case in order to find out whether they had a valid claim. To the extent prisoner litigation is a genuine problem, then, providing prison counsel to filter potential cases and to educate would-be prisoner litigants about the merits or lack of merits of their cases would likely ease existing burdens on both courts and defendants.

Public Advocates or Pro Se Counsel

Courts could do the same on a larger scale for other pro se litigants as well. That is, courts could provide legal assistance to the many pro se litigants initiating civil cases, in the form of a "public advocate" or "pro se counsel" assigned to provide guidance (and assistance with their filings) to pro se litigants—who as noted a large portion of litigants (e.g., Swank 2004). Here too, the purpose of a public advocate or similar counsel would be to provide basic legal assistance to potential litigants towards improving the quality of pro se litigation by filtering out frivolous and bad-faith cases from the system. With respect to frivolous litigation in particular, court staff attorneys assigned to serve as public advocates could discourage the filing of frivolous cases by educating prospective litigants.

The purpose of a public advocate would not be entirely to discourage potential plaintiffs, however. Rather, pro se counsel could serve also to educate potential plaintiffs and to help guide their considerations about whether to file a case and, if so, how best to frame their non-frivolous claims. Often, frivolous cases are frivolous because they are not legally cognizable, although a pro se plaintiff's underlying grievance may be appropriate for other institutions. Where so, public advocates could refer potential plaintiffs to government agencies or to private social service organizations and away from the courts.

Here again, such service need not require substantial new resources from courts. Staff attorneys filing other roles could be designated as public advocates, for example, or could enlist law clerks to serve in such a role. Courts could even increase filing fees for pro se litigants in a modest way to cover any extra costs. While on the one hand filing fees as a general matter can constitute an undesirable limitation on access to the civil litigation system, as will be discussed in chapter 9, on the other hand very modest fees specifically to fund assistance for pro se litigants themselves on balance would seem to promote better access.

Any such assistance would of course have to be provided consistent with legal-ethical rules governing the terms under which attorneys give legal advice and the responsibilities that flow from the attorney-client relationship. But those ethical rules do not pose insurmountable con-straints to providing expressly limited forms of counsel to potential parties who may most need it and, moreover, who are most likely to file frivolous cases. Pro se counsel might provide information at arms' length without entering into a lawyer-client relationship, for example, or alternatively by entering expressly into a limited relationship that ex-pires upon the filing of a complaint. Small claims cases provide a partial analogy, where attorneys at times provide initial legal advice to clients concerning their small claims even in cases where they cannot continue to assist the client by appearing in small claims court. The details here would require some care. But legal-ethical rules are not reasonably un-derstood categorically to prevent courts from facilitating limited legal assistance in the interest of reducing the frequency of frivolous claims.

Some courts have recently developed versions of this proposal. For example, the Settlement Assistance Program for Pro Se Litigants in the Northern District of Illinois provides an instructive example. As explained in greater detail in chapter 9, this program relies on volun-teer lawyers at the Chicago Lawyers' Committee for Civil Rights Under Law who review and filter pro se discrimination cases, and then refer appropriate cases to other volunteer lawyers who provide representa-tion that is specifically limited to settlement negotiations. Other federal and state courts should create similar programs, or develop variations of their own, in the name of curbing undesirable filings. This could be done as extensions of many state courts' recent efforts to make self-help resources available, as also explained in chapter 9. Again, limited rep-resentation to those who file pro se cases improves pro se litigants' ac-cess by giving them the benefit of assistance to sharpen their legitimate claims, while at the same time reducing the costs—borne by defendants and others—associated with meritless cases. In short, pro se counsel can help to ensure that worthy claims are advanced while frivolous or other wholly meritless cases are not. Promoting access and curbing undesir-able litigation can be mutually reinforcing.

Summary

Reducing frivolous and bad-faith litigation is within reach. To be sure, there will always be outlandish cases. An open-court system makes the complete elimination of frivolous cases impossible. But by employing underutilized existing tools and by fashioning new tools, more can be done to reduce litigation that is categorically undesirable. Judges should show increased willingness to impose more costs on parties and their lawyers who bring frivolous litigation or make claims or defenses in bad faith. Where necessary, legislatures should provide courts with appropriate mechanisms statutorily, though courts enjoy considerable authority over their own rules.

At the same time, the legal profession itself can do more to discourage frivolous litigation brought by represented parties. In particular, attorney discipline panels should focus on identifying lawyers who bring demonstrably frivolous cases, and other frequent claims or defenses in bad faith, repeatedly—just as other professions self-regulate violations of their professional norms. The organized bar and attorney discipline boards do this to some extent already, but there is room for the legal profession to bring greater focus to the issue of bad-faith litigation.

While frivolous cases are often filed in bad faith—including virtually all frivolous cases filed by attorneys, who should know better—some frivolous cases filed by pro se litigants may not constitute bad-faith cases because they do not know better. They should be discouraged just the same. Measures to limit or redirect potential claims by pro se litigants that are not appropriate for the legal system, or measures to improve the quality of valid pro se claims, are also possible. Judicial staff could provide increased guidance and assistance to pro se litigants, and in jurisdictions where prisoner litigation is voluminous to prisoner pro se litigants in particular, all in the interest of conserving resources.

None of these proposals to reduce undesirable litigation would require substantial new investments. The case for reform in this area is therefore strong even in the absence of definitive evidence concerning the frequency of unworthy cases. Whether common or uncommon, or somewhere in between, curbing patently meritless litigation would address a perennial criticism of civil litigation, improve the integrity of the litigation system, and reduce litigation costs.

The next chapter focuses on another species of undesirable litigation, one more subtle and likely much more common: the *over-litigation* of legitimate claims.

8

Discouraging Over-Litigation

The costs of litigation are not borne only by those who generate them, another observation rightly emphasized by civil litigation's most influential critics. Setting aside the overhead costs of running court systems, parties also impose litigation costs on each other. To some extent, they do so for entirely legitimate purposes in the course of developing their factual case and advancing their legal arguments. Moreover, many of the costs associated with litigation usefully advance the reliability of the system.

Yet, given that parties do not internalize the full costs of their decisions to litigate, including their marginal decisions to litigate further a case already underway, there is a risk that they will generate excessive litigation costs. These costs may be excessive where the total costs of those decisions, considering the opposing party's costs too, outweigh the benefits, which are likely realized only by the party generating them. Filing a motion requires the opposing litigant to file a response; document requests require the other side to produce documents; noticing a deposition requires the other side to prepare for it; the use of experts requires opposing experts; and so on. In short, the nature of civil litigation, in partial contrast to criminal litigation for instance, ties opposing parties' costs together more tightly, rendering expenditures on one side of the case to necessitate expenditures by the opposing side.

Of course, the relationship between opposing parties' litigation costs is not dollar-per-dollar linear. For example, it is certainly possible for one side to incur much higher costs—or to invest much more in a case—than the opposing side. Still, as a general proposition, one side's cost in a typical civil case is a function of litigation decisions made by the other side, even when both sides generate costs entirely in good faith.

Additionally, and more worrisome, parties sometimes impose litigation costs for illegitimate purposes—that is, *in order to* increase their opponent's costs, to discourage them from advancing their claims, or to obfuscate rather than clarify relevant factual and legal issues. These litigation costs are undesirable; they both impede access (by making access more expensive) and jeopardize the system's reliability. Further, and importantly, these excess costs are by no means limited to claims or defenses made in bad faith at the outset. Parties might well over-litigate claims and defenses that were valid when first stated, but over the course of the case are later revealed to be without merit.

Indeed, it is possible for parties to generate unjustified litigation costs even for claims and defenses that a party considers to be valid and strong—again to discourage the other side from litigating or for other unjustified reasons. And to generalize broadly, whereas frivolous and forms of bad-faith litigation might often be associated with small, unsophisticated parties (although large, sophisticated parties too advance frivolous claims and defenses), over-litigation might be associated especially with larger, sophisticated parties who can readily afford excess litigation expenses themselves and understand well how to manipulate civil process (although small parties too no doubt over-litigate good-faith claims as well). This form of over-litigation—pressing a claim or defense simply too far or otherwise generating unjustified litigation costs—can be difficult to detect, and therefore difficult for courts to police. In any event, it is familiar to any attorney with significant civil litigation experience.

To prepare for consideration of how to reduce over-litigation, recall chapter 6's typology of litigation costs (see figure 8.1).

The question becomes how to deter parties from generating wasteful and especially intentionally wasteful litigation costs, without also impeding parties from their good-faith advancement of reasonable claims. In terms of figure 8.1, litigation costs represented in the bottom right box are fully justified, and those represented by the other three bottom boxes are undesirable (and increasingly so moving left).[1] One way to discourage undesirable litigation expenditures is to allocate, or more precisely to reallocate, some of those costs so that parties who over-litigate, especially at the margin of a case, will bear more of them. This would not only reduce litigation costs (and thus promote access), but also enhance the system's reliability, given that some wasteful litigation obscures the issues at stake, again sometimes intentionally. The following discussion explains.

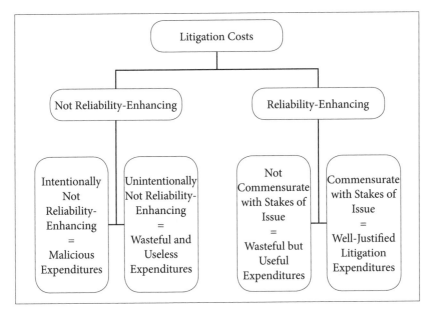

Figure 8.1. Typology of Litigation Costs

"Pay to Impose" and Marginal Decisions to Litigate

As chapter 6 briefly noted, generally speaking, litigation is costly in two ways and at two times. Most litigation costs are incurred during the course of the litigation process; litigants must cover these expenses more or less in real time in order to be able to litigate. These "pay to play" costs include the many out-of-pocket expenditures associated with conducting litigation (for briefs, motions, discovery, documents, experts, investigations, and so on), as well as the costs of legal representation for parties whose attorneys bill periodically and by the hour. Pay-to-play costs are incurred by litigants themselves and at their own initiative, though they are frequently necessitated by the litigation decisions of opposing parties.

In contrast to these pay-to-play costs, litigants might also ultimately bear some costs on an ex post, "pay to lose" basis. Pay-to-lose costs are incurred upon defeat, and they include costs that otherwise would have been incurred by an opposing party. In other words, pay-to-lose costs are the consequence of the civil litigation system reallocating costs from a prevailing party—which typically would be pay-to-play costs for the prevailing party—and imposing them instead on the non-prevailing party. Pay-to-lose costs can be assessed at the end of an entire case, or instead as a result of losing a discrete piece of a case by motion. In any case, unlike pay-to-play costs, paying to lose by definition requires a retrospective determination about which party has prevailed and which has lost the issue in question. For one example already mentioned, Rule 11 and its state analogues permit courts to reallocate the costs of responding to frivolous or wasteful litigation onto the party generating such litigation, on the occasion of that party losing a Rule 11 motion. Attorneys' fee awards available to prevailing parties under certain statutes, as explained in chapter 2, constitute another species of pay to lose.

The current civil litigation system features not only considerable pay to play litigation costs, then, but also some pay to lose costs as well. For another example, in the federal courts—as well as many state courts, as most states have versions of the same rule—prevailing civil litigants can request that the court reallocate their out-of-pocket expenses (not including attorneys' fees, however) to the losing party. Judges have discretion about whether to award such costs, but for instance Federal Rule of Civil Procedure 54 by its terms creates a presumption in their favor, providing that recoverable costs for the prevailing party "should be allowed," though actual practice varies among courts and judges.[2] When Rule 54 and its state counterparts are applied, unsuccessful litigants pay to lose by absorbing the prevailing party's out-of-pocket litigation expenses. For another example, Federal Rule of Civil Procedure 68—and here again many states have analogous rules—allows litigants to make a type of offer known as an "offer of judgment." If rejected, this offer entitles the party making the offer to collect from the rejecting party all costs incurred in the litigation from the point the offer was made going forward (again excluding attorneys' fees), in the event that the rejecting party is awarded less at trial than the amount offered.[3] These rules are examined in detail shortly.

Some state systems take pay-to-lose farther. For one example, Michigan's rules of civil procedure require tort and contract litigants to attempt to settle their cases through a process called "case evaluation," a form of alternative dispute resolution that requires both sides to present their case to a panel of evaluators who thereafter offer an opinion about how much the case is worth. If the evaluators settle on a common figure, as they often do, their valuation of the case is reported to both sides as the amount for which they could settle the case. Both sides are entitled to accept or reject the evaluators' valuation of the case, but if one party accepts the case evaluators' figure and the other party rejects it, the rejecting party must pay the accepting party's costs *and* its attorney's fees, if the rejecting party does no better at trial than 110% of the evaluators' figure (110% is Michigan's threshold). Because the rejecting party risks paying the other side's attorney's fees, this process puts considerable pressure on parties to settle because otherwise paying to lose becomes very expensive. Other states have similarly imposed new forms of pay-to-lose that include attorneys' fees as part of state tort reform (e.g., Carlson 2004).

Even this rule does not constitute the most expansive version of pay-to-lose, however. As explained earlier, the English Rule requires the losing side to pay the prevailing side's attorney's fees as a matter of course, whether or not any offer of judgment or case evaluation has been made. Paying the prevailing party's attorney's fees constitutes a very substantial back-end litigation cost indeed, given that, as discussed, attorneys' fees usually constitute the largest single cost of much civil litigation, often exceeding all out-of-pocket costs combined. While existing pay-to-lose rules take modest potential steps in that direction, the English Rule has not been adopted in U.S. jurisdictions (despite proposals to do so from some litigation reformers) on the grounds that it goes too far (but cf. Di Pietro and Carns 1996; Rennie 2012 (the latter assesses the consequences of Alaska's version of the loser-pays rule)).

There is no doubt that crudely administered, high pay-to-lose costs would have undesirable consequences. Requiring losing parties who litigate entirely in good faith to pay higher costs multiplies their risks of litigation, and thereby substantially impedes access to the courts. Any across-the-board version of the English Rule that prices many parties out of the litigation system would be most undesirable. Bad-faith litigation aside, parties with good-faith claims or defenses should not be discouraged from advancing them, even in cases where they ultimately prove unsuccessful. As established in chapter 3, a just civil litigation system requires access to it, and the English Rule would reduce access dramatically and unjustifiably.

What is more, given that the civil litigation system is not perfectly reliable, sometimes there are cases where the losing parties should have prevailed. Thus, any mechanical application of pay-to-lose would not only discourage good-faith parties from litigating, by increasing their risk, but it also would compound the consequences of the system's inevitable mistakes. So again, any attractive version of pay-to-lose should be administered in the light of its consequences for good-faith and bad-faith litigants alike. Further, the reasonableness of parties' litigating positions should be considered in its application, whatever the ultimate outcome of a case might be.

But—here is the core point—the choice is not all or nothing. In certain circumstances, and when it is properly administered, greater reliance on pay-to-lose *can* serve as a useful tool to incentivize and discipline litigants (e.g., Schwarzer 1992; Fischbach and Fischbach 2005; Issacharoff and Miller 2013), most especially but not only those who litigate in bad faith. Pay-to-lose seems most easily justified to deter nuisance litigation and lottery litigation by parties hoping for undeserved settlements or to benefit from the litigation system's imperfect reliability. But beyond such categorically undesirable litigation, pay-to-lose can also be calibrated to discourage litigants from pursuing claims and defenses that during the course of litigation are revealed to be weak, and especially to discourage litigants from forcing the other side to continue to incur litigation costs in order to defeat clearly weak claims.

That is, parties who file or plead in good faith, but who come to learn more about the doubtful merits of their positions (for example, through pretrial litigation including discovery) should be discouraged from further advancing their claims and defenses—that is, from litigating further at the margin of the case—whenever doing so would no longer be in good faith. Similarly, parties should be discouraged from continuing to litigate at the margins of a case in order to drive up their opponents' costs, or to confuse rather than clarify relevant factual and legal issues, thus threatening the litigation system's reliability. And sometimes even in circumstances where a party's decision to litigate further reflects no bad faith in the narrowest sense, yet constitutes an unambiguously poor decision to expend resources and to force an opposing party to incur additional litigation costs, such a party should be forced to internalize more of the costs of that poor decision too. Accordingly, the discussion that follows proposes a form of judicially administered pay-to-lose—or what might rather be called "pay to impose"—that requires parties to internalize some of the costs of their marginal decisions to litigate where those decisions appear unjustified.

"Pay to Impose" and Rule 54

As noted earlier, Federal Rule of Civil Procedure 54—"Judgment; Costs"—and similar state rules allow a prevailing party to request costs excluding attorneys' fees from the losing party, subject to judicial approval. In practice, however, Rule 54 is very often anemic, as courts often informally limit the extent to which prevailing parties can recover their costs. One possible explanation for judicial hesitance to award costs is that Rule 54 applies equally no matter how strong the losing party's case may have been or how earnestly it was litigated in good faith.

But Rule 54 could and should be applied differently, both much more often and especially in a manner reflecting the strength and reasonableness of litigants' positions and their litigation tactics during the course of a case. If it were, Rule 54 and its state counterparts would provide one useful mechanism for addressing over-litigation. And fortunately, a better application of the rule would not require any amendment to it. First, in cases where courts determine that the losing party's position is far-fetched, either frivolous or otherwise brought in bad faith, perhaps on the hope that the system would err or that the opposing side would settle, courts certainly should award generous costs under Rule 54—that is, higher "pay to lose."

Second, and more importantly here (because courts have other tools for addressing categorically bad-faith litigation, as discussed in the previous chapter), courts should award generous costs under Rule 54 any time a judge determines that the non-prevailing party advanced claims or defenses over the course of litigation farther than was justified. Although distinguishing bad-faith from good-faith litigation—patently frivolous cases aside—can be difficult early on in a case, often judges are well positioned to assess the reasonableness of parties' claims and positions maintained through the course of a case on a retrospective basis. And from such a perspective, sometimes when parties remain committed to such positions over the duration of a case, it is very hard to see that commitment as motivated by anything but an intention to over-litigate, particularly once earlier developments in the case reveal those positions to be weak. In such instances too, courts should rely more on Rule 54 and its state counterparts to reallocate the costs of over-litigation.

To be clear, courts should exercise discretion in doing so, awarding costs on a sliding scale. The more unjustified the non-prevailing party's position, the more litigation costs the party should bear on a pay-to-lose basis. Judges may be especially well positioned to consider the allocation of litigation costs following the resolution of a case by summary judgment or other fact-intensive dispositive motion. That is, upon resolving a summary judgment motion, judges might consider whether the losing party's position was (though perhaps unsuccessful) justified and advanced in good faith, or whether it was instead plainly unjustified and wasteful, in light of what is typically a well-developed record supplied by the parties. Where specific positions or arguments advanced by a litigant seem retrospectively unjustified, judges should impose costs under Rule 54 for those positions and arguments, and not for others advanced by the same party. In the many cases where both sides litigated entirely in good faith and did not over-litigate any portions of their case, but where of course one side or the other had to lose, courts should be most reluctant to impose any costs at all.

Further, where courts do apply Rule 54, they should also reallocate more litigation costs than they often reallocate under current practice. For example, by local court rules, some courts do not allow prevailing parties to recover the costs of depositions taken of expert witness; notwithstanding Rule 54, some courts have by definition deemed expert depositions to be excluded from the costs potentially recoverable under the rule. So, for instance, a plaintiff can in effect force a defendant to pay for the plaintiff's expert's deposition, often a significant cost, even for testimony about a claim that lacks any merit. When the plaintiff thereafter loses the case, the defendant cannot recover the costs of the expert's deposition. In practical terms, this means that the plaintiff does not internalize the costs of the marginal decision to press a meritless claim supported by expert testimony; the plaintiff can externalize part of that cost onto the defendant. On a sliding scale that reflects the strength, reasonableness, and good faith of litigants and the positions they maintain over the course of a case, judges should be more inclusive about the set of costs that can be reallocated under Rule 54's pay to lose principle.

Loser fees are properly assessed against defendants as well. Rule 54 does not distinguish between plaintiffs and defendants, and neither should the administration of greater "pay to impose." Thus, the approach to the rule recommended here would promote access for plaintiffs by lowering their expected costs due to over-litigation by defendants. It would for the same reason discourage over-litigation by defendants, increasing the risk of it as defendants are made to internalize more of the resulting costs

To anticipate an objection to this proposal, some might argue that a more robust Rule 54 (and its state counterparts) would yield too much to proponents of the English Rule. On this view, if courts begin to impose additional costs on losing litigants, adoption of the full-fledged English Rule, including the reallocation of attorneys' fees, may not be far off. But again, "pay to lose" admits of degrees. The civil litigation system already reallocates litigation costs in various ways. The recommendation here is to reallocate costs *somewhat* more often and, in particular, in a way that deters parties from over-litigating. While the English Rule would impede access by good-faith and bad-faith parties alike, forcing all to pay the considerable costs of even their opposing party's attorney's fees, a more nuanced approach to Rule 54 and its state analogues would limit "pay to impose" to out-of-pocket expenses, not attorneys' fees, and moreover would adjust for the faith of the non-prevailing party.

Rule 68 and "Offers to Accept Judgment"

The offer of judgment is another underutilized mechanism that could be used better to discourage wasteful marginal litigation (accord Anderson 1994; Bonney, Tribek, and Wrona 1996; Sherman 1998; Bone 2008; J. Horowitz 2010). As noted, Rule 68 of the Federal Rules of Civil Procedure—"Offer of Judgment"—and its state counterparts (see for example Sumner 2003; Ampulski 2008; and Osevala 2012 (discussing state versions of Rule 68)) reallocate some of the costs of litigation by requiring a plaintiff who has turned down a defendant's offer, but then received at trial an amount less than the offer, to pay the defendant's costs (excluding attorneys' fees) incurred after the offer was rejected.[4]

Rule 68 thus seemingly requires a plaintiff to internalize some of the defendant's costs—that is, costs that the defendant incurs subsequent to the Rule 68 offer as a consequence of the plaintiff's rejection. For example, if a defendant offers a plaintiff $100,000 to settle a case, and the plaintiff rejects that offer and subsequently wins $75,000 at trial, then the plaintiff, having done worse than what the defendant had offered, would have to pay all of the defendant's costs incurred from the point when the plaintiff rejected the $100,000 offer. Although the plaintiff prevailed at trial, the plaintiff had been offered more than the ultimate damage award to resolve the case. The defendants' post-offer costs that the plaintiff must pay thus essentially constitute pay-to-impose costs. Because the trial became a losing proposition for the plaintiff relative to what the defendant offered, the plaintiff must pay some of the costs imposed on the defendant by the trial.

Rule 68 thus illustrates well the crucial distinction emphasized here between a party's decision to litigate in the first place, and that party's decision to litigate further beyond some point. To continue the example, the plaintiff's decision to initiate the case was not misguided; to the contrary, that decision was vindicated when the plaintiff won a favorable judgment of $75,000. But the decision to continue to litigate after the defendant's offer of $100,000 proved wasteful. Not only regrettable from the plaintiff's point of view (because the plaintiff ultimately received less), that decision added marginal, and wasteful, litigation costs for both sides.

Greater use of Rule 68 and its state counterparts could encourage plaintiffs to consider carefully the benefits of litigating beyond a defendant's offer (for economically oriented analyses of the Rule's application, see, e.g., G. Miller 1986; Chung 1996). To be sure, plaintiffs already have an incentive to accept any offer that is greater than what the plaintiff would expect to receive at trial; for self-interested reasons, plaintiffs will aim to calculate their marginal expected costs and expected benefits of going to trial accurately. But the problem is that those calculations do not reflect the defendant's costs of litigating through to trial, costs that are borne by the defendant alone.

Here again, sound application of Rule 68 requires case-by-case judicial analysis. For example, when the plaintiff declines an offer of judgment, the defendant from that point forward may be inclined to incur excessive litigation costs, discounting those costs by the probability that now the plaintiff ultimately will bear them anyway. Judges should be sensitive to such possibilities. Thus there is an inherent trade-off between the potential gains from reallocating litigation costs, by encouraging parties to minimize costs because they might have to internalize them, and the potential inefficiencies from reallocating litigation costs, by encouraging litigants to spend carelessly knowing the other side might have to pay some or all of them.

This trade-off is navigable, however. Courts can monitor the recovery of costs under Rule 68. In fact, they already do. The federal courts, for example, have "Handbooks on Recoverable Costs," which govern costs that parties may collect under Rule 68 and in other circumstances (including under Rule 54, and according to attorneys' fee-shifting statutes that also provide for the recovery of out-of-pocket costs). Courts therefore review the costs that defendants seek to recover from plaintiffs under Rule 68. The problem is that, in some jurisdictions, many costs are excluded from among those recoverable under Rule 68, as noted is the case for Rule 54 as well. And more generally, Rule 68 is not well understood or, thus, widely employed in practice (e.g., Solimine and Pacheco 1997; Shelton 2006). A more rigorous application of Rule 68 would require greater inclusion of the defendant's post-offer costs. Courts should count costs—that is, out-of-pocket litigation expenses— inclusively. In fact, the argument for more comprehensive inclusion of pay-to-lose costs under Rule 68 may be stronger than under Rule 54, given that in the former case the plaintiff affirmatively declined an offer by the defendant, preferring instead to litigate the case further. Nor should plaintiffs recover for their post-offer attorney's fees under fee-shifting statutes that entitle prevailing plaintiffs to recover their attorney's fees from losing defendants—especially when a plaintiff prevailed for less than what a defendant had offered, as the Supreme Court has controversially but from this perspective correctly held.[5]

In addition, Rule 68 should be expanded to apply when the plaintiff loses a case completely. Yet, the Supreme Court has interpreted Rule 68's language to authorize cost-shifting where a plaintiff wins less at trial than the defendant's offer of judgment, but *not* where the plaintiff loses the case outright.[6] Thus, Rule 68 currently does not apply in cases where a plaintiff has turned down a Rule 68 offer and subsequently loses at trial. But the spirit of the rule applies with equal if not greater force in that scenario too. The civil litigation system should discourage continued litigation beyond a defendant's offer of judgment in cases where the plaintiff goes on to lose as well as in cases where the plaintiff prevails. The benefits of the losing plaintiff's marginal decision to litigate beyond the defendant's offer are not apparent.

Where the plaintiff loses outright, defendants might alternatively seek costs under Rule 54 instead. Courts are somewhat more reluctant to require plaintiffs to pay to lose under Rule 54, however, and recoverable costs under Rule 54 are discretionary, not mandatory, and as noted, where available, they may be less complete than under Rule 68. But when a defendant has made an offer of judgment, the case for forcing the plaintiff carefully to consider litigating the case further, by allocating more of the post-offer litigation costs to the plaintiff, seems especially justified. Whether courts do so in reliance on Rule 54 or Rule 68 is not as important as that they do so.

Here again, some will object, arguing that Rule 68's reallocation of litigation costs to plaintiffs is already undesirable and should not be extended to include still more costs or to apply when a plaintiff loses at trial. On one view, Rule 68 already punishes plaintiffs for exercising their right to a day in court. Even where a plaintiff may recover less than what the defendant offered, still there are important process values served by litigating to the very end, and those process values should not be taken lightly. A more robust Rule 68, on this view, thus merely punishes plaintiffs further for litigating. In the earlier example, the plaintiff may value the opportunity of trial—to tell the plaintiff's story—more than the $25,000 difference between what the defendant offered and what the plaintiff ultimately recovered. The benefit of civil litigation is certainly not reducible to recoverable monetary damages, and thus the plaintiff's decision to reject the defendant's Rule 68 offer may have still been the right decision, all things considered. Process values were served.

This objection is not compelling, however. To be sure, the opportunity to seek redress for a legal wrong through telling one's story at trial is an opportunity most litigants value, even when they are ultimately unsuccessful. Focusing only on the bottom line of a damages verdict or a Rule 68 offer misses the procedural benefits of litigation, to be sure. Yet the point must not be taken too far. First of all, there is no abstract right to one's day in court, however common that turn of phrase might be. Civil litigation is possible only where courts and legislatures have seen fit to create causes of action providing remedies to potential litigants who have access to the courts in the first place. (The success of the civil litigation reform movement in recent decades shows all too well that there is no unqualified right to civil litigation).

Second, the suggestion that many plaintiffs might prefer to recover less at trial but have the benefit of the trial process probably assumes too much about plaintiffs. Most plaintiffs would probably prefer to receive a higher settlement award instead. After all, an offer of judgment itself vindicates the plaintiff's position too; the defendant's offer shows that the plaintiff's claims were valid, and to some extent validates the plaintiff's version of events. It is difficult to know what the benefits of presenting one's case through trial are really worth for parties who recover less upon doing so. And a plaintiff might be frustrated by post-offer litigation that leads to an award less than what the defendant had offered; there may be subjective process costs rather than process benefits associated with the post-offer litigation. Further, any satisfaction that the plaintiff realizes from litigating after a Rule 68 offer might be offset by the defendant's own frustration generated from what proves to be needless (because wasteful) additional litigation. In any event, a stronger Rule 68 would not deprive plaintiffs of a day in court, but rather simply require them to internalize more of the marginal litigation costs they impose on defendants resulting from a preference for trial over an offer of judgment, in cases where going to trial means the plaintiff recovers less.

Finally, but not least, Rule 68 should be made equally available to plaintiffs too, as others have also proposed (e.g., Simon 1985; J. Horowitz 2010; cf. Yoon and Baker 2006). In its current form, federal Rule 68 applies only to offers by defendants, and thus it is only triggered, if at all, by a plaintiff's refusal to accept the defendant's proposed judgment. But a bilateral approach would force defendants to internalize their decisions to litigate further too, and also make it more difficult for defendants to exploit the plaintiff's litigation costs by offering plaintiffs too little. Thus, plaintiffs—in state courts and federal courts alike—should be allowed to make a Rule 68–like "offer to accept judgment." In any given case, then, either side or both sides could make such an offer.

This symmetrical offer to accept judgment would apply to defendants similar to the ways in which offers of judgment apply to plaintiffs: a plaintiff could offer to accept a judgment of a specified amount, and if the defendant declines and the plaintiff does better at trial, the defendant would have to pay the plaintiff's marginal litigation costs from the point after the plaintiff's offer was declined. The logic underlying Rule 68 applies equally here. Continued litigation beyond that point, yielding an award greater than the plaintiff would have accepted as a remedy, is wasteful. Defendants should internalize more of those wasteful litigation costs, in the interest of encouraging defendants, too, to focus more carefully on the costs of continued litigation, and to discourage defendants from imposing unnecessary costs on plaintiffs by over-litigating.

Importantly, however, neither plaintiffs nor defendants should be able to discourage their opponents from litigating their cases by making offers of judgment or offers to accept judgment very early in a case. Early preemptive offers, which some defendants attempt by routinely making Rule 68 offers very early on in a case, before the facts of the case are well developed—a practice which likely contributes to some judges' reluctance to allocate many costs under the rule—simply discourage litigation in general, as opposed to marginally wasteful litigation in particular. Rule 68 should not discourage litigation per se, or prevent parties from gathering information about the strength of their cases during discovery or otherwise. Rather, Rule 68 and state versions of the rule should discourage informed but poor decisions to continue litigating once both sides have developed information sufficient to make informed decisions. Thus, Rule 68 should be used to reallocate the costs of litigation to a declining party—plaintiff or defendant—if that party does worse at trial, but *only* when the offer follows the completion of discovery or other adequate fact-finding by the party receiving the offer.

"Pay to Impose" and Civil Discovery

Increased reliance on Rule 68 and its state equivalents will help only in the very small percentage of civil cases that go to trial, whereas Rule 54 and its equivalents cover the larger set of cases resolved by courts short of trial, by summary judgment or other dispositive motion. As chapter 1 explained, often the most time-consuming and costly phase of a case is the discovery process, during which parties develop, clarify, and to some extent test the strength of their factual positions. It is also a phase of litigation that lends itself to over-litigation by parties who, for example, make excessive discovery demands, or disclose voluminous irrelevant materials, or unreasonably refuse to provide requested information without repeated requests and discovery motions—a problem so familiar that it has its own term, "discovery abuse." Fortunately, courts have at their disposal tools to discipline litigants who over-litigate by making poor or unjustified marginal decisions about civil discovery too. And, reallocating the costs of discovery abuse through greater use of pay-to-impose could be done for a much broader set of cases—that is, those for which there is discovery—even for cases that are eventually resolved by settlement or other informal means without final adjudication (and thus without any occasion for application of Rule 54 or 68 at all).

Federal Rule of Civil Procedure 37—"Failure to Make Disclosures or to Cooperate in Discovery; Sanctions"—and its many state counterparts provide for potentially extensive pay-to-lose for any party whose discovery conduct requires the opposing party to seek a motion to compel discovery. In other words, if a party subject to a proper discovery request fails to provide requested information—or likewise fails to comply with an earlier discovery order from the court, or to supplement its earlier discovery disclosures, or otherwise to participate in the discovery process as required—Rule 37 allows the requesting party by motion to ask the court to compel the opposing party to cooperate. Rule 37 provides for several types of sanctions for non-compliant parties, including the possibility that they may have to concede the factual issue in question. Among those remedies, Rule 37 also explicitly calls for the payment of expenses as well as attorneys' fees by the party who loses the motion. Rule 37 thus has the effect of encouraging parties not to refuse to cooperate in discovery, on the one hand, but also not to file unwarranted motions to compel discovery, on the other hand, given that the non-prevailing party on the motion, whichever side, will pay costs and fees. Notably, Rule 37 not only includes attorneys' fees within the scope of its pay-to-lose—in contrast to the rules discussed above—but also says that courts "must" award them to the prevailing party, unless the non-prevailing party's conduct was "substantially justified" or justice otherwise counsels against pay-to-lose.[7]

Rule 37 is thus a powerful potential mechanism for addressing bad-faith or otherwise unjustified positions a party might take during the discovery stage of litigation, imposing wasteful costs on the other side. Its purpose is to force parties whose marginal decisions in a case are unwarranted to internalize the litigation costs associated with those decisions, even if a party's overall position in the case as a whole is justified or even compelling. After all, parties who prevail in a case may very well make some unjustified marginal litigation decisions along the way. Rule 37 usefully decouples the merits of a party's ultimate litigation position from the party's positions taken on discrete discovery issues during the course of litigation. Without it, litigants could easily abuse the discovery process, more than some already do, to generate considerable excess litigation costs for their opponents.

Other procedural rules beyond Rule 37 similarly reallocate costs and attorneys' fees for discovery tactics that generate unnecessary costs for an opposing party. Federal Rule of Civil Procedure 30(g), for example, provides for the recovery of costs and attorneys' fees against parties who fail to attend scheduled depositions or to serve a subpoena on a deponent.[8] Here again, most states have similar rules based on the federal rule, giving state courts similar tools to help ensure that the discovery phase of litigation is not excessively costly. More vigorous and consistent application of all such rules would help to discourage incremental litigation decisions that are wasteful.

Rule 11 and Similar Authorities

Rule 11 provides yet another mechanism to force parties to internalize the costs of over-litigation. As discussed in the previous chapter, Rule 11 allows a court to award costs and fees, as well as other sanctions such as a penalty paid to the court, for filings made to increase an opponent's litigation costs unnecessarily, to advance a frivolous argument, or for other bad-faith purposes. Rule 11 and its state counterparts should be used to allocate costs and, where appropriate, attorneys' fees not only in response to the filing of bad-faith cases at the wholesale level, but also for any position taken during the course of litigation that proves to be completely without merit (accord Cowles 1988). In other words, Rule 11 should be used more often not just for parties who file bad cases or defenses, but also for those who impose unnecessary litigation costs on the opposing side even in the advancement of good-faith claims and defenses. Furthermore, Rule 11 sanctions may be appropriate at any stage of litigation where a party's position is not supported by a reasonable understanding of the law or a good-faith understanding of the facts.

Rule 11 is not the only tool of its type useful for addressing the excessive imposition of litigation costs, however. Section 1927 of Title 28 of the U.S. Code authorizes sanctions in federal litigation for attorneys who needlessly increase litigation costs by "unreasonably and vexatiously" multiplying the proceedings in a case.[9] Thus, under Section 1927, a judge can allocate the costs of redundant pleadings or motions, or those intended to harass opposing parties, to attorneys who generate them. Like Rule 11 and Rule 37, Section 1927 expressly provides for the payment of attorneys' fees as well as costs. Targeted only to attorneys, and not to parties themselves, Section 1927 provides another potential way for courts to address over-litigation.

As chapter 7 observed, many states too have "frivolous" and "vexatious" litigation statutes. While as explained these provisions are useful on the wholesale level for frivolous cases or other cases that should never be filed at all, to some extent they can be used to address over-litigation as well. For example, one practice that can render a claim vexatious is its repetition. That is, even a litigant with a non-frivolous original claim can, by repeatedly litigating the same thing, come within the scope of state prohibitions on vexatious litigation.[10] Likewise, a specific claim brought within a good-faith case may be frivolous and thus within the scope of a state frivolous litigation statute.[11] Because frivolous and vexatious litigation provisions typically require payment of costs and attorneys' fees resulting from them, state courts have these mechanisms too to reallocate the costs of over-litigation. As chapter 7 proposed, courts should apply these tools in appropriate cases, including wherever necessary to deter clearly marginally wasteful litigation.

"Pay-to-Impose" for Other Poor Marginal Decisions to Litigate

Courts should also experiment with other means of imposing greater pay-to-impose costs on litigants who make extremely poor marginal decisions to litigate a case or a particular claim. Whereas Rule 11 and

Section 1927, and to some extent Rule 37, target bad faith by litigants, there is room to experiment with greater pay-to-lose even in cases where parties have not clearly shown bad faith. Of course, Rule 54 and Rule 68 are not limited to those who litigate in bad faith, and their greater use as proposed here would help to curb over-litigation. But generalizing beyond those specific rules, courts should find additional ways to discourage parties from making extremely poor decisions to press claims or defenses farther than is justified beyond a certain procedural point in a case, in particular, the point at which claims or defenses are revealed through the very process of litigation to be very weak. Rather than viewing claims or defenses as "strong" or "weak" from the beginning of a case, when such assessments are difficult not only for judges but for parties themselves, greater attention by judges and other participants in the civil litigation system to the merits of parties' positions *as measured over the course of litigation* would be useful in discouraging excessive litigation. While judges should be initially reluctant to reallocate many litigation costs to losing parties, that reluctance should be overcome in the set of cases where a party's decision to litigate further at the margin of a case is shown to be patently unreasonable.

Procedural Offers

One important way courts should experiment towards combating over-litigation is by encouraging parties to make "procedural offers." Just as parties may make substantive offers to the opposing side proposing to settle a case for a certain amount or under certain conditions, procedural offers would be proposals to agree to a certain amount of civil process—that is, to incur and require the opposing side to incur, only a certain level of litigation costs. The point of a procedural offer would be to reduce, for both sides of a case, the costs of litigation. In particular, parties accepting a procedural offer would agree to curtail discovery, or to limit their pretrial motion practice, or to conduct other forms of abbreviated civil process in order to contain costs.

Chapter 9 proposes several forms of abbreviated civil process, appropriate especially but not only for cases of moderate size. One way a litigant could make a procedural offer is to offer to conduct the case according to one of those processes. Alternatively, a party making a procedural offer could propose any kind of limit to contain the costs of litigating a case. The party receiving such an offer could—just like a party receiving an offer to settle a case—accept it, and thus litigate according to specified parameters to contain litigation costs, or reject it and litigate according to the full suite of rules of civil procedure and civil discovery. But following the resolution of a case, a court could consider whether a party rejecting a procedural offer should incur some of the litigation costs not avoided by virtue of rejecting the offer.

For example, much as Rule 54, Rule 68, and their state counterparts allow courts to reallocate the costs of litigation, courts could consider reallocation of all litigation costs attributable to an offeree's rejection of a procedural offer—that is, the litigation costs that were not avoided—for parties who thereafter lose the case. A court might reallocate such costs even if the judge did not think reallocating all litigation costs would otherwise have been warranted. Where a party lost after having rejected an offer to litigate the same case in a less expensive manner, however, allocating the higher litigation costs that the losing party could have avoided, but did not avoid, may be especially warranted. Here again, litigation costs might be usefully reallocated—in order to encourage litigants to contain them—not on a wholesale basis, but rather on a case-by-case, retrospective, and retail basis. There is ample room for courts, and for parties themselves, to experiment along these lines within existing procedural rules. Chapter 9 returns to this theme.

Greater Judicial Ownership of Litigation Costs

Employing the procedural tools identified here to deter over-litigation would require the judiciary to take a somewhat greater role in the litigation process. For at present, judges do not always exhaust civil litigation's procedural ground rules already available to combat excessive litigiousness. One explanation is that judges may be reluctant to manage litigation closely enough to know when greater pay-to-lose is justified. Such determinations would require judges to consider in some detail the merits of parties' claims, defenses, discovery requests, and various motions. Case-by-case determinations of the appropriateness of reallocating more litigation costs on a pay-to-lose basis would require judges to determine not simply which party should prevail on a given matter, but to make also more fine-grained determinations about the merits of the non-prevailing party's positions and in some sense by "how much" the non-prevailing party lost—that is, whether its arguments were merely unconvincing or instead wholly without merit. Judicial workload, especially in the busiest jurisdictions, may make those kinds of assessments difficult.

Judges might also fear that imposing greater pay to lose in any form may discourage legitimate litigation, including litigation advocating for extensions in the law. One litigant's creative argument may appear to the opposing party to be frivolous. Yet often changes in the law result from advancing novel legal arguments or applying existing legal doctrines to new factual circumstances. Allocating more litigation costs on a pay-to-lose basis therefore could chill or, worse, effectively punish, those who advance innovative arguments entirely in good faith. Many judges no doubt recognize this danger.

These concerns are important, and the imposition of greater pay-to-lose must take into account both the judiciary's institutional constraints and the risks of discouraging legitimate litigation. But neither of these should prevent *somewhat* greater reallocation of litigation costs on litigants who over-litigate wastefully or in bad faith. First, discouraging wasteful litigation would likely have beneficial effects on judicial workloads. Because excessive litigation itself generates more work for courts, which to some degree or another must oversee that litigation, discouraging over-litigation would therefore likely reduce courts' burdens.

Second, and more importantly, judicially administered pay-to-lose— that is, the limited and qualified forms of pay-to-impose proposed here—would not require judges to undertake a fine grained analysis of every civil case. In many civil cases, there is no question that both parties litigated in good faith. While civil litigation necessarily generates losers as well as winners, much litigation is conducted without either side intending to increase its opponent's litigation costs unnecessarily. In other words, in the typical case, judges would not be required to perform any extended analysis for the purpose of reallocating litigation costs. Rather, only where it appears rather clear that a party over-litigated certain claims or defenses would a judge have to consider the validity of potential over-litigation. To be sure, there will be close cases, but there is no reason to expect that the average case will be close.

With respect to discouraging legal creativity, here too the average civil case does not advance novel legal arguments or the application of existing doctrine to new factual circumstances, so this concern will be limited to exceptional cases. But where it is present, judges should err on the side of creative litigants, as suggested in the previous chapter. Rule 11 itself explicitly acknowledges the importance of creative litigation by excluding from the scope of advocacy subject to its sanctions "legal contentions . . . warranted . . . by non-frivolous argument for *extending, modifying, or reversing existing law or for establishing new law*" (emphasis added).[12] Many states' analogous rules echo this same language, as do many states' frivolous litigation statutes. Thus, increased reliance on pay-to-lose should not and need not discourage creative litigation. What is more, over-litigation often takes the form not of creative advocacy but, to the contrary, of needless generation of costs with respect to legal or factual issues for which continued litigation is unjustified precisely because the issues are straightforward. When parties over-litigate by generating straightforwardly unjustified costs, courts should face little difficulty reallocating those costs.

Ultimately, when parties generate excessive litigation costs, they do so under the general authority of the court and in particular the presiding judge. Judges should consider taking a more active role in the civil litigation, then, in part as the best positioned potential supervisors of litigation. And, importantly, the choice for judges is not one between fully passive participants in the litigation process who mobilize only in response to periodic disputes between litigants, on the one hand, and micro-managers of every phase of a civil case, on the other hand. There is much room between these extremes, and many judges already occupy a middle role. Judges should remain above the daily throes of discovery, for example, and allow parties to litigate their cases. At the same time, however, more judges should view themselves as proactive managers of civil litigation whose general and well-understood role to ensure procedural fairness includes, more emphatically and specifically, ensuring the fair and reasonable generation of the costs of litigating a case (see, for example, Gensler 2010; Koeltl 2010), a vision advanced recently and persuasively by Gensler and (*Judge*) Rosenthal (2013) (cf. Hensler and Rowe 2001, which calls on judges to exercise more of their existing authority and discretion in screening class action litigation; and Steinberg

2016, which calls on judges to become more active participants in housing litigation involving low-income individuals, and reporting beneficial results of the same). A conspicuous willingness on the part of judges to reallocate costs in those cases where excessive costs have plainly been needlessly imposed could create better incentives for litigants more generally; discouraging over-litigation does not require judges to reallocate costs in all cases. The proposal here is for judges to encourage litigants not to over-litigate in all cases, by showing a willingness to reallocate excessive costs in some cases.

In addition to increased reliance on pay-to-lose for parties who generate excessive and unjustified litigation costs, courts could do more to discourage over-litigation also by reducing the opportunities for it in the very first place. That is, over-litigation presupposes occasions to over-litigate. Courts might limit those. For example, although the rules of civil procedure limit various discovery requests—limitations on the number of interrogatory requests and the number and hours of depositions, for example—some judges ignore those limits and allow parties to conduct more than what the rules allow. In other words, some judges make discovery more costly by ignoring the limits of discovery contemplated in the rules of procedure. As parties often prefer to request from their opponents more discovery rather than less, discovery raises the costs of litigation. In some cases, more discovery than prescribed by the rules of procedure is necessary. But judges should make that determination on a case-by-case basis, looking with appropriate scrutiny upon the marginal costs of litigation generated. And courts should require the requesting parties to bear those costs when a court allows more discovery that subsequently appears to the court to have been wasteful.

Courts could take still other steps to help contain over-litigation and marginal litigation costs. For one example, in some jurisdictions, better judicial calendar management would reduce the costs of civil litigation. Adjournments of hearings and trials by some judges adds significantly to the costs of legal representation and of expert witnesses, when lawyers and experts appear in court only to be rescheduled to appear another day. In some jurisdictions, courts schedule more motion hearings and more trials at a given time than they can handle, even adjusting for last-minute settlements. Some of this rescheduling is unavoidable, as judges must hear certain matters on emergency bases and cannot possibly predict the set of changing demands on their time. At the same time, some judicially required adjournments require parties to incur litigation expenditures that probably can be avoided or reduced.

To be very clear, the high cost of civil litigation is not the consequence of judicial behavior. The point, rather, is that judges happen to be uniquely well positioned to address it, and in particular to consider not only whether cases are justified on a wholesale basis but also whether and when litigants generate or bear unnecessary litigation costs over the course of a case. Greater judicial oversight and management of litigation—a modest, balanced amount—would therefore help to address the problem of over-litigation. Courts could make litigation more affordable.

And to the extent courts can help to control litigation costs, fewer parties would be inclined to resort to arbitration and formal mediation as an alternative to traditional litigation. As observed in the next chapter, many potential litigants, including sophisticated commercial parties, use arbitration as a less expensive alternative to civil litigation. Arbitration and mediation effectively contain the amount such parties would otherwise spend on full-fledged discovery, extensive motion practice, and other costs associated with traditional litigation, even for parties that can afford it. Increased judicial efforts to control litigation costs and in particular to deter over-litigation would make courts more accessible and more attractive to parties who otherwise have incentives to use a parallel, private system of adjudication instead.

The Boundaries of Zealous Advocacy

Finally, but not at all least, increased professionalism by the bar also could reduce over-litigation. In particular, norms of legal advocacy should be reconsidered wherever they are taken to justify over-litigation. On the one hand, existing rules of professional conduct, including the Model Rules of Professional Responsibility, contemplate on obligation on the part of attorneys to advocate zealously on clients' behalf.[13] This obligation has a distinguished pedigree, as the adversarial system assumes that justice is most likely to be served when parties are represented by zealous advocates.

The trouble, however, is that over-litigation can be too easily justified in the name of zealous advocacy, leading attorneys to advance far-fetched claims and defenses and in turn generate wasteful litigation costs. Taken to the extreme, the obligation to represent one's client zealously could be said to require wasteful litigation whenever it somehow advances the client's narrow interests. And overstating a client's claims or defenses might always be taken to advance the client's narrow interests in some sense; if an opponent must spend additional resources overcoming a far-fetched position, that could be said to show the client's interests were advanced. Wearing an opponent down can always be claimed to advance a client's interests.

Yet even zealous advocacy has an upper bound, and should not serve to justify conduct that needlessly drives up the marginal costs of litigation or undermines the civil litigation system's reliability. Without compromising the responsibility to represent one's client aggressively, there is room for the bar to reconsider poor habits of mind and practice. After all, representing a client with zeal does not override other professional obligations. The rules of professional responsibility also include, explicitly, ethical duties not to advance frivolous claims and contentions, to expedite litigation where possible and in the client's interest, to make honest representations to the court, and to be fair with opposing parties and counsel specifically in connection with discovery.[14] Why these professional obligations must somehow yield to zealous advocacy is far from clear. Instead, zealous advocacy is properly understood in light of these other explicit professional duties, not as a trump of them.

To be sure, balancing zealous advocacy with specific rules of professional responsibility can be difficult in practice. Unqualified reliance on the obligation to represent a client zealously is easier to operationalize. As others have observed, what the rules of professional conduct collectively require, in any specific instance or context, can be indeterminate.[15] The responsibility to advocate zealously lends itself to reflexive invocation likely in part because attorneys' other professional obligations are sometimes imprecise.

But other professional obligations are not second-tier. Attorneys could and should do more to avoid needless litigation costs and the over-litigation even of good-faith claims. After all, over-litigation is a phenomenon facilitated by attorneys, not parties, and there are reasons to worry that cognitive biases and attorneys' "intuition" can lead them to over-litigate (Wistrich and Rachlinski 2013). While the rules of procedure and other legal authorities allow judges to allocate or reallocate litigation costs, reducing over-litigation will ultimately require a change in the behavior of lawyers. This is no small task, and speaks to questions of litigation culture.

How the culture of litigation leads to over-litigation and how the profession might address that problem is a large topic that warrants extended development elsewhere. For present purposes, the relevant point is simply that curbing over-litigation will be accomplished not only by implementing procedural rules that change litigants' incentives externally, but also by influencing lawyers' internal motivations to comply fully with *existing* norms of professionalism. A more vigorous application of the pay-to-impose rules recommended here might foster such behavioral changes. After all, to some extent, litigation culture reflects and is shaped by litigation's ground rules, including those allocating costs. More fine-grained allocation of certain litigation costs might provide a catalyst for litigation cultural change as well.

Summary

Beyond frivolous and bad-faith claims and defenses, excessive litigation costs can take a more subtle form—the over-litigation of issues not raised in bad faith. This form of cost impedes access to the courts by making litigation unnecessarily expensive at the margins of a case. Fortunately, both federal and state courts have at their disposal, and could make much better use of (or expand), several procedural rules allowing for the reallocation of the costs of over-litigation generated by parties whose marginal decisions to litigate seem wasteful—wasteful whether because additional litigation of those issues is not intended to be reliability-enhancing, or is intended to require an opposing party to spend additional resources, or is simply clearly unjustified by the benefits associated with additional litigation. More frequent, calibrated use of "pay to impose" would reduce unnecessary and unjustified litigation costs.

While the case for allocating more litigation costs on parties whose decisions to litigate further at the margin of a case is especially strong for those who do so in bad faith, pay-to-lose should not be limited to bad faith. Parties who make unreasonable—unambiguously wasteful—

decisions to run up litigation costs (their own and their adversary's) also should be subject to more of the costs of that imposition. Subtlety is important here. For up to now, the pay-to-lose debate is usually conducted in terms that are far too crude: "loser pays" need not be all or nothing. Instead, courts should deter over-litigation by focusing on the marginal decisions litigants make over the course of a case. Litigants who insist on litigating plainly past all reasonable points should internalize more of the costs of that insistence, even while judges should reallocate litigation costs cautiously.

Discouraging over-litigation will require more than greater reliance on pay-to-impose, however. In addition to reallocating some of the costs of litigation, and more generally speaking, judges should take a somewhat greater supervisory role in curbing excesses litigation. Without micro-managing civil cases, judges can balance the need to ensure that parties are able to litigate cases as fully as fairness requires, on the one hand, while avoiding excessive and unjustifiable litigation costs, on the other hand. There is room for judges to do so, for example, by showing greater oversight of discovery, better calendar management, and especially a general willingness to manage their cases so that parties have fewer opportunities to engage in excessive litigation.

Yet over-litigation is facilitated by the bar, not the bench. Reducing excessive litigation costs will also require some behavioral change by attorneys themselves. This too is within reach, especially if judges make greater use of procedural mechanisms for reallocating litigation costs, which would helpfully underscore lawyers' professional obligations to expedite litigation where possible, not to advance unjustified claims, and above all to be fair to opposing parties and counsel. Whereas the problem of truly frivolous case filings often (though not always) results from pro se or otherwise unsophisticated parties, over-litigation is sometimes the work of sophisticated attorneys done on behalf of sophisticated clients. The profession at all levels has an important role in combating excessive litigation.

Next, chapters 9 and 10 turn to the problem of access, proposing reforms designed to render the civil litigation system more accessible, in part by reducing the costs of litigating in additional ways.

9

Providing Cheaper Paths to Court

To the extent good-faith litigants with strong legal claims lack access to the civil litigation system, the potential private and social benefits associated with litigation go unrealized. As chapter 6 explained, missing plaintiffs (those who never bring a case notwithstanding they unquestionably suffered legal harm) are difficult to quantify; there are straightforward and compelling reasons to conclude that many potential litigants are priced out of civil litigation. Of course, in some important sense, parties who lack access might lack it "rationally." That is to say, for them, the costs of access outweigh its expected benefits (or else the costs of access do not outweigh its benefits, but some parties simply cannot finance the cost anyway). Even so, if the barriers to access *were* lower, more parties with cognizable claims would be positioned to bring good-faith claims. The circles of the diagram from chapter 2 would overlap more (see figure 9.1).

It must be emphasized that the costs of civil litigation are not all fixed. Nor are they completely determined by market forces. There is a market for legal representation, to be sure, and similarly, there is a market for the many services associated with traditional litigation: deposition

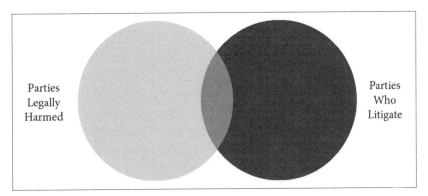

Figure 9.1. Suffer Genuine Legal Harm vs. Initiate Civil Litigation

services, document management, expert testimony, and others. At the same time, however, the costs of litigation depend upon several features of the litigation system itself. These include not least of all the procedural ground rules according to which civil litigation is conducted, and in turn decisions by litigants themselves about how much to spend on a given case. But whereas the previous two chapters addressed litigation costs as a function of litigant decisions, this chapter focuses instead on the costs associated with the institutional structure of civil litigation—with litigation's procedural architecture.

Traditionally, those calling for greater access to justice have focused least on litigation's procedural architecture, and instead mainly on justifying more resources for those who lack access, in particular those who cannot afford representation. But that focus misses an important part of the equation, as greater access can be accomplished also by lowering its price. This chapter argues that the menu of processes for conducting civil litigation should be larger, to include cheaper ways of bringing a case. That is, potential litigants should have more procedural options for advancing their claims, such that they might choose traditional litigation for larger cases, and a less expensive mode of litigation for claims when traditional litigation would be cost-prohibitive. In all cases, litigants should employ procedure better tailored to the stakes of a given case. A wider range of procedural options would benefit potential plaintiffs, but also defendants as well, for whom the costs of defending against claims through traditional civil processes sometimes exceed their benefits too.

It will be important, for reasons explained earlier, that processes less expensive than traditional litigation do not sacrifice reliability in the name of greater access, or at least not too much. Less costly modes of litigation may be undesirable on balance, notwithstanding they are more affordable, if they produce excessive error. But if access *can* be promoted without sacrificing reliability, the argument for greater use of alternative forms of litigation becomes strong indeed. To be sure, as chapter 3 pointed out, reliability can be very difficult to measure, because doing so requires some metric or proxy against which to assess whether the outcome in a given case was correct. On the other hand, if the development of new modes of civil litigation raises no concerns about poor reliability, and moreover if litigating parties could choose to elect those processes—or could tailor litigation processes to their own needs given the stakes of a given case—that might alleviate worries about reliability. In other words, litigants themselves might be well positioned to decide whether a new process were likely to be reliable for them.

Indeed, the establishment of new forms of litigation would constitute a kind of loose test of the proposition advanced here throughout that many parties are, in fact, priced out of traditional litigation: if many litigants employed new, less costly processes, that result would suggest that, in the absence of those new processes, many potential litigants would be priced out. If, on the other hand, new and less expensive processes were employed by few litigants, that would tend to suggest that traditional litigation is not so often prohibitively costly after all.

As explained shortly below, the non-traditional procedures proposed here are costly neither to parties nor to court systems. Because they would employ existing judicial infrastructure, the social cost associated with new processes would be very small. This combination—greater accessibility and low cost—makes the argument for new procedures less expensive than traditional civil litigation stronger still, especially in combination with the reforms prescribed in chapters 7 and 8 to filter more undesirable cases out of the litigation system altogether and to reduce over-litigation at the margins of legitimate cases.

Existing Complements to Traditional Civil Litigation

Calls for cheaper alternatives to traditional civil litigation have been made for decades, gaining more momentum especially during periods of active civil litigation reform. The alternative dispute resolution (ADR) movement of the 1980s reflected efforts to provide litigants with methods of resolving cases without the high costs associated with traditional litigation. By now, ADR has seen wide institutionalization in both state and federal courts in the form of various mandatory and elective processes (e.g., Hensler 2003). For another example, "health courts," which have not yet seen wide adoption, have been proposed as a response to alleged shortcomings of medical malpractice litigation. Finally, although they may be easy to overlook as an alternative to traditional civil litigation given their ubiquity, small claims courts promote access to the courts with a process designed especially for litigants whose cases present very low stakes. Small claims courts now exist in nearly all jurisdictions, and the use of them—and experimentation with new features of them, as explained later—should be encouraged. What links all of these is an underlying effort to provide less costly yet reliable alternatives to traditional civil litigation. While no doubt important, they are not enough to provide a sufficiently wide range of less expensive alternatives to traditional litigation to ensure meaningful access to the courts.

Alternative Dispute Resolution

On the whole, ADR has much to recommend it. Parties employing a dominant form of ADR—mediation—present arguments informally to a trained mediator, who then facilitates communication between the parties in an effort to settle the case without taking any hard position respecting the merits of opposing parties' contentions. Mediation is thus especially useful in cases where, for whatever reason, opposing parties are not well situated to negotiate over the terms of settlement themselves. A successful mediation is consummated by a settlement of the dispute. Thus, the figures mentioned in chapter 1 about the portion of filed cases that are resolved by settlement instead of by courts reflect, in part, mediated settlements (though not all mediated settlements follow the formal filing of a case).

Arbitration is another common ADR process, in which opposing sides present more formal arguments or even legal briefs to an arbitrator or panel of arbitrators, who then render a decision. Arbitration, often used by parties who had some relationship prior to their legal dispute (such as parties to a contract), and thus who had an opportunity to agree in advance to employ arbitration for any future disputes, comes in nonbinding and binding forms. The various forms of both mediation and arbitration have inspired still other subspecies of ADR, some of which were developed specifically as part of civil litigation reform initiatives. For example, "case evaluation" requires litigating parties, prior to trial, to present their cases to a three-person case evaluation panel, empowered to issue a settlement figure for the case. Either side can then accept or reject the panel's settlement figure, but those who reject must do better at trial or else pay their opponent's attorney's fees. Case evaluation, then, is designed not simply to provide a mechanism for dispute resolution, but to discourage continued litigation through trial.

While ADR has been the subject of extensive commentary and extended analysis of it is thus unnecessary here, several quick observations relevant to present purposes are in order. First, the proliferation of ADR confirms that traditional litigation is often costly; otherwise, ADR would not constitute a widely employed alternative. In addition, and however, most forms of ADR presuppose that litigants enjoy some access to the civil litigation system in the first place. That is, ADR processes are designed mostly as a less costly pathway for parties who could otherwise litigate—an optional path to traditional litigation, to which the parties might otherwise resort. Indeed, ADR is often used only after a civil case has already been filed.

In fact, to some extent, ADR is employed by parties as an integral part of the traditional litigation process, not as a complete alternative to it. For example, many judges encourage or even require parties to participate in mediation of their case following the discovery phase of a case before going to trial. Such mediation is convened by a mediator chosen by the parties, often from a list provided by the court. Here, mediation may be a cost-savings mechanism that is cheaper than trial, but one designed for parties already deep into the traditional litigation process, not those who lack access altogether.

To be sure, some forms of binding arbitration, in contrast to mediation, require parties to arbitrate their disputes rather than to litigate at all. Here, arbitration is binding not only in the sense that the parties must accept the arbitrator's decision, but also in that the parties must employ the arbitration process to resolve their dispute instead of litigation; where binding arbitration contracts govern, a party cannot resort to traditional litigation instead. This form of ADR thus does not provide an alternative path to traditional litigation so much as it displaces altogether, barring even parties who might prefer traditional litigation from filing a case in court. Binding arbitration where one side or the other would prefer litigating thus impedes rather than promotes access to the courts, and for that reason is the most controversial form of ADR—especially when binding arbitration is required of an unsophisticated party through a boilerplate contract.

The proponents of binding arbitration counter that the mechanism does reduce litigation costs. At least where binding arbitration is elected between sophisticated parties who understand arbitration and are well positioned to negotiate over its terms, that argument has considerable force. On the other side, opponents of binding arbitration see binding arbitration as the unjustified denial of access to the courts for parties who may enter into arbitration contracts unaware of their terms, when for instance consumer suits are prohibited by binding arbitration clauses in standardized form contracts. However that may be, the important point here is that most ADR processes either presuppose that sophisticated parties would have access to the civil litigation system in the first place, or they prevent unsophisticated parties from resorting to traditional litigation even if they would prefer it. In either scenario, ADR is not a complete solution for those who lack access to the courts, although its voluntary use seems completely unobjectionable.

That leaves some ADR-like services available to parties who cannot afford traditional litigation but for whom some form of informal dispute resolution may be useful. These include community-based mediation services, which offer free counseling and mediation to parties without the means to secure legal representation, usually relying on volunteer mediators. Such services, somewhat like expanded self-help services offered by some local courts as discussed shortly, provide useful assistance to parties who lack other resources. As useful as they may be, however, ensuring greater access to justice cannot depend on the services of volunteer mediators. Unless parties can resort to litigation where mediation is unsuccessful, they will have little bargaining power during mediation or any other informal ADR process. In contrast to those who rely on ADR as a cost-savings measure, then, those for whom volunteer mediation services constitute their *only* means of resolving a legal dispute are not very well positioned to advance their legal rights and interests. Modes of litigation through which would-be litigants could, if necessary, advance their interests in court are also needed.

Health Courts

As noted in chapter 4, one proposed reform of the civil litigation system is the establishment of "health courts." Recent proponents of health courts—from litigation-reform groups including Common Good and the American Medical Association—propose new courts for what they see as the principal defect of medical malpractice litigation, which is that juries prove unreliable in such cases. According to these reformers, juries, moved by excessive sympathy for plaintiffs and unable fully to understand the medical-scientific issues at stake, often decide cases in favor of medical malpractice plaintiffs when they should not. And even when juries prove reliable, the costs of defending against a medical malpractice case successfully are so high that they make liability insurance for doctors excessively expensive and sometimes therefore reduce the availability of medical care. Worse still, according to some reformers, plaintiffs' attorneys are often overcompensated in medical malpractice cases, while damage awards are often too high—especially for punitive damages and pain and suffering—and the evidentiary standards for proving malpractice are too susceptible to manipulation especially as a result of unscrupulous medical experts. The establishment of health courts to adjudicate medical malpractice cases would, according to some, avoid or reduce these problems (Barringer 2006; Barringer et al. 2008).

The proposal to create health courts for medical malpractice litigation is not entirely new, however. Proposals to create quasi-administrative health courts or pilot programs were raised as early as the 1970s, repeated later in the 1980s, and resurfaced again in 2005 at both the state and federal levels in the form of reform legislation (Chow 2007). In the late 1980s, Florida and Virginia created health courts restricted specifically to cases involving alleged medical malpractice leading to cognitive impairment for infants. Although by the mid-2000s those particular programs suffered from lack of legislative funding, the core idea has gained traction more recently as a result of national health-care reform.

The most distinctive feature of a health court is the potential replacement of lay jurors with expert juries. In one variation, juries would be comprised of an expert panel of doctors. In another variation, motivated in part by constitutional concerns given the constitutional right to trial by jury, lay jurors would receive special training before hearing a medical malpractice cases. In still another, an expert judge would sit along a lay jury to provide medical-scientific help and instruction to jurors. Many health court proposals contemplate court appointment of a neutral expert to assist the court and jury more generally, all in the name of ensuring more reliable outcomes consistent with the relevant medical science.

Another element of many health court proposals is the establishment of "ACEs"—"automatically compensable events" or "avoidable classes of events" (Bovbjerg and Tancredi 2005). Here the idea is that the occurrence of certain medical mistakes would entitle plaintiffs to compensation, on the grounds that medical malpractice would be assumed or granted without additional procedure or evidence. This aspect of health court proposals is intended to provide recovery for certain categories of plaintiffs without any dispute over whether the defendant violated the liability standard, although the extent of a plaintiff's resulting harm might still be subject to dispute. Even in that latter case, though, proponents emphasize that litigation costs would be lower for plaintiffs, and some remedy more easily available.

Other aspects of proposed health courts have sparked more controversy. For example, some leading proponents have also called for changes in the applicable liability standard, combining liability reform with litigation reform. For example, Common Good calls for changing the negligence standard applicable to medical malpractice cases to a weaker "avoidability" standard. (The current liability standard conditions recovery on a violation of the relevant standard of medical care.) Setting aside the likely imprecision of such a new standard, it is not clear why the current liability standard should be replaced in a health court that would already otherwise address reformers' concerns about medical malpractice litigation. If health courts with informed juries were to work, presumably they could reliably adjudicate questions about whether a defendant violated the relevant standard of medical care.

For another example reform, advocates of health courts have also proposed establishing schedules for non-economic damages, and lower caps on the contingency fee rate that plaintiffs' attorneys may charge. With respect to the former, the desirability of damages schedules for injuries such as pain and suffering will depend on the level of allowable recovery, and on whether the savings resulting from not litigating the issues of damages outweighs the disadvantage of damage awards not calculated for individual plaintiffs. If damage schedules simply seek to reduce the amounts that successful medical malpractice plaintiffs recover—low damages caps in disguise—then they are deservedly controversial on the grounds that they may deprive successful plaintiffs of full compensation.

With respect to lower caps on contingency fees, here again the reason why health courts constitute a proper forum for regulating contingency fees is not apparent. If litigation in new health courts proves less expensive, as intended, that should put downward pressure on contingency-fee contracts, just as plaintiffs' lawyers often charge lower contingency amounts for less complicated litigation in other administrative or quasi-administrative courts (such as for workers' compensation and social security cases). If litigation in new health courts is not as straightforward as its proponents predict, there would likely be less downward pressure on attorneys' fees. Presumably the legal market would settle that question one way or the other.

But more fundamentally, as chapter 5 explained, the premise underlying recent proposals to establish health courts—that medical malpractice litigation is unreliable and imposes excessive costs—remains unproven. Again, the evidence taken as a whole shows to the contrary that medical malpractice is not over-litigated, and indeed that some medical malpractice never generates litigation at all (see generally T. Baker 2005). As chapter 5 also observed, plaintiffs lose medical malpractice cases roughly 75% of the time, do not receive especially high damage awards relative to their average injuries, and punitive damages awards against doctors are uncommon. Thus, the imperative to establish health courts is not at all clear (Chow 2007; Peters 2008).

All of this said, continued experimentation with health courts (or similarly motivated institutional reforms; see Mello et al. 2014) seems worthwhile, given the potential to increase reliability and lower litigation costs simultaneously. For one thing, experimentation with the civil litigation process seems desirable in the abstract, without which improvements to that process may be too few and infrequent. Innovations designed to render medical malpractice juries more informed and thus more reliable would certainly be desirable, if that can be accomplished at a reasonable cost. Lower litigation costs would also mean that more potential plaintiffs would have access to pursue their claims. The designation of "automatically compensable events" in particular may reduce litigation costs while providing access to deserving plaintiffs. Further, if adequate damages schedules rendered defendants less motivated to contest liability, for fear—well founded or not—of exorbitant damage awards, such an effect also would likely avoid needless litigation.

On the other hand, whether the ACE proposal constitutes a meaningful change from existing medical malpractice law, which already imposes liability for obvious errors (although not named "automatically compensable") under existing legal doctrines, is subject to question. In other words, automatic recovery for such plain misfeasance may not provide medical malpractice plaintiffs with much that is new. And there are other potential drawbacks. For one, capping attorneys' fees may well reduce rather than expand access, as fewer attorneys may be willing to take medical malpractice cases. For another, unlike other forms of ADR, some versions of health courts would require some investment in new legal infrastructure. New resource commitments raise important questions of cost and financing, and experiences in Florida and Virginia suggest such challenges may be difficult. On the other hand, it is not clear why some variations of health courts could not mostly piggyback on existing courts. While permanently empaneling expert juries probably would require significant new investments, providing ordinary juries with expert guidance is not so dissimilar to judicial use of "special masters," "judicial experts," and other useful features of existing litigation processes.

Concerning the ultimate desirability of health courts, then, more experimentation and study is needed. To the extent a version of health courts may make medical malpractice litigation less expensive and thus truly more accessible, while promoting reliability along the way, health courts could be a welcome complement to traditional forms of litigation. Indeed, it is possible that experimentation with specialty courts for other types of civil cases (such as asbestos cases, intellectual property cases, or other types of litigation for which expertise may be useful towards promoting reliable outcomes) would be useful as well. On the other hand, to the extent health courts deprive deserving parties of a meaningful opportunity to recover—for example, by making it more difficult for medical malpractice victims to find legal representation or by permitting plaintiffs to seek only partial compensation for genuine injuries— they would likely make bad matters worse. Such questions cannot be resolved in the abstract; they require trial, error, and evaluation. Any complement to traditional litigation that might lower the costs of litigation and promote greater reliability as well as provide more access warrants further development and continued consideration.

Small Claims Courts and Legal Self-Help

Although this fact is not always fully appreciated, cases brought in small claims courts constitute a substantial percentage of *all* civil litigation. According to available data, out of a total of some 17 million civil cases per year of all types (i.e., not just general civil cases as defined in chapter 1), over 40% constitute cases brought in small claims courts. There are jurisdictional ceilings on the size of monetary damages that small claims plaintiffs may seek to be eligible for small claims court jurisdiction—in most states around several thousand dollars, from a low of $1,500 (in Kentucky) to a high of $25,000 (Tennessee), with a modal amount of $5,000. The fraction of small-claim cases out of all civil cases within a state varies accordingly. But even given that variance, it is clear that small claims constitute a substantial portion of all civil litigation both within and across all states. More should be done to encourage small claims, including experimentation with making small claims courts even more accessible.

Parties to small claims cases typically represent themselves. In some jurisdictions, lawyers are barred from appearing in small claims proceedings, while in others they are permitted though often not used by parties seeking precisely to resolve their cases without the expense of legal representation. The formal rules of evidence do not apply in small claims courts. Nor may parties engage in civil discovery. Indeed, that is the very purpose of small claims adjudication—to resolve small cases quickly and informally, without lawyers and the other costly trappings of traditional litigation. A party's cost thus consists mainly of the time it takes to appear in small claims court.

Small claims court judges or trial court judges or magistrates hear the small claim (jurisdictions vary); there are no juries. Not constrained by formal evidentiary rules, presiding judges hear testimony from the parties and review any documentary materials or other informal evidence a party may wish to submit. There are no witnesses in small claims trials, or formal testimony as such. Instead, the presiding judge freely questions the parties; communication during a small claims trial thus flows informally between the bench and the litigants. After having heard the parties' arguments and any informal evidence they wish to provide, the judge renders a final decision, usually resolving the case on the spot.

Judges may also recommend mediation to the parties before rendering a final decision. In most jurisdictions, a small claims court decision is not appealable, though in some jurisdictions the defendant can appeal. Thus, small claims proceedings often provide closure on the dispute. The decision provided in a small claims proceeding is enforceable just like any other judicial order.

By providing a forum in which the costs of litigation are extremely low, small claims courts provide access to justice for an important set of prospective litigants—those with good-faith claims whose potential damages are modest, so small indeed that they may be worth neither significant litigation costs nor even the social costs associated with mobilizing a jury. Common small claims involve, for example, landlord-tenant disputes, small contract cases, and small real property cases.

In most states, litigants can elect to bring a case in small claims courts in lieu of the general trial court. Filing in small claims court is usually elective, however, not mandatory; a party with a small claim can choose to file in the general trial court instead. In other words, small litigants face a trade-off between the benefits and costs of traditional litigation in the general-jurisdiction trial courts, on the one hand, and the advantages and disadvantages of proceeding in less rigorous but much less expensive small claims courts, on the other hand.

In more practical, economic terms, however, small claimants often have no real choice to make. Given the size of the stakes, contingency-fee lawyers generally will not take any case small enough that it could be filed in small claims court. And given the size of the stakes, litigants likewise cannot afford to pay for legal representation by the hour, which would quickly consume the potential benefit of the case. In short, often it is small claims court or nothing, which is why small claims courts were developed in the first place—to provide a venue for litigants in cases where the total stakes are small relative to the costs of traditional litigation. Thus, it is unsurprising that the institution of small claims court is well regarded among citizens, and not only plaintiffs, as defendants too benefit from the opportunity to litigate small disputes at low cost.

Given that small claims courts provide access to litigants who would otherwise lack it, more should be done to promote small claims proceedings. Fortunately, various legal services organizations and many courts themselves have aimed to provide greater access to justice by making it easier for individuals to represent themselves in certain circumstances, including small claims actions and similar forms of legal self-help. These initiatives manifest themselves in several ways, including among others user-friendly websites and court forms for pro se litigants, and in some places, court "small claims advisors." Many organizations have also developed legal kiosks—installed in courts, but also in libraries, community centers, and places like women's shelters—as well as interactive websites providing guidance for common legal needs and telephone legal hotlines targeting low-income persons. The goal of all of these initiatives is to facilitate legal self-help for persons who will represent their own interests without legal representation. Such initiatives also include in-person counseling by paralegals, members of social and religious organizations, and law students, often through community aid organizations. Several large cities also have created one-stop consumer counseling centers that include legal assistance. Some centers provide legal triage, assigning routine cases to paralegals and more complicated cases to attorneys. Some also review self-prepared legal documents for common errors.

All of these initiatives constitute welcome improvements to the civil litigation system (see generally Engler 2010). Assistance for litigants who cannot afford legal representation, whether it is simply assistance to prepare small claims or otherwise, promotes access to justice (Van Wormer 2007). For parties who have little chance of finding legal representation, any possibility of protecting their legal rights depends on their ability to navigate the civil justice system on their own. Fostering their ability to do so therefore seems especially desirable, which explains why such initiatives have been met with little resistance.

The organized bar constitutes a partial exception, however. That is, the American Bar Association (ABA) together with many state bars has resisted some of these self-help initiatives, on the grounds that some of them constitute or else encourage the unauthorized practice of law. The bar's basic argument is that legal advice and counsel from non-lawyers can be harmful to the recipients of such advice. In some instances, the unauthorized practice of law has even led to prosecutions under unauthorized-practice statutes. As an alternative to non-lawyer assistance for the unrepresented, the bar prescribes instead increased pro bono representation by licensed attorneys, as reflected in the ABA's

Model Rule of Professional Conduct 6.1, which calls for lawyers to spend at least fifty hours per year representing those who cannot afford representation.

The bar's resistance notwithstanding, however, it is hard to see how elementary legal assistance could be harmful to those who have little or no prospect of securing legal representation; very few of those served by counseling initiatives would otherwise hire an attorney, and attorneys would not be willing to take such cases on contingency. Nor can the volume of unmet legal needs realistically be absorbed only through increased pro bono commitments by the bar (Charn and Zorza 2005). And because lawyers are, in some jurisdictions, prohibited from small claims court, other types of assistance aimed at small claimants seem especially justified.

Facilitating legal self-help is also inexpensive. Legal kiosks and legal hotlines do not require substantial new investments or long-term costs. The cost of developing user-friendly court forms, which benefit litigants generally, is small too. And much of the legal counseling provided to pro se parties is undertaken by volunteers. In fact, many legal information and counseling services are provided by organizations that have recently added legal counseling to the services they already offer. Such efforts thus do not require new infrastructure or any other significant investment, nor do they tax the public. For this reason too, promoting legal self-help for those filing in small claims court or for those seeking to represent themselves otherwise seems worthwhile in the interest of promoting access, especially given that such assistance is likely to reduce outlandish claims brought by self-represented litigants. This latter observation warrants emphasis; fostering legal self-help through basic counseling seems likely to avoid the filing of some far-fetched claims that pro se litigants might, in the absence of counseling, otherwise file.

In addition to basic counseling, and the greater use of touch-screen or other electronic assistance and user-friendly court forms, still more should be done to encourage legal self-help and small claims in particular. For one, case-filing fees—requiring litigants to pay for "entering" the civil litigation system at all—charged at the time a plaintiff files a case, should be restructured. In addition to case-filing fees, many state courts also impose fees for filing any motion in a case already commenced, and likewise many courts require litigants who go to trial to cover the costs associated with convening a jury, including paying the jury's per diem payment as well daily court fees for trials. Motion fees too should be restructured better to accommodate pro se litigants.

Although most states, like the federal courts, waive filing fees for truly impecunious litigants, access fees for resorting to the courts should be curtailed more generally for small claimants. Indeed, why litigants should be assessed what are essentially user fees for accessing the court system at all is not clear. Presumably, litigants are required to pay filing fees and jury costs on the premise that those who employ the civil litigation system should be taxed for doing so, perhaps like those who pay fees to enter public parks or pay tolls to access certain highways. But taxing access to the courts makes no more sense than taxing access to other institutions of government. It would be difficult to imagine, for example, charging fees to citizens who write letters to their elected representatives in order to cover the costs of responding to them, or likewise those who lobby legislators or engage in grass-roots legislative politics to pay a larger portion of society's costs of maintaining a legislature. But this raises the question why access to the judicial branch of government is properly taxed through user fees. As a general proposition, access to the courts should not require payment (setting aside vexatious or other types of bad-faith litigants, as addressed in chapter 7).

On the other hand, given that filing fees are now an important part of the operating budget of many state courts, their elimination may be unrealistic in the short run. But again, such fees should be restructured to the extent court systems can afford to do so. For example, wherever small claims or other pro se plaintiffs are required to pay fees for merely accessing the civil litigation system, those fees might be refunded to a prevailing plaintiff and levied instead against the losing defendant—another form of pay to lose. Such an arrangement would conserve total resources for state and local courts that depend on filing fees, but would lower the costs of access to litigants who represent themselves in meritorious cases. Courts should employ any reasonable means of lowering the barriers to court for small claimants. This theme is developed next.

A New Court of Medium Claims, and Other Less Costly Paths to Court

Continued experimentation with health courts and greater assistance to pro se litigants do not exhaust the ways to make the civil litigation system more accessible. Much to the contrary. It is possible to develop additional procedures allowing litigants to advance their claims at a cost more commensurate with the size of those claims, especially but not only moderate claims for which traditional litigation is cost prohibitive. Such new forms of litigation would be desirable in the interest of promoting access to the courts *while* curbing litigation costs.

Accordingly, in the interest of making the civil litigation system more accessible, the discussion below proposes four reforms. These include the greater use and adaptation of small claims courts; the establishment of a new court of *medium* claims; the greater use of a revived form of expedited trials; and more generally the use of litigation procedures tailored to the stakes of a given case in any type of civil proceeding. These reforms would provide a greater range of litigation procedures from which litigants could choose, according to the size and significance of a given case. All of them warrant experimentation and development along the lines outlined here.

Expanding the Use of Small Claims Court and Small Claims Juries

The path to small claims court should be expanded for more cases not large enough to justify the costs of traditional litigation. Not only are small claims cases inexpensive to litigate, the resolution of small claims by judges rather than jurors also is likely to avoid any worry about unreliable jurors. Indeed, it seems quite likely that judges are reliable adjudicators of small claims in particular, as judges are well positioned to draw from their considerable experience in evaluating the credibility of opposing parties and the strength of parties' factual positions. Judges are also well positioned to know when a small claimant is bringing a meritless case, and can respond appropriately to plaintiffs who litigate excessively.

In other words, small claims courts are advantageous to defendants and not only plaintiffs. In fact, given the advantages of small claims court as a forum for resolving cases presenting low stakes, defendants too should be allowed to proceed in small claims court for cases within the jurisdictional limits. That is to say, when a plaintiff files a case in a general trial court that could have been brought in small claims court, the defendant should have the right to "remove" the case to small claims court instead. In short, proceeding in small claims court should be available to either side of any case within applicable jurisdictional limits. Defendants should be able to elect small claims proceedings for the same reason plaintiffs do—to avoid the costs associated with traditional litigation for a case presenting low stakes. Furthermore, the ability to move to small claims courts would give defendants a way to respond to small nuisance cases, by litigating in the low-cost forum of small claims court instead of settling small cases to avoid higher litigation costs.

Given that many states provide a right to a jury in civil cases (as the U.S. Constitution's Seventh Amendment does in the federal judicial system), plaintiffs may be able to insist that a case remain in the general trial court over a defendant's preference to remove it to small claims court. Likewise, under current practices in most places, defendants can insist that plaintiffs proceed in a general trial court instead of small claims court, as jury trial rights extend to defendants as well as to plaintiffs. In other words, either side might trump the other's preference for litigating in small claims court.

Nevertheless, states should encourage both plaintiffs and defendants to use small claims courts. Among other ways, they could do so by requiring higher filing fees for parties who insist on litigating what would constitute a small claim through a more expensive process instead. While filing fees in general constitute an undesirable surcharge on access to the courts, fees specifically for litigants who insist on litigating small cases in a relatively expensive forum when a less expensive forum is available and preferred by the opposing party, as discussed above, seem well justified. And litigants making that choice would be those most unlikely to be adversely affected by filing fees.

In addition, litigants who move a small claims case to a general trial court should also be made to pay some amount of "loser fees" in the event they lose the case. As with reallocated filing fees, here again the idea is that litigants whose decisions to litigate in a more expensive forum when a less expensive forum is readily available—and thus, imposing higher costs on their opponents as a result of that choice—should bear more of the costs of their decisions when they do not prevail. If the reform proposed here to allow defendants to remove cases to small claims court were adopted, for example, non-prevailing plaintiffs who trumped that decision should be made to pay for having imposed higher and avoidable costs on their opponents. This reallocation of costs would provide a significant incentive for both sides of a small dispute to employ the cheaper litigation process that small claims proceedings offer.

More fundamentally, states could go further and preserve jury trial rights even in small claims cases, by empaneling new small claims court juries. That is, although small claims courts currently involve no juries, state and local courts should consider experimenting with juries for small claims. A small claims court could use every *other* feature of small claims litigation—including the absence of attorneys and the waiver of civil discovery and the formal rules of evidence—and thus conduct small claims litigation much as it is now conducted, but rely on juries instead of judges to resolve contested factual questions, though judges could and should remain actively involved in the proceedings in the interest of reliability and procedural efficiency. This would combine all of the advantages of small claims litigation while protecting litigants' constitutional right to a civil jury where one party or the other preferred a jury but was otherwise willing to use the small claims process.

One benefit of creating small claims juries would be to preempt the removal of cases out of small claims proceedings and into more expensive, traditional proceedings by litigants who demand jury trials. Such an advantage would hold not just when litigants are motivated to litigate in general trial courts instead of available small claims courts in order to increase costs for their opponents, but also when litigants genuinely desire a jury to hear their cases. Put differently, small claims juries may bring legitimacy as well as efficiency benefits for litigants who seek to exercise jury-trial rights.

A new small claims jury could be convened for a single day—or slightly more or less—in order to hear several small claims cases within that short period. In other words, a single small claims jury should, for reasons of efficiency, hear multiple small claims. This approach would resemble grand juries in criminal law, which hear multiple cases within a set period for the purposes of issuing indictments, though here on a smaller and much shorter scale. As there is no reason why juries are incompatible with the other features of small claims court, state and local courts should consider pilot experimentation with small claims juries in the interest of expanding the capacity of, and access to, their small claims tribunals. However, courts can encourage litigants to bring cases eligible for small claims courts into that forum—towards expanding access and minimizing costs—seems warranted.

Establishing a New Court of Medium Claims

Even with an expanded use of small claims court (and certainly without), many civil cases will fall between small claims, on the one hand, and claims large enough to justify the costs of traditional litigation, on the other. For cases in that wide middle, greater access to justice would be achieved by the creation of new *medium* claims courts. Such courts could go far to provide greater access to justice for litigants who would state claims too high for the jurisdictional ceilings of small claims court, and yet whose expected recovery may not be high enough to offset the more or less fixed minimum costs of ordinary litigation. In contrast to small claims litigation, the process for medium claims would have some of the features of traditional litigation, but fewer than full-fledged civil litigation conducted under the rules of procedure, including civil discovery, and the rules of evidence.

Like small claims courts, medium claims courts too would be subject to jurisdictional limits (although, as discussed below, there are strong reasons to make them available more generally as well for parties that so elect). These jurisdictional limits would be defined by a maximum recoverable damage award some multiple above the ceilings for small claims court, perhaps up to $50,000 or more, for example—in one sense, then, "small claims heavy." Also like small claims courts, medium claims trials would be short, though longer than most small claims proceedings. But unlike small claims courts, parties would be typically represented by counsel (unless, like in any case, they chose to represent themselves), one distinguishing feature of medium claims cases. The presence and expense of counsel can be justified and may be desirable given that medium claims cases could involve significant stakes—the possibility of recovery and liability beyond existing small claims ceilings.

Among other things, attorneys could offer short, time-limited opening and closing statements during a medium claims trial or hearing. Attorneys would also submit documentary and other informal evidence on behalf of their clients, and generally participate in the proceeding by speaking on behalf of their clients.

In further contrast to small claims cases, medium claims would be subject to truncated discovery, such as a very limited number of depositions per party and likewise a limited number of written interrogatories or document requests, both restricted to plainly central questions of the case at hand—in this sense, then, "traditional litigation light." Parties would likewise be limited to at most a single expert. Robust discovery, which characterizes much traditional litigation and to which many of the high costs of traditional litigation are attributable, is not justified by the moderate stakes of medium claims. Discovery should instead be commensurate with the size of a medium claims case.

Also in contrast to small claims cases, most of the ordinary rules of civil procedure governing traditional litigation would apply to a medium claims case, apart from those providing for robust civil discovery, but excluding also rules providing for summary judgment or summary disposition. This means, for example, that after a medium claims case commences upon the filing of a complaint, a defendant could move to dismiss a case on the initial pleadings (just as in traditional civil litigation, as explained in chapter 1) and the judge would rule on that motion. Unlike small claims, then, some medium claims cases could be resolved against the plaintiff through an early motion. But given both abbreviated discovery and the simplicity of any trial, medium claims should not be subject to summary judgment with its significant associated costs. Medium claims should not be subject to post-trial motions or other rules of procedure that govern post-trial processes either. As in small claims cases in most jurisdictions, there should be very limited, if any, appeal of medium claims verdicts, here too in the interest of providing closure at low cost.

The moderate size of a medium claim justifies avoiding the costs associated with the rigors of formal evidentiary rules as well, again to keep the litigation costs of medium claims low, and in particular to make medium claims cases less laborious for counsel and thus more likely that medium claimants can find legal representation. As in small claims courts, informal evidence would be given whatever weight the presiding judge deemed appropriate. Put differently, although none of the formal rules of evidence would apply, medium claims judges would, at their discretion, filter informally rendered evidence through the lens of traditional evidentiary practices as well as common sense. Here once again, trial judges are very well positioned to assess the credibility of witnesses, for example, and also to determine the weight to be given to evidence introduced informally.

Like in an ordinary small claims case, the judge would be the default fact finder: medium claims cases would be short-bench trials resolved quickly without post-trial legal briefing. Given the moderate stakes of a medium claims case, the costs and time associated jury selection and jury trial may not be justified in many cases. And given that the medium claims court judge is already playing a more active role in the case, it makes sense for the judge to resolve all factual questions. That said, parties to a medium claims case might elect juries if they so choose or if one side insists on exercising jury-trial rights.

Not that every, or even most, cases would go all the way to trial. Rather, it is likely that many medium claims cases would settle, just as conventional civil cases and indeed even some small claims cases settle after a complaint is filed but before any hearing. Parties to a medium claims case, like litigants in any civil proceeding, would have an incentive to settle whenever they reasoned that the risks of an adverse judgment, and in light of the costs of continued litigation, counseled in favor of settling their claims. To be sure, one great advantage of a medium claims procedure is that its lower litigation costs would make either side's threat of continued litigation smaller; fewer parties would be discouraged from litigating due to high litigation costs. This means that nuisance claims and defenses, and other forms of bad-faith litigation, would not plague medium claims proceedings to the extent that they plague traditional civil litigation. This too would be a substantial advantage of this form of proceeding.

But while parties to a medium claims case would not have the wrong incentives to settle their claims—simply to avoid litigation costs notwithstanding the strength of their positions—they might have just the right incentives to settle. Abbreviated litigation and limited discovery might well reveal important information about the relative strengths and weaknesses of opposing litigants' positions, and thereby encourage settlement. The core purpose of a new medium claims civil action would not be to hold lots of trials, but rather to provide a relatively inexpensive procedure for litigants to air their claims and defenses. When doing so might lead medium claims litigants to settle in advance of trial, so be it. Otherwise, parties to a medium claims case could have their case decided by the judge in a relatively quick, streamlined, and, thus, accessible proceeding.

Above all else, medium claims litigation should be designed to limit the amounts parties would—or indeed possibly *could*—spend on litigation. Medium claims trials likewise would be abbreviated and inexpensive. In contrast to small claims cases, parties through their attorneys should be allowed to examine a very limited number of witnesses at trial, as well as to cross-examine adverse trial witnesses. As in small claims court, however, judges as well as attorneys could ask questions of witnesses (which is allowed in traditional litigation in many jurisdictions, though is seldom done). Greater judicial involvement would compensate for the lack of procedural and evidentiary formality, and would further promote reliability.

By limiting discovery, avoiding extensive motion practice, and eliminating the formal rules of evidence and limiting trial testimony, medium claims proceedings would to some extent cap the amount of time attorneys could spend litigating a case, and therefore put some limit on the cost of legal representation. In traditional litigation, ethical rules for lawyers that require strong advocacy, as well as concerns about potential legal malpractice liability for taking shortcuts, can motivate attorneys to spend incur substantial litigation expenses that may or may not prove cost-justified. For example, if there is some small chance that a potential witness may have relevant information about a case, or a chance that documents might contain information that could be used in a case, litigators may have professional-ethical incentives to exhaust all avenues of civil discovery, even if their likely yield is low. Likewise, trial lawyers often will enlist and prepare rebuttal witnesses for testimony that they may never require in trial. They may file pretrial motions that are unlikely to succeed.

In short, traditional litigation can be costly because litigants and especially their attorneys do not always have incentives to economize. A medium claims procedure would lower litigation costs by allowing—indeed requiring—litigants to prioritize and economize through abbreviated civil procedure, limitations on discovery and trial witnesses, and the use of informal evidence.

Toward that purpose, then, and to put this in concrete terms, a plaintiff with a claim seeking monetary damages for, say, $45,000 should be able to file a complaint to initiate what the plaintiff expressly designates to be a medium claim. This would trigger the medium claims court process and require the defendant to answer, with both parties represented by counsel (if they so choose). The defendant could thereafter ask the medium claims court to dismiss the case for failure to state a claim or on a similar ground. If that initial motion were denied, the judge would issue a standard order resembling a typical scheduling order in traditional litigation, though designed especially for medium claims cases, requiring that limited civil discovery be completed within a short and specified period of time, such as one or two months.

Parties could be allowed to take one or perhaps two depositions, such as the deposition of the opposing party plus another. They could also make document requests, but again only a limited number and only for documents they intend to submit to the judge at trial. Parties should not be allowed request documents or other discovery from third parties (that is, non-parties to the case) unless shown to be crucial to a given case. That said, within established parameters, the details of discovery and potentially of trial in a medium claims civil action could and should be determined by litigants themselves. Parties to a medium claims case could thus agree, under the supervision of the presiding judge, to undertake particular amounts of civil discovery or to call a prescribed number of witnesses, again within established caps, in order to shape the process according to the factual complexity and stakes at hand.

In cases that proceed to trial, counsel would appear with their clients to present each side's case to the court, with a trial limited anywhere from an hour up to half of a day, as appropriate for the case and to be determined by the judge together with the parties (as in traditional litigation). At trial, parties could introduce documentary and other evidence informally. Each side could call a limited number of witnesses (perhaps two or three, but only one expert witness) and counsel would have a time-limited opportunity to cross-examine adverse witnesses under oath, but with no redirect examinations. In place of redirect examinations, the trial judge could question witnesses, parties, and their counsel, in much the same manner of informal give-and-take that characterizes small claims courts. At the close of trial, attorneys could give short statements, after which the judge would decide the case on the spot or after short deliberation and without post-trial motions.

Within these general parameters, the more particular features of a new mediums claims civil action could be left to local courts. And just as the procedures and practices both for small claims and also for traditional litigation vary somewhat from jurisdiction to jurisdiction, there is room here too for flexibility and variance according to the needs of local litigants and local courts. But the above general features of a medium claims process, however further detailed or expanded, should reflect its central purpose: to provide an abbreviated and thus less expensive form of civil litigation that allows parties in cases involving moderate stakes to advance their legal interests at costs that are not disproportionate to the size of those stakes. Thus, some version of truncated civil discovery, curtailed motion practice, informally presented evidence, limited number of trial witnesses, and time-limited, informal trials would promote cost-justified access to the courts for medium sized cases.

The choice to litigate in a medium claims court should be available to defendants as well as to plaintiffs. Of course, if the plaintiff prefers a general trial court, the plaintiff can seek damages for a claim exceeding the medium claims court's jurisdictional ceiling. But otherwise, defendants should be encouraged not to remove cases from medium claims courts to the general trial courts. By the same token, when a plaintiff files a complaint in the general trial court seeking an amount in damages that would make the case eligible for a medium claims jurisdiction, the defendant should be allowed to propose removing the case to medium claims court.

That is, medium claims processes should allow either side to move to litigate within the specified jurisdictional limits of the medium claims court, for all of the reasons explained, with respect to small claims. For again, the central purpose of a court of medium claims is to contain the costs of litigation for *all* parties in cases presenting moderate stakes, and it is hard to see how plaintiffs would be disadvantaged by a rule allowing defendants to remove medium-sized cases to medium claims courts.

Thus, when one party or the other insists on litigating a case eligible for a medium claims court in the general trial court instead, here again that party should absorb more costs in the form of increased pay-to-impose fees, just as previously proposed for small claims courts.

There is much to recommend the development of new medium claims courts. Above all, medium claims courts would provide access for a class of potential litigants who lack it. Furthermore, medium claims bench trials would likely be at least as reliable as conventional trials, especially given the more active role judges could take in medium claims procedures by questioning parties and witnesses. Nor would reliability be threatened by parties' ability to advance bad-faith claims and the pressure of opposing litigants to settle. That is to say, as noted, given the relatively small costs of medium claims litigation, defendants should feel less pressure to settle in order to avoid the high costs of litigating to victory. Indeed, neither nuisance cases nor nuisance defenses would likely be a significant problem—nor would lottery litigation or bad-faith claims in general, given the accessibility of a medium claims forum. And, just as courts can assess costs in traditional litigation, judges in medium claims cases should exercise their discretion to assess some costs against losing parties as necessary to create incentives against over-litigating. For several reasons, then, medium claims courts could provide greater access to the courts while promoting reliability in a judicially managed venue.

That said, as proposed above in connection with small claims, courts could also consider experimenting with juries for medium claims courts. That is, in order to preserve the forum of medium claims courts for litigants who would otherwise remove a medium claim to the general trial court in order to exercise their jury trial rights, courts could empanel medium claims juries as well, though even then judges should continue to play an active role in the proceedings by questioning witnesses and otherwise. Here too, empaneling one jury to hear multiple medium claims cases would make the most sense; medium claims would not warrant mobilizing a jury for a single case. In the short run, however, simply establishing courts of medium claims resembling existing small claims courts but with abbreviated discovery and limited procedural formality would constitute a desirable and substantial first step. Medium claims cases heard and resolved by judges would provide potential litigants with a new forum in which to litigate cases of moderate size in an economical way. The case for creating new courts of medium claims is compelling.

Fortunately, it is also readily achievable. Establishing such a new court would require neither new courthouses nor new judges. Rather, medium claims cases could and should be heard by existing courts, simply sitting in the capacity of a medium claims court. For example, existing small claims judges (or magistrates, depending on the jurisdiction) could be authorized to hear medium claims as well, applying the corresponding procedural rules for cases filed as medium claims actions. Alternatively, general trial court judges, who may hear small claims already depending on the jurisdiction, could hear medium claims, again simply sitting in the capacity of a medium claims court. Upon the filing of a medium claim, the presiding judge would employ the procedural rules designed for such a claim. Local courts could designate judges to hear medium claims actions however they see fit, and as most appropriate given their own jurisdictional rules and existing court structure.

Medium claims actions could be authorized and governed by state or local court rules, much as small claims cases are currently. Although legislation creating medium claims proceedings would not be necessary in most jurisdictions, legislators too should consider establishing them. As an initial step, state supreme courts or county judicial systems (depending on how administrative power within a state judiciary is allocated) should pilot new medium claims procedures. They might do so by inviting litigants to participate, including perhaps litigants who file ordinary civil actions, and soliciting feedback from participating parties and judges. California's "limited jurisdiction" proceeding for claims under $25,000, which allows for more economical discovery practice, pleading rules, and evidentiary standards, provides a ready model.[1] By piloting new medium claims procedures, state court systems could learn through experience which specific process rules are best suited for cases of moderate size, and how best to accomplish reliable outcomes through procedures accessible to a class of litigants who likely would otherwise be priced out of ordinary litigation.

Greater Use of Expedited Jury Trials

Medium claims proceedings would find a cousin in a recent form of "summary jury trials," or "expedited jury trials" as they are known in some jurisdictions, which provide another cheaper alternative to traditional civil litigation and, therefore, warrant greater use. Expedited jury trials are not entirely new, but have recently been revived in a new and successful form. Much like a new medium claims court, expedited jury trials would promote access for a class of litigants whose claims and defenses, moderate in size, are often outweighed by the costs of traditional civil litigation.

The first substantial experiment with summary jury trials dates to the 1980s in federal court. With some forum-to-forum variation, this first generation of summary jury trials had several features. As their name suggests, they were short. In some jurisdictions, litigants had to finish their trials within an hour, giving them little more than a short opportunity to summarize their cases to the jury, perhaps with a few exhibits. More commonly, summary jury trials could last up to one full day.

Their short duration was made possible because many of the formal rules of evidence were relaxed. For example, for most purposes, lawyers could read deposition transcripts to the jury in place of presenting live witnesses, which (with some exceptions) is not permitted in ordinary trials. Lawyers could read the deposition testimony of friendly witnesses, for instance, or have that testimony supplied by a stand-in "witness," such as a paralegal pretending to be the deponent, by reading aloud deposition answers to the jury in response to being asked the deposition questions by a lawyer. In other words, these witnesses essentially reenacted before the jury portions of a deposition taken previously, as if the deponent were testifying live. Alternatively, lawyers could simply summarize deposition testimony to the jury, even during closing arguments.

The evidentiary rules governing hearsay were also relaxed. For example, medical hearsay was often permitted, allowing parties to report to the jury the contents of medical records, or what a doctor said about a particular issue. Relaxing the rules of evidence in this way too saved time, allowing parties to move quickly to the core of their evidentiary case without first establishing foundations and authenticating records, and likewise without calling numerous witnesses, all of which are often required in traditional litigation. No less importantly, this relaxation also allowed parties to avoid paying witnesses to appear in court, which is to say travel to court and wait until they were called to testify. In short, the summary jury process was designed to be not only quick, but also inexpensive.

A judge presided over the summary trial, as in an ordinary case, though the judge's role in ensuring proper application of the rules of evidence was diminished. Otherwise, the judge functioned as in an ordinary trial—ruling on motions, instructing the jury, and so on. While the jury functioned as an ordinary jury would, usually summary jury trials were heard by mini-juries, sometimes by as few as four jurors. After deliberation, the jury rendered its verdict. Often, the jury was instructed to render a verdict on liability and damages separately, and to assess damages even if it found no liability. The jury's assessment of damages even when it found no liability gave litigating parties the benefit of more information about the strengths of their cases.

In the end, the parties to a summary jury trial could elect to adopt the verdict rendered, or not. In other words, the summary jury trial of the 1980s was not binding. This was true even though the process was, in the few federal jurisdictions where it existed, also involuntary, another defining feature of the early experiment with summary jury trials. That is, some federal judges required parties to participate in summary jury trials before they could try their cases before an ordinary jury. For a time, such a requirement proved controversial, and more so than other forms of mandatory alternative dispute resolution in that same time period. In fact, some commentators at the time argued that federal judges lacked the power to require litigants to participate in summary jury trials. Congress eliminated that specific objection in the Civil Justice Reform Act of 1990, which explicitly authorized the use of mandatory summary jury trials, provided that judges employed the procedure as part of some comprehensive case management plan.

The original proponents of the summary jury trial advocated for its use on two main grounds. First, summary jury trials were supposed to help with docket control. Especially during the 1980s, when many argued that civil dockets were overburdened, resolving cases through summary jury trials, like other forms of ADR, was seen as a significant potential advantage. Second, the summary jury trial was supposed to encourage settlement by giving litigants the benefit not only of presenting and thus testing their own cases, but also of hearing the other side's case as well. As a result, both sides could reassess the strength of their own case in light of their opponent's presentation to the summary jury. Litigants could then make more informed—and more realistic—settlement calculations following a summary jury's verdict.

But the summary jury trial of the 1980s never saw use beyond a small number of federal jurisdictions, even while the use of many other forms of ADR grew substantially during the same period. The process faded in large part because summary jury trails did not reduce dockets or promote settlement as their proponents had hoped. According to a leading contemporaneous study, Judge Richard Posner (1986) argued that available data, though sparse, did not show that summary jury trials led to a decrease in ordinary trials, an increase in settlements, or a decrease in the total time it took to resolve civil cases, although proponents subsequently marshalled such evidence (Connolly 1999).

In recent years, however, a new version of the original summary jury trial has emerged in a number of states, with far more promising results. Charleston County, South Carolina provides perhaps the best example (Croley 2008), and several other states have since adopted versions of this model. There, the local plaintiff and defense bars collaboratively developed a version of the summary jury trial that reduces litigation costs, promotes access, and resolves cases quickly and efficiently.

Charleston's "expedited" jury trial differs from that of the 1980s in two crucial ways. First, it is entirely voluntary, and thus employed only by willing litigants. Second, for parties who elect to have a summary jury trial, it is binding, not simply an exercise to promote settlement as urged by some of the proponents of the original summary jury trial (Metzloff 1992, 1993). In other words, whereas the original federal summary jury trial likely added to the costs of litigation because it constituted an additional, pretrial step in the traditional litigation process, Charleston's expedited jury trial instead replaces the traditional trial fully, and is used only by parties who choose to be bound by the summary trial verdict.

Once the parties to a case agree to use the expedited trial process, they file a stipulated motion requesting the judge in their case to designate a "special judge" to preside over the summary jury trial. In Charleston County, opposing counsel agree on other lawyers to serve as the special judges presiding over expedited jury trials—essentially as deputized judges—but judges of the local trial court could do the same. Jurors used in Charleston's expedited jury trials are drawn from the same pool of prospective jurors summoned for ordinary trials.

The new expedited jury trial procedure resembles that of the 1980s. Although Charleston's process trial has no time limit, in fact most expedited trials last a day, and most of those that last longer than a day are completed during the second day. Litigants, not facing tight time constraints, may call live witnesses if they choose. They may instead summarize the testimony a witness would give if called, based on the absent witness's prior deposition testimony, which litigants are allowed to summarize or read to the jury. The ability to read or summarize witness testimony instead of calling live witnesses means that the only live witnesses tend to be the parties themselves.

The rules of evidence are relaxed in other ways too. Litigants can make some hearsay objections, for example, which are ruled upon immediately from the presiding judge. But hearsay in the context of medical reports and medical opinions, including the opinions of experts, is also allowed. Thus, parties need not pay a doctor or another expensive medical expert to appear and testify in court. Nor must litigants spend resources on the many facets of pretrial witness preparation—such as reviewing testimony, preparing witness exhibits, conducting mock examinations and cross-examinations, and so on.

Lower trial and pretrial costs are not the only reason expedited jury trials are inexpensive relative to traditional litigation. Because expedited jury trials relax the rules of evidence, litigants do not spend a lot of time filing and responding to pretrial evidentiary motions either, although expedited jury trial litigants can file motions to circumscribe what evidence the opposing litigant will be allowed to introduce at trial. Discovery is also much less expensive in a case for which the parties select an expedited jury trial. Parties may elect the expedited jury trial early on in the life of a case, which they often do, and they then limit their discovery accordingly. In other words, and importantly, the lower costs of cases employing the expedited trial process extend backwards in a case, long before trial itself.

Because expedited jury trials are not only binding, but also final, South Carolina's summary jury trials are not recorded by a court reporter. Because there is no appeal, there is no need for a record, and thus the parties do not enlist a court reporter. Once the jury has rendered its verdict, the case is fully over, with nothing left to be done but carry out the judgment. There are no post-trial motions. Once finished, a case resolved by expedited jury trial is recorded on the official circuit court docket as "resolved by settlement" much like any other case resolved by private settlement.

This new incarnation of the summary jury trial provides access to the civil litigation system for plaintiffs who, given the small size of their claims relative to the costs of traditional litigation, would otherwise lack access. In fact, it was designed for cases presenting small stakes, such as potential monetary damages in the low dozens of thousands of dollars. Whereas proponents of the summary jury trial of the 1980s viewed that process as perfectly suitable for complex, high-stakes litigation, that is not the type of case for which summary jury trials are intended or principally used in South Carolina or the several states that have also developed summary jury trials. Rather, their paradigm case is a simple torts case—involving an automobile accident or a slip and fall—in which a plaintiff allegedly suffered significant but not life-altering injuries as a result of the defendant's conduct. Potential damages in such cases typically include some lost wages, medical bills, and some pain and suffering, but they are not so high to make finding contingency-fee representation easy against the expected costs of traditional litigation. Expedited jury trials are well suited for moderately sized contracts cases as well. What plaintiffs with legal claims of moderate size need is some opportunity to litigate liability and damages at a cost that does not approach their expected relief. Expedited jury trials provide that opportunity.

But they are attractive to many defendants too, for similar reasons. In the typical case in Charleston, for example, the defendant is covered by a liability insurance policy, usually with a fairly low policy limit. The nominal defendant may be an alleged tortfeasor, but the tortfeasor's insurance company faces liability up to the policy limit. Were the plaintiff to prevail and be awarded damages exceeding the coverage amount, the defendant would be liable for the amount of damages exceeding the policy limit, and the insurer would be liable up to the policy limit.

In most cases tried through the expedited jury process in Charleston, however, the plaintiff and defendant agree in advance to "high/

low" damages, a potentially attractive but by no means essential feature of summary jury trials that depends on the parties' willingness to bind themselves in this way. If the plaintiff prevails, the plaintiff receives whatever amount the jury awards, unless that amount is higher than the specified "high" or lower than the "low." In other words, the parties agree in advance to floor and ceiling damages, which is to say they have already settled the case for an undetermined amount within a determined range. The agreed upon "low" is typically in the mid-single digit thousands of dollars, presumably an amount to cover a portion of the plaintiff's out-of-pocket costs for this inexpensive form of litigation. The "high" is typically an amount equal to the defendant's insurance policy limit. Therefore, the defendant's own exposure is virtually always zero, for even if the defendant loses the expedited jury trial, damages are capped by agreement at the policy maximum. Of course, individual defendants still prefer not to lose, as there are collateral consequences— higher insurance rates for drivers, the stigma of having been sued and lost, and so on. But their immediate economic exposure is minimal. So the expedited jury trial is attractive to defendants, as well as to plaintiffs who also risk virtually nothing with a "high/low" that covers their out-of-pocket litigation costs.

The insurance companies who finance the legal defense benefit too. They enter into volume contracts with local defense firms to resolve claims made against their policies. When a defendant prevails, the insurance companies pay nothing. When a plaintiff prevails on liability but the jury returns a small verdict on damages, the insurance companies pay something, but less than the amount of their exposure. What the insurance companies require, then, are local counsel who can try the cases and minimize the total amounts the companies have to pay. Because the expedited jury trial process is fast and inexpensive, insurance companies enjoy an inexpensive process to advance their legal interests in order to minimize their liability. Moreover, local defense firms pass on part of the litigation savings to the insurance companies. They do so by making smaller bids for the companies' volume contracts than they would make if they had to litigate and try all cases through traditional processes. In short, expedited jury trials provide low-cost access to defendants and insurance companies too, which is what led the defense bar in Charleston to develop and promote the new process in the first place.

Individual defendants and their insurance companies enjoy a related benefit as well. Given that expedited jury trials involve lower litigation costs, defendants have less incentive to entertain nuisance settlements. Even though defense attorneys bill their clients by the hour, the possibility of a summary jury trial to resolve cases that do not settle is not so costly that defendants view nuisance settlements as economically rational. Summary jury trials thus avoid one type of undesirable settlement for defendants.

Of course, defendants might instead attempt to price plaintiffs out of litigation that defendants believe plaintiffs cannot really afford, or for the same reason, attempt to force plaintiffs to accept nuisance settlements. Plaintiffs likewise might demand settlements and otherwise seek to increase a defendants' litigation costs in order to encourage the defendant to settle. In general, where litigation may be high enough to overtake the expected benefit either side would get from litigating successfully, litigation becomes a contest about which side can credibly signal that it can afford to litigate, and is prepared to litigate, further. But the process developed by plaintiffs' attorneys and the defense bar in Charleston provides one way to avoid that battle of attrition while giving both sides an opportunity to make their case to a jury. Undoubtedly, different kinds of litigation incentives may operate over different types of cases. But while not all cases go to summary jury trial in Charleston, in one study it appeared that approximately half of *all* civil trials in Charleston were summary jury trials during the period examined (Croley 2008), suggesting that many litigants view the process to be in their interest.

This considerable level of participation supports the inference that this new summary jury trial promotes access while lowering litigation costs. Nor are there reasons for concern that the new summary jury trial is unreliable. The "high/low" that parties establish in advance eliminates completely any risk of outlier damage awards by a summary jury, and moreover reduces the uncertainty of damages where a jury finds liability. Thus, expedited jury trial verdicts do not produce big surprises for either side.

And here again, parties might choose to settle a case that would be tried through the expedited jury trial process if it were to proceed to trial. In other words, nothing about this new procedure commits parties in a given case to litigate all the way through trial. The central virtue of this relatively inexpensive litigation process is that litigants otherwise priced out of traditional litigation enjoy access to the litigation system in the first place. Given that the expedited jury trial process makes even trial more affordable, parties may well find trial in particular attractive. But they need not, and some parties may find settlement preferable following the initial stages of litigation in a case employing the expedited process.

To promote greater access and reduce litigation costs for both sides of cases that present moderate stakes, other jurisdictions should develop their own versions of expedited jury trials. Like medium claims courts, expedited jury trials would provide greater access to the courts for a class of litigants who might otherwise fall between the jurisdictional requirements of small claims court and the practical economics of traditional litigation. Expedited jury trials like South Carolina's have seen recent adoption in parts of ten states, including California, Florida, and New York (Hannaford-Agor and Waters 2012). Other states should pilot expedited jury trial processes as well, and the federal courts should revive the federal summary jury trial, although in a voluntary and binding form.

As with the establishment of medium claims courts, legislation would not be necessary for any of the above. County courts can experiment with summary jury trials at the initiation of willing litigants. Most state supreme courts have inherent authority to pilot summary jury trials, especially for litigants who may elect to use them, as several state high courts have done. At the federal level, too, Congress has already allowed federal judges to require summary jury trials, as previously noted, so clearly voluntary summary jury trials would be well within federal judges' authority. Federal judges too should exercise that authority by experimenting with expedited jury trials in appropriate cases.

Tailored Litigation Processes

A more general prescription remains. While greater use and innovative development of small claims proceedings, the creation of a new court of medium claims, and wider use of expedited trials all could go very far to promote the civil litigation system's accessibility, greater procedural flexibility across all types—and sizes—of cases would as well. That is, litigants should be able to shape the litigation process according to the needs, complexity, and especially the stakes of a given case, even in traditional civil litigation. This would mean, for one thing, that parties take on a much more active role in determining how much discovery and motion practice is necessary, and of what sort, and on what timetable in order to litigate their cases (see Moffitt 2006 for an excellent analysis along the same lines). Judges, for their part, should more actively supervise parties to encourage them to economize where possible, and to ensure that neither side engages in excessive discovery, unnecessary motion practice, or other unreasonable litigiousness. In small and large cases alike, courts could do more to fashion proceedings to meet the needs of litigants, especially but not only unsophisticated litigants who are not represented (for a compelling analysis, see Steinberg 2015).

To a limited degree, this is done already. In the federal system, for example, the Federal Rules of Civil Procedure, and likewise the Local Rules of federal courts, require or encourage litigants to confer and to propose scheduling orders, discovery orders, and even trial orders that govern the case. And state procedural rules commonly mimic the Federal Rules in these respects. Federal Rule of Civil Procedure 16, for instance, authorizes courts to order parties to a conference for the purpose, among others, of "expediting disposition of the action" and to ensure "that the case will not be protracted because of lack of management," and to "discourage wasteful pretrial activities."[2] Some Local Rules requiring attorney "civility" similarly require attorneys to confer about appropriate case management. And judges routinely ask parties to fashion civil discovery according to the needs of a given case.[3] To some extent, then, civil litigants do tailor civil procedure to fit the circumstances of their cases (see, for example, Grenig 1999); parties litigating through the ordinary litigation process enjoy some control over the contours of procedure in a given case.

But considerably more could be done to promote litigation processes better tailored to the individual case. Too often, litigating parties are not constrained in how much process they "consume" in a case, and the default limits on discovery expressed in the rules of procedure (such as ten depositions or twenty-five interrogatories in the federal system) are treated as the norm rather than an upper limit.[4] Some parties by motion seek to exceed those limits as well, and some judges who consider themselves to be "full discovery judges" routinely grant motions for discovery beyond the limits set forth in the Federal Rules. Indeed, conventional wisdom holds that litigants often use discovery not to economize on litigation, but to increase costs for their opponents. There is thus room for better tailoring of the litigation process to suit the needs of the particular case, and increased supervision by judges might foster such tailoring (cf. Woolf 1996).

Part of the attraction of creating a court of medium claims and promoting a more widespread use of expedited jury proceedings is that these modes of civil litigation would provide "off the shelf" alternative processes for litigants to employ. Any potential litigant who might otherwise be priced out of traditional litigation could proceed through these ready procedures. But while a medium claims action and the expedited jury trial process are especially well suited for controversies of moderate size, there is no reason why litigants in cases involving higher stakes might not elect by stipulation to economize by using them, or variants of them, as well. That is, even parties who could afford expensive, discovery-intensive traditional litigation might sometimes choose these simplified procedures anyway.

Whether they might do so could depend on litigants' expectations about, for example, the extent to which application of all the formal rules of evidence would be important to the case at hand, perhaps especially for factually complex cases. For legally and factually straightforward cases, which just happen to involve high potential damages, it is possible parties may prefer to resolve their dispute through processes much less expensive than traditional litigation. Of course, parties do so routinely, by resolving cases through mediation and types of ADR. The availability of a medium claims court process and expedited jury trials would simply add to the existing menu of civil processes available to parties for resolving their disputes within rather than outside of the judicial system.

But whether or not they elect off-the-shelf alternative civil processes, litigants should be affirmatively encouraged to tailor their process to fit the needs of their specific case in any event. As explained, parties who employ the expedited jury trial process in South Carolina do this already—further specifying procedural details as part of their stipulated order governing the case. In other words, even that innovative process is commonly furthered tailored to meet the needs of particular cases as the circumstances warrant. Likewise, parties to a medium claims proceeding could do so as well. And again, traditional litigation also already allows for some tailoring.

But the civil litigation system at present plainly does not exhaust all means of encouraging parties to tailor civil process to the case at hand. One mechanism for doing so is to require parties who insist on more rather than less civil process to pay something for their decisions not to economize. For example, as suggested in the previous chapter, if a party proposed limiting depositions, document requests, trial witnesses, or other ways to shorten and simplify—and thus reduce the costs of—the litigation process, and the opposing party refused, an argument can be made that a non-prevailing refusing party should sometimes bear more of the offering party's costs resulting directly from refusal of that "procedural offer." More generally, increasing use of "pay to impose" mechanisms should be applied to litigants' decisions about what procedural rules they will employ, and insist that the opposing side employ, in a given case.

As noted, much of the same logic underlying existing mechanisms that require losing parties to pay costs when they refuse offers to settle a case would apply also to procedural offers about how to economize on the litigation process itself. Judges as well as parties could make procedural proposals, with *some* costs to be potentially reallocated if one side but not the other refused to accept a judge's procedural proposal, under the authority of existing cost-allocation rules of civil procedure. In short, litigants who unreasonably refuse to economize should be made to absorb more of the costs directly resulting from that refusal, where the refusing party does not prevail on the issue in question notwithstanding its insistence on more rather than less procedure. In any mode of civil proceeding—including ordinary civil litigation—parties should have greater incentives to tailor the litigation process according to the needs and stakes of a given case.

Summary

Meaningful access to the courts requires that potential litigants have some opportunity to advance their claims. And the availability of litigation processes for which the costs are commensurate with the benefits of litigating is important for defendants and plaintiffs alike. Fortunately, new forms of civil litigation could be established—with feasible changes in rules of pleading and procedures, and without large institutional investments—to provide access to litigants whose claims and defenses of moderate size fall within the gap between small claims and major cases.

By the way of summary, table 9.1 captures what a more complete choice of civil litigation processes would look like, and notes the main features of each. Between traditional civil litigation's features suitable for parties in cases that may involve very high stakes, on the one hand, and small claims proceedings designed for parties who represent themselves in cases of limited stakes, on the other hand, medium claims court and expedited jury trials provide attractive alternatives in the middle of what is best understood as a procedural continuum. To different degrees, these new procedures would forgo some of the ordinary rules of civil procedure, including civil discovery and the formal rules of evidence. But there is nothing sacrosanct about those aspects of litigation; relaxing them specifically for cases of moderate size, or where parties elect to do so, should be unobjectionable. As noted, conventional forms of alternative dispute resolution, and likewise health courts and small claims courts, already substantially alter or eliminate the traditional procedural rules through which parties resolve their disputes. Thus, innovative expansion of small claims courts, the creation of new medium claims courts, and the increased use of the new form of expedited jury trials would not be unprecedented in their abbreviation of traditional civil procedure. But beyond such innovations, civil litigants in all types of civil proceeding should be allowed—and affirmatively encouraged—to tailor the litigation process to reflect the size of their cases.

To be clear, none of this is to call into question the efficacy of the formal rules of evidence and procedure, or the advantages of full civil discovery, or the merits of extended motion practice, or of long jury trials in high-stakes litigation for which these are necessary and affordable. The point, rather, is that where the traditional procedural architecture of civil litigation requires costs that overtake the expected benefits of litigating, the case for developing new, less expensive modes of litigation becomes very strong. Judges and policymakers should therefore make available less costly, more accessible procedures available to potential litigants.

Next, chapter 10 argues for promoting greater access to the courts in additional ways as well.

TABLE 9.1. Expanded Forms of Civil Litigation

Features of Process:

Type of Civil Process:	Duration:	Who Elects:	Dollar Ceiling:	Legal Representation:	Fact Finder:	Discovery:	Civil Procedure:	Rules of Evidence:	Examination/Cross Examination:
Small Claims Court	Very brief	Either Party	Low	No	Judge	No	No	No	Judge
Medium Claims Court	½ Day	Either Party	Medium (e.g., $50K)	Yes	Judge	Very limited	Motion to dismiss only	No	Attorneys and Judge
Expedited Jury Trials	1 Day	Both Parties	As parties desire	Yes	Jury	Yes, but tailored to expedite trial	Yes	Selective relaxation of rules of evidence	Attorneys
Traditional Civil Litigation	Unlimited	Plaintiff	Unlimited	Yes	Jury or Judge	Yes—Full	Yes—Full	Yes—Full	Attorneys

10

Supporting Greater Access

The previous chapter argued for lowering the fixed costs of litigation in the name of access, whereas chapters 7 and 8 argued for filtering undesirable cases out of the litigation system and reducing the variable costs of litigation, in the name of lower cost. The litigation system could be rendered more accessible for plaintiffs and defendants alike through the development of new procedures and a realistic adaptation of existing litigation processes.

Promoting greater access to the civil litigation system is possible and desirable on the demand side as well. That is to say, providing more resources to cover more of the costs for potential parties who otherwise lack sufficient resources to initiate litigation also would increase access. One way to accomplish this is through increased social funding for organizations that provide access for those who cannot afford it. Such support promotes access largely by funding the costs of legal representation, which is economical given that compensation for attorneys employed by legal services organizations is not enough. Greater social support might take more decentralized forms as well.

In addition, increased resources for those who lack access might come from lawyers in particular, who provide representation without compensation as a matter of professional commitment or because their membership in the bar comes with a heightened responsibility to ensure that the civil litigation system works well. In other words, as a complement to increased support for full-time legal services attorneys who represent only non-paying clients, increased commitments to pro bono representation by attorneys whose compensation comes from their paying clients is another means of promoting access. Finally, greater access to the courts might be achieved also through certain cross-subsidies among groups of civil litigants and their lawyers, as well as from defendants in certain cases. This chapter proposes all three approaches—increased financial support for legal services, increased pro bono commitments from the bar, and cross-subsidies between certain classes of civil litigants—all in the interest of providing increased access to the civil litigation system for those likely to be priced out of it.

Social Support for Access to the Courts

The social benefits of litigation, in particular the beneficial externalities associated with litigation, justify some amount of resources to finance litigation for those who lack the means to cover litigation's costs. From a different point of view, however, traditionally emphasized by proponents of greater access to justice, access to the civil litigation system is required because it—much like education, housing, or health care—is a right that everyone should be entitled to at some basic level. But the stronger case for greater access is that civil litigation is socially beneficial, and should be supported not as part of a larger program of *distributive* justice, but because it advances social interests by reinforcing the law's obligations. That said, the case in favor of supporting access in order to advance social interests and the imperative to entitle vulnerable individuals to some minimal level of access may carry similar policy implications.

For example, the American Bar Association's House of Delegates in 2010 passed a policy resolution calling for greater access to the civil litigation system.[1] Specifically, the ABA resolution calls for "legal counsel as a matter of right at public expense to low-income persons in those categories of adversarial proceedings where *basic human needs are at stake*" (original emphasis; see generally Schwinn 2008). The resolution goes on to define basic human needs to include "shelter, sustenance, safety, health, or child custody." Such a right to legal representation— somewhat analogous to the constitutional "Gideon" right to representation for criminal defendants—would have to be conferred by state statute, and paid for somehow. But providing legal representation in cases where basic human needs are at stake would likely yield significant returns, as studies referenced in chapter 2 show, and as one might expect. Given that unmet basic human needs strain public and private institutions in various ways, providing legal representation when individuals' housing, safety, and sustenance are at risk seems likely to mitigate socially costly problems.

The bar has also long supported access to the courts more generally. The ABA's Standing Committee on Pro Bono and Public Service, for one example, promotes access for the unrepresented and under-represented, and provides informational and other resources to encourage pro bono representation. That Standing Committee's affiliate, the ABA's Center for Pro Bono, provides pro bono standards of practice, a library of materials for pro bono initiatives, and a variety of technical support for pro bono activities. It also promotes coordination across jurisdictions among organizations that support pro bono representation. The ABA also provides grant support to entities to expand access to the litigation system. All such efforts deserve greater support from the bar's membership, law firms, and courts.

Other organizations that provide legal services to those who have little access to the civil litigation system should likewise be supported. As noted in chapter 6, Congress has in recent decades decreased funding for the Legal Services Corporation (LSC)—which provides grants to entities providing legal services for individuals at or below 125% of the federal poverty level—by more than half over the last decade, adjusting for inflation. As a result, a majority of the poor's civil legal needs continue to go unmet. Because the likely returns on taxpayer investments justify greater support for LSC and its activities, lawmakers should provide greater funding for LSC, again not narrowly for redistributive purposes but rather as a matter of good social policy.

Increased resources for legal aid organizations beyond those supported by LSC funds would also likely see significant returns on investment. Many such legal aid organizations provide legal assistance to those who lack access to the courts. The National Legal Aid and Defender Association's Division of Civil Legal Services provides support and information to such organizations, and maintains a list of funding opportunities for legal aid organizations. Entities providing access for those who lack it constitute worthy beneficiaries of philanthropic support as well, including from foundations focused on the needs of populations that also most often lack legal representation as well as those that emphasize community and neighborhood development.

In addition to the organized bar and civil legal assistance organizations, many states and state supreme courts also promote greater access through state "access to justice commissions" and similar entities that promote greater representation for those who lack access to the litigation system. Many of those efforts are facilitated by the National Center for State Courts (NCSC), an independent nonprofit coordinating body that provides statistical information and identifies best practices among state courts, and which houses a Center on Court Access for Justice for All to provide informational resources and technical support for state and local courts. The NCSC works closely with state supreme courts and state court administrators to leverage its resources and outreach. The NSCS and its Center promote not only simplified court forms and court rules to benefit self-represented litigants, but also the expansion of pro bono representation. States' efforts in this area should find financial support from state legislators and others, and states that lack access-to-justice commissions or similar entities (which is, at present, almost half of the states) should create them, which could be done by state supreme courts. Many federal courts too provide increased assistance to pro se litigants, although modest additional investments would likely provide substantially more assistance (see generally Stienstra, Bataillon, and Cantone 2011).

Finally, greater support to promote access to the courts could target individuals rather than organizations. Such support could take the form of individual income tax incentives, in particular for low- and moderate-income individuals who purchase legal contingency insurance (see Logue forthcoming). For individuals who are likely to be priced out of the market for legal services, tax incentives for purchasing insurance to cover the cost of legal representation for certain legal contingencies, especially legal harms for which contingency-fee representation is unlikely, could promote access for those who need it most. Much like income tax subsidies for health insurance plans, supplemental health insurance plans, and retirement and educational savings plans—all intended to encourage individuals to make what are considered to be socially beneficial investments—tax-favored insurance premiums to cover the costs of legal representation required for specified legal contingencies could encourage more individuals to secure legal representation. In principle, employers could offer group legal service plans as well. Short of the American Bar Association's civil Gideon proposal, but in the same spirit, favorable federal and even state income tax treatment for legal service insurance could increase representation for those with important but otherwise unmet legal needs.

Increased Commitment from the Profession

The organized bar, legal services organizations, and state access commissions and similar organizations taken together provide a significant organizational infrastructure for expanding access to the courts. But that infrastructure, without greater participation by legal professionals, is insufficient. Individual lawyers and law firms could and should do more to provide greater access. To be very clear, individual lawyers, major law firms, and many corporations already do much to provide legal representation and thereby promote access. But in truth the legal profession's investment here is uneven, with some doing a substantial share and others contributing little. As a result, the distribution of legal resources remains heavily weighted towards those who can afford high hourly fees (e.g., Rhode 2004a, 2004c). The importance of greater commitment from the profession to providing access to the courts has been well articulated by others (e.g., Rhode 2004a). The following discussion accordingly recommends what would be largely new or extended forms of such commitment.

Legal "Urgent Cares"

For one example, law firms of sufficient size should consider establishing "legal emergency rooms" or "legal urgent cares." A legal urgent care, modeled loosely on small, neighborhood urgent medical care clinics that provide emergency health care on a walk-in basis for persons with certain types of medical problems, might similarly target income-eligible persons within a specified geographical area requiring urgent legal assistance. Legal ERs would be free for anyone with one of a number of specified legal problems. Such an initiative might be limited in scale, yet still helpful to those most in need.

The suggestion is not unrealistic. Unlike medical emergencies, which can involve innumerable problems given the complexities of the human body, and which can require specialists and specialized medical equipment, most civil legal emergencies fall into one of a few categories. Parties requiring urgent civil legal services might face imminent eviction from their housing, for example. Or, their income may be unexpectedly reduced or eliminated. Or, they fear domestic abuse. Urgent legal needs presuppose a crisis threatening one of life's necessities: food, housing, personal safety. Beyond those, civil legal needs may be very important, but they are not usually emergencies. Law firms should consider providing representation for parties requiring truly urgent legal services for a manageable but important set of legal needs. Such efforts would resonate with the ABA's civil Gideon proposal, in that legal ERs would address legal emergencies that affect life's basic needs.

This could be done on a modest yet meaningful scale. Legal urgent cares might be open to anyone residing in a particular neighborhood or certain city blocks. In addition, or alternatively, a legal ER could service only persons with a specified list of civil legal problems. Or, a legal urgent care might provide services to a limited number of people per week or per month, on a first-come basis. Income requirements or limitations with respect to the legal relief to be sought might further ensure that the beneficiaries were those who could not otherwise secure legal representation.

The financial commitment required need not be great. After all, most neighborhood legal aid shops operate on small budgets. And many large law firms already pay hundreds of thousands per year to finance their pro bono programs. Although in some instances firm pro bono programs provide mostly representation for capital punishment cases or free transactional services to charitable organizations, other firms make broad and significant commitments to providing legal representation to those who otherwise would lack access to the courts. Sponsoring neighborhood legal ERs would accomplish similar goals. In addition to recruiting and other collateral business benefits, firm-sponsored legal ERs could provide valuable hands-on litigation experience for new lawyers. Importantly, by establishing neighborhood legal ERs, law firms would go to where legal needs arise.

There is recent partial precedent here. For example, in California, New York, and Wisconsin, state court access groups, foundations, and law schools have developed mobile law clinics that provide legal services to individuals who lack legal resources and the ability to travel to legal aid clinics. By establishing part-time legal ERs, law firms could similarly provide legal assistance in areas where individuals with legal needs and little access are likely to be concentrated. They might do so even with the support of local governments, which could for example provide office space in under-utilized city or county properties. The details of such an initiative could be left to innovation. The more general point is that new forms of pro bono representation, beyond law firms' conventional pro bono programs—as valuable as those are—are feasible in the interest of expanding access. Just as courts should innovate with new self-help procedures to enable potential litigants to find greater access to the courts, so too the legal profession should experiment with new ways to deliver legal services to those who need it most.

Legal Disaster Relief

For another example, lawyers and law firms should do more to provide ad hoc legal services in times of serious localized crisis. That is, natural disaster or economic disaster often creates legal disaster as well. Thus, in addition to increased efforts to provide greater access on an ongoing basis, attorneys should also provide greater access on a temporary basis in circumstances where crises make representation both especially important, and otherwise unlikely. Hurricane Sandy, the California drought, or the recent large backlog of Veterans Administration benefits cases, for example, might create acute needs for targeted and time-limited legal assistance to specific populations.

Here too, there is precedent to inform innovation. The ABA's model "Katrina Rule," adopted in 2007, would alter the usual unauthorized-practice rules in state legal ethics codes.[2] Under this model rule, an emergency within a given jurisdiction—including a major disaster such as "a hurricane, earthquake, flood, wildfire, tornado, public health emergency, or an event caused by terrorists or acts of war"—can trigger an allowance for out-of-jurisdiction lawyers to provide pro bono representation for parties in the jurisdiction where there is an emergency. In other words, local bar admission requirements can be waived for attorneys from outside jurisdictions for the purpose of assisting individuals in response to an emergency. Several states have adopted versions of this rule, and others are considering it as well. Meanwhile, the ABA now works with the Federal Emergency Management Agency to provide legal assistance in the wake of a federal disaster.

The Katrina Rule has much to recommend it. Attorneys from out-of-state jurisdictions should be permitted to practice anywhere in times of crisis when substantial legal needs will otherwise go unmet. Because, by hypothesis, attorneys within the jurisdiction cannot possibly meet such needs, they can have no selfish complaint against attorneys from other jurisdictions doing so. More states should therefore adopt versions of the rule, and attorneys should take advantage of it by establishing legal disaster relief programs. Through coordination with local legal aid organizations, out-of-state attorneys could likely provide meaningful assistance without leaving their home states, providing timely access to the courts for those who would otherwise lack it in the wake of disaster.

Expanded Referrals

Lawyers also can do more individually to promote access. For example, individual attorneys could agree to take more case referrals from courts and legal service organizations. Many courts maintain referral lists, used where judges believe an attorney could provide useful assistance to a pro se litigant, as pro se claims are very common in both state and federal courts, as noted in chapter 6. Many legal services organizations do too, to make referrals for potentially deserving would-be clients who do not qualify for legal assistance due to income eligibility or legal subject matter, or where a legal services entity lacks enough capacity to accept more clients. Courts and legal assistance organizations thus provide useful screens for attorneys willing to take referrals, determining which claims or clients have sufficient potential merit to justify a referral. As court practice here varies widely, more judges should maintain current lists of attorneys willing to take civil cases by court appointment without compensation, and more attorneys should agree to be listed. Referral lists provide a well-established mechanism for individual attorneys to provide representation for those who otherwise lack access.

But this familiar approach too can be extended in new ways. For example, retired lawyers constitute an important potential new source of referral lawyers. The ABA has therefore provided assistance to states to facilitate pro bono representation by retired lawyers, and has encouraged states to waive some or all of their bar licensing requirements specifically for lawyers whose practice consists only of volunteer representation. While more than half the state bars have done so, many have not. Waiving licensing requirements for retired attorneys, in order to promote greater access and given the volume of potential parties who lack representation, is well justified (accord Rhode 2011).

Attorneys licensed to practice in jurisdictions other than where they reside provide another group of lawyers who also should be allowed to provide representation where they reside. In 2013, New York became the first state to allow this practice, by waiving bar admission requirements for in-house counsel providing pro bono representation to those who otherwise lack access to the courts. That is, because many in-house attorneys do not appear in court or file pleadings or motions in court, they are not required to maintain bar memberships where they may live and work. But given the number of attorneys employed by corporations or other organizations to serve as in-house legal counsel, forbidding them from appearing in court on a pro bono basis for clients who otherwise would lack representation is in effect to shrink the population of attorneys available to provide pro bono representation. New York's high court thus waived New York bar admission requirements for in-house counsel providing pro bono representation, and other states should do the same in order tap the substantial human resources of in-house lawyers.[3] With the help of state bars and state courts taking steps to empower more attorneys to provide legal representation for those who lack it, attorneys on an individual level can do more to promote greater access to the civil litigation system.

An innovative program authorized by the federal court for the Northern District of Illinois provides another instructive example. There, the court created a "Settlement Assistance Program for Pro Se Litigants," according to which attorneys agree to represent pro se litigants to settle discrimination cases of a wide variety.[4] The pro se litigants' cases are screened initially by the Chicago Lawyers' Committee for Civil Rights. Thereafter, program-trained local attorneys (the Mayer Brown law firm helped to pilot the program) are appointed by the court to represent pro se litigants in cases for which representation would be useful. They do so pursuant to a "limited appointment" order from the court, which allows an attorney to withdraw from representation if a settlement is not reached after diligent efforts. The attorney provides advice and counsel about settlement, the strengths and weakness of a pro se litigant's case, its expected monetary value, and how the pro se client should approach settlement. By providing limited yet important legal representation to those with potentially meritorious claims, this program promotes greater access. Other courts and law firms should develop variations of it.

Cross-Subsidizing Access

Greater access to the civil litigation system can be achieved also by subsidizing the costs of litigation across classes of litigants and potential litigants. The costs of supporting increased access need not, and should not, fall entirely on taxpayers or foundations, state and local courts themselves, and the good will of pro bono lawyers and law firms. Indeed, as the ABA itself recently concluded, even given expanded efforts in this area, vast civil legal needs remain completely unmet, and promoting greater access therefore requires additional methods (American Bar Association 2014). For one, in unusual cases where civil litigants or their lawyers see very high windfalls or secure high rents as a result of litigation, committing portions of those high windfalls and rents to support greater access seems justified. In addition, in certain cases where statutes allow, courts should not be hesitant to allocate the costs of legal representation otherwise borne by plaintiffs or by nonprofit legal organizations to defendants instead.

Punitive Damages

For example, punitive damages provide one potential source to finance greater access. As noted in chapter 4, as a result of civil litigation reform many states now tax punitive damages, in some instances heavily. Some of these states use the proceeds to fund greater access to justice, while others do not commit the proceeds to any particular use. While taxing punitive damages simply to discourage litigation by making it unattractive for plaintiffs' attorneys is not justified, in appropriate circumstances using punitive damages to finance greater access to the courts can be.

Also noted in chapter 4, one resilient criticism of punitive damages is that they constitute a windfall for undeserving litigants and their attorneys: Although punitive damages may be necessary adequately to deter or even to punish legal wrongdoers, why—the critics challenge—should plaintiffs, once fully compensated for their loses, receive those extra damages necessary to deter or punish? Defenders of punitive damages respond that the availability of punitive damages is necessary to incentivize some types of litigation, and furthermore that there is no reason not to award punitive damages to those who incur the trouble and expense—and often considerable economic risk—of bringing litigation to discourage egregious legal misfeasance.

Yet defenders of punitive damages should not resist every version of reform. So long as allocating punitive damage awards to fund greater access preserves the incentives to bring desired litigation, no harm and much good might be accomplished. To do this sensibly, the effective tax rates on punitive damages must not be too high, and certainly not constant. Some states' practices that tax punitive damages very heavily, for example, seem excessive, removing too much of the incentive to bring socially beneficial litigation against legal wrongdoers. Instead, a *progressive* punitive damages tax rate is appropriate. That is, parties receiving up to some high dollar threshold in punitive damages should pay no portion of their award towards an access fund, while parties receiving high punitive awards should pay some share, increasing along specific dollar thresholds, while multi-million or multi-billion dollar punitive awards should pay still higher rates. Thus the higher the punitive award, which is to say the greater the potential windfall to prevailing litigants *and* the lesser the need for litigants to receive full awards in order to motivate litigation, the greater the portion of the award that should be taxed. And there is little reason to worry that a graduated tax rate for truly blockbuster punitive damage awards will discourage litigation. Once a plaintiff has received a very large punitive damages award, the case for awarding that plaintiff a still higher amount becomes unclear. As between fully compensated plaintiffs, on the one hand, and could-be plaintiffs who might otherwise be unable to afford access and who would benefit from a share of a large punitive windfall, on the other hand, the argument for allocating some of very large punitive awards to the latter through contributions to state access funds seems strong.

That is, taxing punitive damages to support access to the courts really means that certain successful litigants would subsidize other would-be litigants' access. The subsidy runs from one class of plaintiff to another. This benefits plaintiffs as a whole, as it is hard to see how risk-averse *potential* plaintiffs—unaware of whether someday they would receive a punitive award or instead benefit from a punitive award subsidy—would object to such a subsidy. Moreover, such a subsidy seems justified by a logic similar to that which underlies the contingency fee: using some of the gains received by successful litigants enables more parties to have access at all. If anything, the case for the cross-subsidy among plaintiff classes might be stronger for punitive damages than for compensatory damages, given that the latter by definition take from awards necessary to make plaintiffs whole, as opposed to punitive damages, which by definition exceed what is necessary to compensate plaintiffs, though the underlying economics are similar. That said, blockbuster punitive damages are not paid only to plaintiffs in personal injury cases, as chapter 6 observed. Business plaintiffs in contracts cases, for example, sometimes collect very large punitive awards—beyond what is necessary to compensate plaintiffs fully and to compensate their attorneys generously. Progressively taxing exceptional punitive damage awards should be done across all types of civil cases.

To anticipate one objection, some may argue that dedicating punitive damages specifically to promote access to the courts, instead of to states' general funds, amounts to taxpayer subsidies of litigation, because state funds are lower than they would otherwise be and thus taxpayers will have to make up the difference. That point can easily be taken too far, however. While it is of course true that where resources are used one way they cannot be used another, it is also true that using punitive damage taxes to finance greater access is not the same as taxing state citizens generally or creating any entitlement that state taxpayers must bear. Nor is it clear why taxpayers as such would be *entitled* to punitive awards, which makes unsurprising that traditionally punitive damages were never paid to the state at all. Using part of very large punitive awards for the purpose of financing civil litigation by those who lack access would constitute an appropriate use of such awards. Policymakers should therefore create graduated tax rates to commit exorbitant punitive damage awards to state access-to-justice funds.

Contingency Fees

As discussed in chapter 4, contingency fees are another common focus of the civil litigation system's critics; the image of plaintiffs' lawyers profiting enormously from contingency fees is a favorite among reformers.

The suggestion is that plaintiffs' lawyers routinely make millions of dollars, which, in turn, fuels excessive and even frivolous litigation. While matters are far more complicated than that, at the same time, in certain circumstances, contingency fees also should be used to promote greater access, here again by dedicating a portion of very high fees to state access-to-justice funds or other institutions supporting access to the civil litigation system.

First, using part of contingency fees in exceptional cases where fees provide extremely large profits for plaintiffs' lawyers—in the many thousands or tens of thousands of dollars per hour—seems justified. Here, policymakers should require plaintiffs' lawyers to commit some amount of such large fees to finance initiatives providing greater access. Courts could do so, for example, as a condition of approving an extremely large settlement, a proposed consent decree, or a proposed class action fee award. There is little reason to worry that taxing some very high fees in this way will create any significant disincentives for plaintiffs' lawyers to bring high-damages cases; after some point, multi-million contingency fees effectively constitute rents.

Committing some portion of such rents must be done on a case-by-case basis, however. In most cases, contingency fees provide fair even if sometimes generous compensation for plaintiffs' lawyers. In the *typical* contingency fee case, there is no justification for requiring plaintiffs' lawyers to finance improved access to the civil litigation system. But where such awards unambiguously constitute enormous rents for plaintiffs' attorneys (as in certain class action cases, or instances where a quick settlement yields millions in fees), some portion of contingency fees should be dedicated to financing greater access.

Some will object that plaintiffs' attorneys should not be singled out for the purposes of financing a subsidy. According to this objection, plaintiffs' lawyers often undertake significant economic risk, for which contingency fees constitute a fully justified return. Moreover, the objection continues, the contingency fee arrangement is just what enables potential plaintiffs in effect to pool their resources, by shifting some of the gains successful plaintiffs would otherwise realize—paid instead as contingency fees to their lawyers—to finance litigation by other plaintiffs who are therefore able to find willing legal representation even though they cannot afford representation by the hour. Taxing contingency fees, from this point of view, therefore would simply undermine the very advantages that contingency fees bring with respect to promoting access.

This objection is compelling for the vast majority of contingency fee cases. But in the exceptional case where the size of the contingency fee far exceeds what any plaintiff's attorney would demand or could reasonably expect as generous compensation for incurring substantial risks, the objection loses force. Sometimes, civil litigation results in contingency fee payments that swamp any reasonable level of compensation. This is true particularly in certain class action cases, where courts actively review proposed settlements precisely to ensure that the interests of the class are not jeopardized by class counsel in exchange for high fees. Such judicial vigilance is necessary only because, in some cases, there is a recognized threat of excessive fees. Again, this argues for a case-by-case approach. Rather than tax all contingency fees at specific rates, judges instead should consider whether, in appropriate cases, some portion of a very large contingency fee—large not only in absolute terms but also and especially relative to the amount of work or risk involved for the contingency fee lawyer—should be committed to state access funds.

Moreover, while using contingency fees would affect plaintiffs' attorneys and not the defense bar, as a general proposition defense-oriented law firms more often contribute to pro bono representation and other forms of commitment to legal services. There is room for more of that, but the bar's responsibility for promoting access to the courts should be shared widely. Plaintiffs' lawyers should not bear it alone, but nor should they be exempt. Where committing some portion of extremely high contingency fee awards would promote more access to the courts, all relevant considerations on balance argue in favor of doing so.

Unclaimed Class Action Awards

Dedicating portions of punitive damages and contingency fees in certain cases to finance greater access provide two ways to move some of the high gains from successful litigation to parties unable to afford litigation. Several states (including California, Georgia, Illinois, Maryland, Michigan, and Texas) now promote another mechanism as well—allocating unclaimed class action proceedings to state access-to-justice funds. This is a welcome development, and other states should do the same.

Like interest on lawyers' trust accounts, unclaimed class action awards and class action settlement amounts must be allocated somewhere. It would make no sense to return unclaimed damages to the defendants who pay them, nor proper to distribute them to already-compensated class action plaintiffs. Class action attorneys cannot keep them either; they are already compensated. But, legal doctrines borrowing from the law of trusts and estates can authorize the designation of unclaimed portions of class action awards to nonprofit legal aid organizations. An argument can be made that such a use comports fully with the rules of procedure creating class actions in the first place (for example, see Maryland Access to Justice Commission 2012), as the purpose of class litigation is to facilitate representation to those who could not feasibly bring individual cases.

Furthermore, courts may be more likely to approve class action settlements in the first place when it is clear how unclaimed portions of such awards will be used. For that matter, defense counsel might also be slightly more inclined to settle cases if it is understood that unclaimed portions of awards will be dedicated to state access funds. Dedicating unclaimed awards to state access-to-justice funds requires a proposal to do so by class counsel or presiding judges themselves. More should propose such a use. In several states, access funds have received significant contributions from unclaimed class action awards or settlements. Although usually the amount of unclaimed portions of successful class action cases is modest, nevertheless allocating those resources to finance state access funds provides another desirable means of financing greater access to the civil litigation system.

Robust Statutory Fee-Shifting

Finally, greater access to the civil litigation system requires more than cross-subsidies from one class of litigants or their attorneys to another. Socially beneficial litigation is, at times, appropriately financed by the same defendants whose conduct gave rise to litigation in the first place. As chapter 2 explained, certain statutes provide for the recovery of attorneys' fees by prevailing plaintiffs from non-prevailing defendants. Litigation to enforce the civil rights laws provides the most common example, but other statutes have similar provisions. The section of federal law that provides for attorneys' fees in successful civil rights litigation also has been interpreted by some courts to allow prevailing defendants in civil rights cases to collect fees when the litigation was frivolous or otherwise brought in bad faith, a desirable disincentive to bad-faith civil rights litigation.[5] As further explained in chapter 2, attorney fee awards must be reviewed by the presiding judge based on evidence submitted by prevailing plaintiffs. Approved awards allow prevailing plaintiffs to recover attorneys' fees at or near prevailing market rates, and based on reasonable amounts of time devoted to a case.

Attorneys' fee provisions should be interpreted broadly, consistent with their underlying purpose. For example, cases such as *Buckhannon*, discussed in chapter 2, in which civil rights plaintiffs are prevented from recovering fees when defendants moot a case by providing the relief a plaintiff seeks, warrant reconsideration.[6] Again, attorneys' fees constitute an important mechanism to finance access where potential monetary recovery is insufficient to motivate contingency fee litigation, such that without the availability of attorneys' fees, there might be little or no litigation. Fee awards are especially desirable where civil litigation is necessary to effectuate social purposes, such as in the civil rights and environmental context where the legislature has created private causes of action in order to motivate private litigation to enforce the law. In such cases, and where the defendant's underlying conduct was deemed to violate applicable law—as the plaintiffs must prevail to be eligible for attorneys' fees—the case for attorneys' fees is strongest.

In addition to attorneys' fee provisions for federal civil rights litigation and litigation to enforce certain environmental statutes against private parties, the Equal Access to Justice Act provides for the recovery of attorneys' fees for litigation against the federal government wherever the government's position was not substantially justified.[7] The Freedom of Information Act (FOIA), for another example, also provides for the recovery of attorneys' fees.[8] Here again, in the absence of such fees, the FOIA would likely be under-enforced, because although parties could sue for its violation, those suits would seek injunctive relief, which is to say that the FOIA would tend to be enforced only by parties who could afford to pay hourly fees. Reasonable fees for successful plaintiffs often are necessary to finance socially desirable litigation in these contexts too.

And between the federal government, on the one hand, and plaintiffs bringing litigation to enforce federal law, on the other, the government seems better situated to incur the costs of meritorious litigation when necessary to incentivize claims. Attorneys' fee awards ultimately constitute a version of "pay to lose," and where a plaintiff prevails in litigation against a defendant judged to have violated socially important legal obligations, the case for "pay to lose" may be strongest. To be sure, given that courts are not perfectly reliable, some defendants lose cases where attorneys' fees are available, and in close cases, courts should take the merits of the defendant's position into consideration before awarding fees, as the Equal Access to Justice Act expressly requires. But when it is clear that the defendant violated important legal obligations, "pay to lose" in the form of robust statutory attorney fee awards is warranted for certain types of civil cases.

Summary

Promoting greater access to the civil litigation system justifies not only devising cheaper litigation procedures on the supply side, as chapter 9 proposed, but also promoting greater support for would-be litigants unable to cover the costs of litigation themselves. Greater social support for legal services, enhanced and innovative pro bono commitments, and the partial use of extremely high punitive damage and contingency fee awards all would helpfully promote increased access to the courts. To be sure, these would not "solve" the access problem. But that is not the right test. Their cumulative impact would be significant, especially if they were implemented in combination with more accommodating modes of civil procedure. The case in favor of greater accessibility becomes all the more compelling given a civil litigation system that can plausibly be rendered less costly in the many ways proposed in previous chapters. Policymakers should therefore support reforms to reduce costs and to promote access—in tandem.

Conclusion

In Pursuit of Civil Justice

Civil justice is a worthy aspiration. It requires that legally injured parties have some meaningful opportunity to seek redress of their harms, and that courts reliably give injured parties their due. So central is this aspiration that it is reflected in many state constitutions. Yet the vindication of civil wrongs is important not only for individual litigants, but more broadly as well. Righting civil wrongs reinforces the law's substantive commitments. Indeed, the maintenance of those commitments requires remedies in response to their breach. Civil litigation is the central institution through which most of the law's (non-criminal) obligations are maintained.

This is not the prevailing view of civil litigation, however. Or at least it competes with the widespread perception that civil litigation very commonly rewards unscrupulous litigants and those who represent them, with undesirable consequences. As a result of that perception, civil litigation reform is never out of fashion, and the dominant reform program calls for increasing the barriers to civil litigation in various ways. And yet, the evidentiary support for the most influential view of civil litigation does not match its influence. Civil litigation reformers have not demonstrated that the civil litigation system is fundamentally defective as much as they have insisted it is so. Nor have they adequately addressed how otherwise to implement the law's substantive obligations when civil litigation is made harder rather than easier.

That said, some influential criticisms of the civil litigation system do have merit; the critics of civil litigation need not be either all right or else all wrong. First, some litigants may advance claims they should not—frivolous claims, bad-faith claims, and various forms of undesirable cases, claims, and also defenses. These threaten the system's reliability and undermine its integrity. They should be filtered out of the civil litigation system as far as practicable.

Second, the costs of litigation, in particular the costs of non-frivolous litigation, are indeed often excessive, in part because litigants sometimes press claims farther than they should, while externalizing some of the costs of doing so on their opponents. Such litigants should be made to internalize more of those costs. But more generally, civil litigation's substantial costs mean that many potential litigants lack practical access to the courts. This is true most especially for those with modest good-faith claims, for whom the expected benefits of litigation may not justify its costs—an observation virtually implied but not emphasized by civil litigation's most influential critics, though well understood by those who focus on the system's accessibility.

The central claim of this analysis has been that the civil litigation system should be made both more accommodating to those who lack access to it, and less costly for those who have access. The existing litigation system most likely sees at once too few cases *and* too much litigation. Fortunately, legal reformers need not choose between widening the gates both for desirable and undesirable litigation at once, on the one hand, and creating barriers that make civil litigation more costly for both good-faith and bad-faith litigants alike, on the other. Instead, the civil litigation system can be made more accessible, even while the costs of litigation can be better managed both to reduce categorically undesirable litigation and to require litigants who generate unjustified costs to internalize more of them.

First, courts should rely more on available mechanisms to reduce the costs of undesirable cases first by filtering more of them out of the litigation system entirely; more can be done to rid the civil litigation system of bad-faith litigation. In addition, courts should administer under-utilized procedural rules to reallocate more of the costs of litigation to parties who litigate beyond reasonable points, measured against a judge's well-informed, retrospective assessment—a more subtle yet no less important task. While most litigants should not be routinely required to "pay to lose" their good-faith litigation, parties who over-litigate at the margin of a case should be required to pay more of the excessive costs that they impose, which would discourage excessive litigation and the costs associated with it. Reducing undesirable cases at the wholesale level and discouraging over-litigation would likely have the fortunate consequence of shrinking the number of claims by parties seeking to benefit from the litigation system's mistakes (which prompts them to bring bad-faith cases and to press weak claims at all), in turn promoting the system's reliability.

In addition, the civil litigation system can be made more accessible in part by developing less costly litigation processes suited especially for cases involving moderate stakes, as well as greater support for those who lack access. Accordingly, policymakers should support, and courts should establish less expensive and flexible new litigation procedures designed for parties with moderate claims. New civil processes for cases involving moderate stakes would require very little investment within the existing judicial infrastructure, while increasing access substantially. Policymakers together with the bench and bar also should promote accessibility more broadly as well, including in cases that involve substantial stakes by creating better incentives for all parties to tailor civil processes according to the circumstances of their cases. And finally, given the social benefits resulting from litigation, greater social resources to support access and certain subsidies accomplished from within the civil litigation system itself are also warranted.

Such reforms of the civil litigation system should be undertaken from a holistic perspective. That is to say, some changes in the way litigation is conducted may make other changes more important, or may inform the contours of other reforms. For instance, the better the civil litigation system becomes at discouraging undesirable litigation, the stronger the case for making it more accessible, for its greater accessibility would more often accommodate only good-faith claims. By a similar token, the more accessible litigation becomes, the more parties may be tempted to advance frivolous claims or claims in bad faith, and thus greater steps to curb such claims become especially important. More generally, the more accessible litigation becomes, the more important it will be to contain litigation's costs. Thus, for example, while a mechanical application of pay-to-lose would have very undesirable consequences on access-to-justice (holding everything else equal), a targeted application of pay-to-impose in the forms proposed here may make considerable sense against the background of a litigation system otherwise rendered much more accessible.

A final point remains, which concerns from where innovative reforms of the civil litigation system consistent with those proposed might come. Promising reform along the lines proposed here seems likely to come more often from the bottom-up, rather than from the top-down. That is to say, highly centralized reform seems at once less likely and less necessary than localized experimentation with ways to promote access and reduce the costs of litigation. Support for this generalization is found, among other places, in state experimentation with health courts; the creation in recent years of access-to-justice commissions by state supreme courts; the revival of the summary jury trial by plaintiffs' lawyers and defense counsel in several states; the establishment of limited representation for pro se litigants by an Illinois federal court in partnership with large law firms and an organization committed to greater access; the New York high court's liberalization of bar admissions requirements for in-house corporate lawyers to provide pro bono counsel; and the ABA's ad hoc "Katrina" rule to allow out-of-state attorneys to assist with disasters. Even individual state and federal judges can do much on their own, by piloting new programs and no less by using longstanding rules of civil procedure, which already give judges considerable discretion to encourage desirable litigation and discourage its opposite.

In the end, however, there is no doubt that a perfect civil litigation system is not possible in an imperfect world. Even were all of the reforms proposed here adopted, civil litigation would remain too costly for some, inaccessible to some, and sometimes unreliable. But the steps collectively recommended in this book would promote civil justice by making the existing civil litigation system less costly and more accessible. Realizing civil justice's aspiration more fully will require continued assessment of where the litigation system falls short, and continued experimentation towards its improvement.

NOTES

CHAPTER 1. THE CIVIL LITIGATION SYSTEM

1 *Bell Atlantic Corp. v. Twombly,* 550 U.S. 544 (2007); *Ashcroft v. Iqbal,* 556 U.S. 662 (2009).

2 548 U.S. 903 (2006).

3 To be sure, there is some variation here across different types of civil cases. For example, in civil rights cases, more than one-third of all cases settle, while only 5% are abandoned, and a slightly higher percentage, 4 to 8%, are tried. But the differences in how cases are resolved across types of civil cases are surprisingly small, and 2 to 6% is a fair estimate of the trial rate across all types of civil litigation.

4 See generally National Center for State Courts, Court Statistics Project, Examining the Work of State Courts 2005: A National Perspective from the Court Statistics Project (2006) (hereafter cited as "NCSC 2006"), 16, 22; National Center for State Courts, Court Statistics Project, Examining the Work of State Courts 2007 (2008) (hereafter cited as "NCSC 2008"), 12–13; National Center for State Courts, Court Statistics Project, Examining the Work of State Courts: An Analysis of 2010 State Court Caseloads (2012) (hereafter cited as "NCSC 2012"), 3–4. Precise estimates of general civil litigation are difficult given that civil case volumes in states with uniform-jurisdiction or "single-tiered" courts include both general civil cases and small claims or other specialty cases that are, in other states (i.e., those with both general-jurisdiction and limited-jurisdiction courts), brought in limited-jurisdiction courts. In other words, counting civil cases across all states is somewhat over-inclusive—by the number of specialty cases brought in uniform/single-tiered courts. Still, 7 million is likely a fair estimate. For 2010, NCSC counts 9.2 million civil cases, taking general-jurisdiction courts (6.6 million) and uniform/single-tiered courts (2.5 million) together (NCSC 2012). Adding general civil cases brought in federal court does not change the estimates, given that federal civil cases number only in low hundreds of thousands.

5 National Center for State Courts, Examining the Work of State Courts 2002 (2003) (hereafter cited as "NCSC 2003"), 30; NCSC 2006, 31, 36; National Center for State Courts, Caseload Trends in State Courts, 1996–2005 (2007) (hereafter cited as "NCSC 2007"), 12–13; NCSC 2008, 17, 21, 25; NCSC 2012, 11.

6 See Administrative Office of the United States Courts, Judicial Business of the U.S. Courts: Annual Report of the Director (2013), Table C-2A.

7 NCSC 2006, 27; 2007, 31; 2008, 24.

8 NCSC 2008.

9 NCSC 2003, 2006, 2007, 2012.

10 NCSC 2006, 29; NCSC 2012; see online tables at www.courtstatistics.org.

11 Bureau of Justice Statistics, Special Report: Civil Justice Survey of State Courts, Tort Cases in Large Counties 1992 (Apr. 1995).

12 NCSC 2008, 23.

13 National Center for State Courts, Caseload Highlights: Examining the Work of State Courts (2005).

14 National Center for State Courts, Caseload Highlights: Examining the Work of State Courts (1995).

15 See, for example, Bureau of Justice Statistics, BJS Bulletin: Federal Tort Trials and Verdicts, 2002–2003 (2005), which provides data from 1970 through 2003.

16 Administrative Office of the United States Courts, Annual Report of the Director: Judicial Business of the United States Courts, Table X-5 Class Action Civil Cases (2000–2004 data).

17 See, for example, Administrative Office of the United States Courts, Annual Report of the Director: Judicial Business of the United States Courts, Table C-7 (2013).

18 See Bureau of Justice Statistics, Special Report: Civil Rights Complaints in U.S. District Courts, 1990–2006 (2008). See also Bureau of Justice Statistics, Special Report: Civil Rights Complaints in U.S. District Courts, 1990–1998 (2000).

CHAPTER 2. THE BENEFITS OF CIVIL LITIGATION

1 See, for example, *State Farm Mutual Automobile Insurance Co. v. Campbell*, 538 U.S. 408 (2003).

2 42 U.S.C. §1983, for example, provides for attorneys' fees for prevailing plaintiffs in certain kinds of civil rights litigation.

3 The Equal Access to Justice Act provided that the federal government's position was not substantially justified.

4 *Buckhannon Board and Care Home v. West Virginia Department of Health and Human Resources*, 532 U.S. 598 (2001).

5 *Evans v. Jeff D.*, 475 U.S. 717 (1986).

CHAPTER 4. INFLUENTIAL CRITICISMS OF CIVIL LITIGATION

1 American Tort Reform Association, Lawsuit Abuse Reform Coalition, "The Federal Lawsuit Abuse Reduction Act, Why It's Needed, How It Will Help, and Why It Has Broad Support," www.atra.org.

2 For example, *Daubert v. Merrell Dow Pharmaceuticals*, 509 U.S. 579 (1993), and its progeny generally require that expert testimony be grounded in scientific knowledge.

3 31 U.S.C. §§3729–3733.

4 See as well the American Tort Reform Association, "State and Federal Tort Reform Map," www.atra.org.

5 538 U.S. 408 (2003).

6 509 U.S. 579 (1993).

7   See F.R.E. 702.

8   Pub. L. 104–134, 110 Stat. 1321, codified at 42 U.S.C. §1997e. See generally Legal Services Corporation, Office of Government Relations and Public Affairs, Statutory Restrictions on LSC-Funded Programs (2007).

9   For one example, Wisconsin Statutes 802.05(4).

10 Pub. L. 104–134, 110 Stat. 1321, codified at 48 U.S.C. §§18, 20, 28.

11 Pub. L. 104–67, 109 Stat. 737, codified in scattered sections of 15 U.S.C.

12 Pub. L. 105–353, 112 Stat. 3227, codified in scattered sections of 15 U.S.C.

13 Pub. L. 109–2, 119 Stat. 4, codified at 28 U.S.C. §§1332(d), 1453, 1711–715.

14 See *Bell Atlantic v. Twombly*, 550 U.S. 544 (2007); and *Ashcroft v. Iqbal*, 556 U.S. 662 (2009). For subsequent developments in the antitrust class action context, see, for example, *Comcast Corp. v. Behrend*, 133 S. Ct. 1426 (2013).

CHAPTER 5. THE UNSUBSTANTIATED CASE FOR LITIGATION REFORM

1   See U.S. Chamber, Institute for Legal Reform, Lawsuit Abuse Impact, www.instituteforlegalreform.com.

2   See Pacific Research Institute, "Jackpot Justice: The True Cost of America's Tort System," (2007), www.pacificresearch.org.

3   American Tort Reform Foundation, www.atra.org.

4   American Justice Partnership, www.americanjusticepartnership.org.

5   American Medical Association, www.ama-assn.org.

6   Doctors for Medical Liability Reform, www.kintera.org.

7   American Enterprise Institute, www.aei.org.

8   Cato Institute, Overlawyered: Chronicling the High Cost of Our Legal System, www.overlawyered.com; Center for Legal Policy, www.manhattan-institute.org.

9   Manhattan Institute, "Trial Lawyers, Inc.," www.triallawyersinc.com.

10 Faces of Lawsuit Abuse, www.facesoflawsuitabuse.org.

11 See, for example, "Man Who Says He Was Denied Napkins May Sue McDonald's," Orlando Sentinal (Mar. 3, 2014), www.orlandosentinel.com; "Man Sues McDonald's for $1.5 Million Because He Was Only Given One Napkin," Business Insider (Feb. 28, 2014), www.businessinsider.com.

12 Avila et al., "The $67 Million Pants," ABC News (May 2, 2007); Lee, "Dry Cleaner Calls $54 Million Lawsuit Over Pants a 'Nightmare,'" New York Times (Jun. 14, 2007); Lee and Sabar, "Judge Tries Suing Pants Off Dry Cleaners," New York Times (Jun. 13, 2007); Sheehan, "Dry Cleaning Case Presents Frivolous Lawsuit," Collegiate Times (Jun. 27, 2007).

13 "Flying Shrimp Killed Man, Family Claims in Suit," Associated Press (Jan. 12, 2006); Kilgannon, "Jury to Decide if Flying Sizzling Shrimp Led to Man's Death," New York Times (Feb. 8, 2006).

14 American Tort Reform Association, "ATRA Condemns Multimillion-Dollar 'Pantsuit' as 'Outrageous Manipulation' of D.C.'s Consumer Protection Law," (Jul. 24, 2007).

15 "N.Y. Jury Tosses Family's Claim that Thrown Shrimp Led to Death," Insurance Journal (Feb. 13, 2006). The *Insurance Journal* also covered the "missing pants" case. See Takruri, "Plaintiff Who Lost Pants Loses $54 Million Suit Against Dry Cleaner," Insurance Journal (Jun. 27, 2007).

16 National Legal and Policy Center, "Legal Services Monitor," www.nlpc.org.

17 Cauvin, "Court Rules for Cleaners in $54 Million Pants Suit," Washington Post (Jun. 26, 2007).

18 Fisher, "Judge Who Seeks Millions for Lost Pants Has His (Emotional) Day in Court," Washington Post (Jun. 13, 2007).

19 "Benihana Wins Flying Sizzling Shrimp Case," New York Times (Feb. 10, 2006).

20 In 2013, for example, in federal court, more than half of all trials took one day or less, while about 40% took from two to nine days, with approximately 3% taking ten days or more. See Administrative Office of U.S. Courts, Judicial Business of the United States Courts, Annual Report 2013, Table T-2 (Lengths of Civil and Criminal Trials Completed). Typically, trials in state courts in general are shorter than federal trials.

21 See Bureau of Justice Statistics, Special Report, Civil Justice Survey of State Courts, Civil Jury Cases and Verdicts in Large Counties, 1992 (July 1995) (hereafter cited as "BJS 1995"); BJS Bulletin, Civil Justice Survey of State Courts, Civil Jury Cases and Verdicts in Large Counties, 1996 (Sept. 1999) (hereafter cited as "BJS 1999"); BJS Bulletin, Civil Justice Survey of State Courts, Civil Jury Cases and Verdicts in Large Counties, 2001 (Apr. 2004) (hereafter cited as "BJS 2004").

22 Bureau of Justice Statistics, BJS Bulletin, Civil Justice Survey of State Courts, Tort Bench and Jury Trials in State Courts, 2005 (Nov. 2009) (hereafter cited as "BJS 2009a").

23 See generally Bureau of Justice Statistics, Civil Justice Survey of State Courts, Contract Trials and Verdicts in Large Counties, 1996 (Apr. 2000) (hereafter cited as "BJS 2000"); BJS Civil Justice Survey of State Courts, Contract Trials, and Verdicts in Large Counties, 2001 (Jan. 2005) (hereafter cited as "BJS 2005"); BJS Civil Justice Survey of State Courts, Contract Trials and Verdicts in Large Counties, 2005 (Sept. 2009) (hereafter cited as "BJS 2009b").

24 BJS 1995, 1999, 2004.

25 See generally Bureau of Justice Statistics, BJS Special Report, Civil Rights Complaints in U.S. District Courts, 1990–2006 (Aug. 2008) (hereafter cited as "BJS 2008").

26 BJS 1995, 1999, 2004, 2008, 2009b.

27 BJS 1995, 1999, 2004, 2008, 2009b.

28 BJS 2008.

29 See Bureau of Justice Statistics, BJS Special Report, Civil Justice Survey of State Courts, Civil Bench and Jury Trials in State Courts, 2005 (Oct. 2008); 2009a.

30 BJS 2009a.

31 BJS 2004.

32 See BJS 2009a, 2009b.

33 BJS 2008.

34 BJS 1995, 1999, 2004, 2008; BJS Special Report, Punitive Damage Awards in State Courts, 2005 (Mar. 2011) (hereafter cited as "BJS 2011").

35 Bureau of Justice Statistics, BJS Selected Findings, Civil Justice Survey of State Courts, Punitive Damage Awards in Large Counties, 2001 (Mar. 2005) (hereafter cited as "BJS 2005a"); 2011.

36 BJS 2009b.

37 BJS 2005a.

38 See, for example, BJS 2005a, 2008.

39 See, for example, Bureau of Justice Statistics, BJS Bulletin Federal Justice Statistics Program, Federal Tort Trials and Verdicts, 2002–03 (Aug. 2005) (hereafter cited as "BJS 2005b").

40 According to the National Center for State Courts' statistical comparison of joint BJS-NCSC data and data from verdict reporters "reveals that [verdict reporters] often omit defense verdicts and low-dollar plaintiff awards. . . . Plaintiff win rates were 9% high in the jury verdict reporter data, and damage awards were systematically skewed toward high compensatory and punitive awards" (NSCS 2005, 3).

41 BJS 2009a.

42 BJS 2005a.

43 BJS 2005b.

CHAPTER 6. REAL THREATS TO CIVIL JUSTICE

1 Administrative Office of U.S. Courts (AOUSC), Judicial Business of the United States Courts, Annual Report 2013, Table C-13 (Civil Pro Se and Non-Pro Se Filings). It is clear that most pro se cases filed in federal court are not prisoner cases, because, as noted in chapter 1, the AOUSC compiles information about civil cases, which are filed and terminated by subject matter, and the number of cases involving prisoner petitions concerning civil rights or prison conditions constitute significantly fewer than one-third the number of pro se case filings. Compare AOUSC, Judicial Business of the United States Courts, Annual Report 2013, Table C-13 (Civil Pro Se and Non-Pro Se Filings) with AOUSC, Judicial Business of the United States Courts, Annual Report 2013, Table C-4 (Civil Cases Terminated by Nature of Suit).

2 Administrative Office of U.S. Courts, Judicial Business of the United States Courts, Annual Report 2013, Table C-2A (Civil Cases Commenced by Nature of Suit); BJS 2005, 2009.

CHAPTER 7. REDUCING UNDESIRABLE CASES

1 Fed. Rule of Civ. Proc. 11(b).

2 Fed. Rule of Civ. Proc. 11(c).

3 Fed. Rule of Civ. Proc. 12(b).

4 New Jersey Statutes Annotated, 2A:15–59.1(a)(1).

5 Wisconsin Statutes §802.05.

6 South Carolina Statutes and Codes §15–36–10.

7 South Carolina Statutes and Codes §15–36–10 (I) and (M).

8 See, for one example, Connecticut Judicial Branch Law Libraries, Vexatious Litigation in Connecticut (2014), which summarizes common law and statutory prohibitions on vexatious litigation, the tests for vexatious litigation, and available remedies.

9 See generally Issue Brief 2012–212, "Vexatious Litigation," The Florida Senate (Sept. 2011).

10 See California Code of Civil Procedure §391; Florida Statutes §68.093(3); Hawaii Revised Statute §634J-7(a).

11 This is the case in Ohio, for example. See Ohio Revised Code §2323.51.

12 Ohio Revised Code §2323.51, "Frivolous Conduct in Filing Civil Claims" (which defines frivolous conduct to be, among other things, litigation filed with malice and intended to harass the opposing party, and applicable to plaintiffs and defendants). See also *Busocio v. Oborn* (Ohio Common Pleas, Civil Division, Case No. CV-2006–05–3153, Feb. 20, 2007).

13 This is the case in Florida, for example. See Florida Statutes §68.093(3)(b).

14 Texas Statutes and Codes Title 2, Chapter 11.

15 California Code of Civil Procedure §391.

16 Connecticut General Statutes §52–568.

CHAPTER 8. DISCOURAGING OVER-LITIGATION

1 Figure 8.1 represents the types of litigation costs commonly incurred in civil litigation, but it does not exhaust all conceptual possibilities. For example, a litigant might incur costs that are reliability-enhancing and commensurate with the stakes at hand—and thus fully justified—but might do so unintentionally (i.e., by mistake).

2 Fed. Rule Civ. Proc. 54(d).

3 Fed. Rule Civ. Proc. 68.

4 Id.

5 *Marek v. Chesny*, 473 U.S. 1 (1985).

6 *Delta Airlines, Inc. v. August*, 459 U.S. 349 (1981).

7 Fed. Rule Civ. Proc. 37(a)(5)(B), (b)(2)(C), (c)(2), and (d)(3).

8 Fed. Rule Civ. Proc. 30(g).

9 28 U.S.C. §1927.

10 See, for example, *Boggs v. Doe Defendants* (Hawaii 2003) (the vexatious litigation provision applies to specific claims within a case, not only to completely new litigation).

11 See, for example, New Jersey Statutes Annotated, sec. 2A:15–59 (which notes the frivolous litigation provision is potentially applicable "if the judge finds *at any time during the proceedings* or upon judgment that *a* complaint, counterclaim, cross-claim or defense of the non-prevailing person was frivolous") (emphasis added).

12 Fed. Rule Civ. Proc. 11(b)(2).

13 Model Rules of Professional Conduct, Preamble and Scope, ¶¶ 2, 8–9.

14 See Model Rules of Professional Conduct, 3.1–3.4.

15 Model Rules of Professional Conduct, Preamble and Scope, ¶ 9.

CHAPTER 9. PROVIDING CHEAPER PATHS TO COURT

1 California Code of Civil Procedure, Sections 85–100.

2 Fed. Rule Civ. Proc. 16(a)(1)–(3).

3 More generally, multidistrict litigation in the federal system also reflects an effort to economize by avoiding the high costs that would be associated with decentralized litigation of similar complex civil cases.

4 Fed. Rule Civ. Proc. 30(a)(2)(A); 33(a).

CHAPTER 10. SUPPORTING GREATER ACCESS

1 American Bar Association, Basic Principles of a Right to Counsel in Civil Legal Proceedings (2010).

2 American Bar Association, Model Court Rule on Provision of Legal Services Following Determination of Major Disaster (2007).

3 See State of New York, Court of Appeals, In the Matter of the Amendment of the Rules of the Court of Appeals for the Registration of In-House Counsel (C.J. Lippman) (Nov. 15, 2013); State of New York, United Court Systems, Press Release, "New Rule Permits Thousands of Out-of-State Lawyers Employed as In-House Counsel in N.Y. to Provide Pro Bono Legal Services on Behalf of N.Y.'s Needy" (Dec. 2, 2013).

4 See U.S. District Court for the Northern District of Illinois, Settlement Assistance Program for Pro Se Litigants; U.S. District Court for the Northern District of Illinois, Amended General Order (J. Holderman) (Nov. 6, 2006); Chicago Lawyers' Committee for Civil Rights Under Law, Inc., Settlement Assistance Project.

5 42 U.S. C. §1988.

6 *Buckhannon Board and Care Home v. West Virginia Department of Health and Human Resources*, 532 U.S. 598 (2001).

7 5 U.S.C. §504; 28 U.S.C. §2412.

8 5 U.S.C. §552.

REFERENCES

Abel, L. (2009). "Keeping Families Together, Saving Money, and Other Motivations Behind New Civil Right to Counsel Laws." Loyola L.A. L. Rev. 42:1087.

—— (2010). "Evidence-Based Access to Justice." U. Pa. J. L. & Soc. Change 13:295.

Abel, L., and S. Vignola (2010). "Economic and Other Benefits Associated with the Provision of Civil Legal Aid." Seattle J. Soc. Justice 9:139.

Abel, R. (1987). "The Real Tort Crisis—Too Few Claims." Ohio St. L. J. 48:443.

—— (2006). "General Damages Are Incoherent, Incalculable, Incommensurable, and Inegalitarian (But Otherwise a Great Idea)." DePaul L. Rev. 55:253.

Alexander, J. (1991). "Do the Merits Matter? A Study of Settlements in Securities Class Actions." Stan. L. Rev. 43:497.

Allen, M. P. (2006). "A Survey and Some Commentary on Federal Tort Reform." Akron L. Rev. 39:909.

American Bar Association (ABA) (1984). Action Commission to Reduce Court Costs and Delay. "Attacking Litigation Costs and Delay."

—— (1994). Consortium on Legal Services and the Public. "Legal Needs and Civil Justice: A Survey of Americans."

—— (1995). "Legal Needs among Low-Income and Moderate-Income Households: Summary of Findings of the Comprehensive Legal Needs Study."

—— (1996). Consortium on Legal Services and the Public Final Report on the Implications of the Comprehensive Legal Needs Student. "Agenda for Access: The American People and Civil Justice."

—— (2006). Resolution of the House of Delegates.

—— (2009). Member Survey on Costs.

—— (2014). "Accessing Justice in the Contemporary USA: Findings from the Community Needs and Services Study."

Ampulski, J. E. (2008). "Offers of Judgment and Rule 68." Bench and Bar of Minnesota 65:32.

Anderson, D. (1994). "Improving Settlement Devices: Rule 68 and Beyond." J. Leg. Stud. 23:225.

Apelbaum, P., and S. Ryder (1998). "The Third Wave of Federal Tort Reform: Protecting the Public or Pushing the Constitutional Envelope." Cornell J. L. & Pub. Pol'y 8:591.

Arlen, J. (2010). "Contracting Over Liability: Medical Malpractice and the Cost of Choice." U. Pa. L. Rev. 158:957.

Avraham, R. (2006a). "Database of State Tort Law Reforms (DSTLR 2nd)." Northwestern University Law and Economics Research Paper No. 06–08.

——— (2006b). "Putting a Price on Pain-and-Suffering Damages: A Critique of the Current Approaches and a Preliminary Proposal for Change." Nw. U. L. Rev. 100:87.

Avraham, R., and M. Schanzenbach (2010). "The Impact of Tort Reform on Private Health Insurance Coverage." Am. Law & Econ. Rev. 12:319.

Baker, J. L. (2004). "Another New Law, Another Slap in the Face of California Business." McGeorge L. Rev. 35:409.

Baker, L., and C. Silver (2002). "Introduction: Civil Justice Fact and Fiction." Tex. L. Rev. 80:1537.

Baker, T. (2005). The Medical Malpractice Myth. Chicago, University of Chicago Press.

Baker, T., and S. Griffith (2009). "How the Merits Matter: Directors' and Officers' Insurance and Securities Settlements." U. Pa. L. Rev. 157:755.

Barber, K., D. Honig, and N. Cooper (2004). "Prolific Plaintiffs or Rabid Relators? Recent Developments in False Claims Act Litigation." Ind. Health L. Rev. 1:135.

Barendrecht, M., J. Mulder, and I. Giesen (2006). "How to Measure the Price and Quality of Access to Justice?" Available at SSRN.com/abstract=949209.

Barnett, A., and T. Terrell (2001). "Economic Observations on Citizen-Suit Provisions of Environmental Legislation." Duke Envtl. L. & Pol'y F. 12:1.

Barringer, P., III (2006). "A New Prescription for America's Medical Liability System." J. Health Care L. & Pol'y 9:235.

Barringer, P., D. Studdert, A. Kachalia, and M. Mello (2008). "Administrative Compensation of Medical Injuries: A Hardy Perennial Blooms Again." J. Health Pol. Pol'y & L. 33:725.

Bass, M. (2006). "Dangerous Liaisons: Paramour No More." Valparaiso L. Rev. 41:303.

Bernstein, D. (2004). "Hostile Environment Law and the Threat to Freedom of Expression in the Workplace." Ohio N. U. L. Rev. 30:1.

Black, B., D. Hyman, C. Silver, and W. Sage (2008). "Defense Costs and Insurer Reserves in Medical Malpractice and Other Personal Injury Cases: Evidence from Texas, 1988–2004." Am. Law & Econ. Rev. 10:185.

Blasi, G. (2004). "How Much Access? How Much Justice?" Fordham L. Rev. 73:865.

——— (2009). "Framing Access to Justice: Beyond Perceived Justice for Individuals." Loy. L.A. L. Rev. 42:913.

Boehm, K. F. (1997). "The Legal Services Program: Unaccountable, Political, Anti-Poor, Beyond Reform, and Unnecessary." St. Louis U. Pub. L. Rev. 17:321.

Bogus, C. T. (2001). Why Lawsuits Are Good for America: Disciplined Democracy, Big Business, and the Common Law. New York, New York University Press.

——— (2004). "Fear-Mongering Torts and the Exaggerated Death of Diving." Harv. J. Law & Pub. Pol'y 28:17.

Bone, R. (2008). "To Encourage Settlement: Rule 68, Offers of Judgment, and the History of the Federal Rules of Civil Procedure." Nw. U. L. Rev. 102:1561.

Bonney, L., R. Tribeck, and J. Wrona (1996). "Rule 68: Awakening a Sleeping Giant." Geo. Wash. L. Rev. 65:379.

Booth, R. (2007). "The End of the Securities Fraud Class Action as We Know It." Berkeley Bus. L. J. 4:1.

——— (2008). "Taking Certification Seriously: Why There is No Such Thing as an Adequate Representative in a Securities Fraud Class Action." Villanova University Legal Working Paper No. 108.

——— (2009). "The Paulson Report Reconsidered: How to Fix Securities Litigation by Converting Class Actions into Issuer Actions." J. Securities Law, Reg. & Compl. 2:244.

Boston Bar Association (2014). Investing in Justice: A Roadmap to Cost-Effective Funding of Civil Legal Aid in Massachusetts. Boston, Statewide Task Force to Expand Civil Legal Aid in Massachusetts. www.bostonbar.org.

Bovbjerg, R., and L. Tancredi (2005). "Liability Reform Should Make Patients Safer: Avoidable Classes of Events Are a Key Improvement." J. L. Med. & Ethics 33:478.

Boyle, J., and A. Chiu (2007). Financial Impact Study of Legal Health Services to New York City Hospitals. New York, Legal Health, A Division of the New York Legal Assistance Group. www.legalhealth.org.

Brickman, L. (1989). "Contingent Fees without Contingencies: Hamlet without the Prince of Demark." UCLA L. Rev. 37:29.

——— (2003a). "Effective Hourly Rates of Contingency-Fee Lawyers: Competing Data and Non-Competitive Fees." Wash. U. L. Q. 81:653.

——— (2003b). "The Market for Contingent Fee-Financed Tort Litigation: Is It Price Competitive?" Cardozo L. Rev. 25:65.

——— (2004). "Early Offers: A Proposal to Counter Attorney Fee Gouging by Aligning the Contingent Fee System with Its Policy Roots and Ethical Mandates." Point of Law (blog). Available at www.pointoflaw.com.

——— (2011). Lawyer Barons: What Their Contingency Fees Really Cost America. Cambridge, Cambridge University Press.

Brickman, L., M. Horowitz, and J. O'Connell (1994). "Rethinking Contingency Fees." New York, Manhattan Institute.

Brill, A. (2008). "Rights Without Remedy: The Myth of State Court Accessibility after the Prison Litigation Reform Act." Cardozo L. Rev. 30:645.

Brodoff, L. (2008). "Lifting Burdens, Proof, Social Justice, and Public Assistance Administrative Hearings." NYU Rev. L. & Soc. Change 32:131.

Bronsteen, J. (2006). "Against Summary Judgment." Geo. Wash. L. Rev. 75:522.

Burbank, S. (2004). "Vanishing Trials and Summary Judgment in Federal Civil Cases: Drifting Toward Bethlehem or Gomorrah?" J. Empir. Leg. Stud. 1:591.

Burke, T. (2002). Lawyers, Lawsuits, and Legal Rights: The Battle over Litigation in American Society. Berkeley, University of California Press.

Cantril, A. H. (1996). "Agenda for Access: The American People and Civil Justice." Final Report on the Implications of the Comprehensive Legal Needs Study. Chicago, American Bar Association.

Carlson, E. (2004). "The New Texas Offer-of-Settlement Practice: The Newest Steps in the Tort Reform Dance." S. Tex. L. Rev. 46:733.

Carlton, D., and R. Picker (2014). "Antitrust and Regulation," in Economic Regulation and Its Reform: What Have We Learned? (N. L. Rose, ed.). Chicago, University of Chicago Press.

Cassingham, R. (2005). The True Stella Awards. New York, Plume.

Charn, J., and R. Zorza (2005). "Civil Legal Assistance for All Americans." Bellow-Sacks Access to Civil Legal Services Project. Cambridge, MA, Harvard Law School and the Hale and Dorr Legal Services Center.

Chen, C. (2004). "The Prison Litigation Reform Act of 1995: Doing Away with More than Just Crunchy Peanut Butter." St. John L. Rev. 78:203.

Choi, S. (2004). "The Evidence on Securities Class Actions." Vand. L. Rev. 57:1465.

Chow, E. (2007). "Health Courts: An Extreme Makeover of Medical Malpractice with Potentially Fatal Complications." Yale J. Health Pol'y L. & Ethics 7:387.

Chung, T. (1996). "Settlement of Litigation Under Rule 68: An Economic Analysis." J. Leg. Stud. 25:261.

Clermont, K., and T. Eisenberg (2007). "CAFA Judicata: A Tale of Waste and Politic." U. Pa. L. Rev. 156:1553.

Cohen, H. (2005). "Medical Malpractice Liability Reform: Legal Issues and Fifty-State Survey of Caps on Punitive Damages and Noneconomic Damages." Washington, DC, Congressional Research Service Report for Congress.

Connolly, J. (1999). "A Dose of Social Science: Support for the Use of Summary Jury Trials as a Form of Alternative Dispute Resolution." Wm. Mitchell L. Rev. 25:1419.

Cowles, J. (1988). "Rule 11 of the Federal Rules of Civil Procedure and the Duty to Withdraw a Baseless Pleading." Fordham L. Rev. 56:697.

Crier, C. (2003). The Case Against Lawyers: How the Lawyers, Politicians, and Bureaucrats Have Turned the Law into an Instrument of Tyranny, and What We as Citizens Have To Do about It. New York, Broadway.

Croley, S. (2008). "Summary Jury Trials in Charleston County, South Carolina." Loy. L.A. L. Rev. 41:1585.

Daniels, S., and J. Martin (1986). "Jury Verdicts and the 'Crisis' in Civil Justice." Justice Sys. J. 11:321.

——— (1990). "Myth and Reality in Punitive Damages." Minn. L. Rev. 75:1.

——— (1995). Civil Juries and the Politics of Reform. Chicago, Northwestern University Press.

Davis, W. (1999). "International View of Attorney Fees in Civil Suits: Why Is the United States the Odd Man Out in How It Pays Its Lawyers." Ariz. J. Int'l & Comp. L. 16:361.

Del Rossi, A. F., and W. K. Viscusi (2010). "The Changing Landscape of Blockbuster Punitive Damages Awards." Am. Law & Econ. Rev. 12:116.

Di Pietro, S., and T. Carns (1996). "Alaska's English Rule: Attorney's Fee Shifting in Civil Cases." Alaska L. Rev. 13:33.

Dunworth, T., and J. Rogers (1996). "Corporations in Court: Big Business Litigation in U.S. Federal Courts, 1971–1991." Law & Soc. Inq. 21:497.

Eisenberg, T. (2009). "U.S. Chamber of Commerce Liability Survey: Inaccurate, Unfair, and Bad for Business." J. Emp. Leg. Stud. 6:969.

Eisenberg, T., and H. Farber (1997). "The Litigious Plaintiff Hypothesis: Case Selection and Resolution." RAND J. Econ. 8:28.

Eisenberg, T., J. Goerdt, B. Ostrom, D. Rottman, and M. Wells (1997). "The Predictability of Punitive Damages." J. Leg. Stud. 26:623.

Eisenberg, T., P. Hannaford-Agor, M. Heise, N. LaFountain, G. Munsterman, B. Ostrom, and M. Wells (2005). "Juries, Judges, and Punitive Damages: Empirical Analyses Using the Civil Justice Survey of State Courts 1992, 1996, and 2001 Data." J. Emp. Leg. Stud. 3:263.

Eisenberg, T., V. Hans, and M. Wells (2006). "The Relation Between Punitive and Compensatory Awards: Combining Extreme Data with the Mass of Awards." Cornell Law School Legal Studies Research Paper No. 06–026.

Eisenberg, T., and M. Heise (2009). "Plaintiphobia in State Courts? An Empirical Study of State Court Trials on Appeal." J. Leg. Stud. 38:121.

Eisenberg, T., M. Heise, N. Waters, and M. Wells (2010). "The Decision to Award Punitive Damages: An Empirical Study." J. Leg. Anal. 2:577.

Eisenberg, T., M. Heise, and M. Wells (2010). "Variability in Punitive Damages: Empirically Assessing Exxon Shipping Co. v. Baker." J. Inst'l & Theo. Econ. 110:5.

Eisenberg, T., and J. Henderson Jr. (1992). "Inside the Quiet Revolution in Products Liability." UCLA L. Rev. 39:731.

Eisenberg, T., N. LaFountain, B. Ostrom, D. Rottman, and M. Wells (2002). "Juries, Judges, and Punitive Damages: An Empirical Study." Cornell L. Rev. 87: 743.

Eisenberg, T., and C. Lanvers (2009). "What Is the Settlement Rate and Why Should We Care?" J. Emp. Stud. 6:111.

Eisenberg, T., and G. Miller (2004). "Attorney Fees in Class Action Settlements: An Empirical Study." J. Emp. Leg. Stud. 1:27.

——— (2005). "Incentive Awards to Class Action Plaintiffs: An Empirical Study." UCLA L. Rev. 53:1303.

Eisenberg, T., and M. Wells (2006). "The Significant Association Between Punitive and Compensatory Damages in Blockbuster Cases: A Methodological Primer." J. Emp. Leg. Stud. 3:175.

Elwart, L., N. Emerson, C. Enders, D. Fumia, and K. Murphy (2006). Increasing Access to Restraining Orders for Low-Income Victims of Domestic Violence: A Cost-Benefit Analysis of the Proposed Domestic Abuse Grant Program. Madison, State Bar Association of Wisconsin.

Engler, R. (2010). "Connecting Self-Representation to Civil Gideon: What Existing Data Reveal about When Counsel Is Most Needed." Fordham Urb. L. J. 37:38.

Engstrom, D. (2012). "Harnessing the Private Attorney General: Evidence from Qui Tam Litigation." Colum. L. Rev. 112:1244.

Erichson, H. (2007). "CAFA's Impact on Class Action Lawyers." U. Pa. L. Rev. 156:1593.

Farmer, A. and J. Tiefenthaler (2003). "Explaining the Recent Decline in Domestic Violence." Contemp. Econ. Pol'y 21:158.

Feelhaver, R., and J. Deichert (2007). The Economic Impact of Legal Aid of Nebraska (unpublished report). University of Nebraska at Omaha, Center for Public Affairs Research.

Feierman, J. (2006). "The Power of the Pen: Jailhouse Lawyers, Literacy, and Civic Engagement." Harv. CR-CLL Rev. 41:369.

Finigan, M., J. Mackin, T. Allen, M. Waller, and J. Weller (2010). "Civil Right to Counsel, Phase II Pilot Study: Needs Assessment and Cost Elements." Report to Northwest Justice Project and the Civil Right to Counsel Leadership and Support Initiative. www.npcresearch.com.

Fischbach, J., and M. Fischbach (2005). "Rethinking Optimality in Tort Litigation: The Promise of Reverse Cost-Shifting." BYU J. Pub. Law 19:317.

Fitzgerald, D. (2008). "Saving Alternative Dispute Resolution in Patent Law: Countering the Effects of the Patent Troll Revolution." Ohio St. J. on Disp. Resol. 23:345.

Florida TaxWatch (2010). The Economic Impact of Legal Aid Services in the State of Florida. Maitland, Florida Bar Foundation. www.thefloridabarfoundation.org.

Galanter, M. (1974). "Why The 'Haves' Come Out Ahead: Speculations on the Limits of Legal Change." Law & Soc. Rev. 9:95.

—— (1993). "News from Nowhere: The Debased Debate on Civil Justice." Denv. U. L. Rev. 71:77.

—— (1996). "Real World Torts: An Antidote to Anecdote." Maryland L. Rev. 55:1093.

—— (2001). "Contract in Court; Or Almost Everything You May or May Not Want to Know about Contract Litigation." Wis. L. Rev. 2001:577.

—— (2004). "The Vanishing Trial: An Examination of Trials and Related Matters in Federal and State Courts." J. Emp. Leg. Stud. 1:459.

—— (2006). "Planet of the APs: Reflections on the Scale of Law and its Users." Buffalo L. Rev. 53:1369.

Galanter M., and M. Cahill (1994). "'Most Cases Settle': Judicial Promotion and Regulation of Settlements." Stan. L. Rev. 46:1339.

Galligan, T., Jr. (2005). "The Risks of and Reactions to Underdeterrence in Torts." Mo. L. Rev. 70:691.

Garry, P., C. Spurlin, D. Owen, W. Williams, and L. Efting (2004). "The Irrationality of Shareholder Class Action Lawsuits: A Proposal for Reform." S. Dakota L. Rev. 49:275.

Gensler, S. (2010). "Judicial Case Management: Caught in the Crossfire." Duke L. J. 60:669.

Gensler, S., and L. Rosenthal (2013). "The Reappearing Judge." Kansas L. Rev. 61:849.

Gilles, M., and G. Friedman (2012). "After Class: Aggregate Litigation in the Wake of 'AT&T v. Concepcion'" U. Chi. L. Rev. 79:623.

Gordon, J. S. (2006). "Punitive Damages." The American Heritage Blog. www.americanheritage.com.

Gramatikov, M. (2009). "A Framework for Measuring the Costs of Paths to Justice." J. Jurisprudence 2:111.

Green, E., and A. Smith (2005). "Conduct and Its Consequences: Attempts at Debiasing Jury Judgments." Law & Human Behavior 29:505.

Greiner, D. J., and C. Pattanayak (2012). "Randomized Evaluation in Legal Assistance: What Difference Does Representation (Offer and Actual Use) Make." Yale L. J. 121:2118.

Grenig, J. (1999). "Stipulations Regarding Discovery Procedure." Am. J. Trial Advoc. 21:547.

Guthrie, C. (2000). "Framing Frivolous Litigation: A Psychological Theory." U. Chi. L. Rev. 67:163.

Hadfield, G. (2000). "The Price of Law: How the Market for Lawyers Distorts the Justice System." Mich. L. Rev. 98:953.

—— (2004). "Where Have All the Trials Gone? Settlements, Non-Trial Adjudications, and Statistical Artifacts in the Changing Disposition of Federal Civil Cases." J. Emp. Stud. 1:705.

—— (2005). "Exploring Economic and Democratic Theories of Civil Litigation: Differences Between Individual and Organizational Litigants in the Disposition of Federal Civil Cases." Stan. L. Rev. 57:1275.

—— (2010). "Higher Demand, Lower Supply? A Comparative Assessment of the Legal Resource Landscape for Ordinary Americans." Fordham Urb. L. J. 37:129.

Haltom, W., and M. W. McCann (2004). Distorting the Law: Politics, Media, and the Litigation Crisis. Chicago, University of Chicago Press.

Hannaford-Agor, P., and N. Waters (2012). "The Evolution of the Summary Jury Trial: A Flexible Tool to Meet a Variety of Needs." National Center for State Courts, Future Trends in State Courts. www.ncsc.org.

—— (2013). "Estimating the Cost of Civil Litigation." National Center for State Courts and Conference of State Court Administrators, Court Statistics Project, www.courtstatistics.org.

Hans, V. P. (2000). Business on Trial: The Civil Jury and Corporate Responsibility. New Haven, CT, Yale University Press.

—— (2007). "Judge, Juries, and Scientific Evidence." J. Law & Pol. 16:19.

Hantler, S., M. Behrens, and L. Lorber (2004). "Is the Crisis in the Civil Justice System Real or Imagined?" Loy. L.A. L. Rev. 38:1121.

Hantler, S., and R. Norton (2004). "Coupon Settlements: The Emperor's Clothes of Class Actions." Geo. J. Legal Ethics 18:1343.

Helland, E., and A. Tabarrok (2006). Judge and Jury: American Tort Law on Trial. Oakland, CA, Independent Institute.

Henagen, C. (1998). "False Claims of Sexual Harassment in Education: The Path to an Appropriate Remedy for the Wrongly Accused." Wash. U. L. Q. 76:1431.

Hensler, D. (1988). "Researching Civil Justice: Problems and Pitfalls." Law & Contemp. Prob. 51:55.

—— (1993). "Reading the Tort Litigation Tea Leaves: What's Going On in the Civil Liability System?" Justice Sys. J. 16:139.

—— (2003). "Our Courts, Ourselves: How ADR Is Transforming the U.S. Court System." Penn. St. L. Rev. 108:165.

Hensler, D., N. Pace, B. Dombey-More, B. Giddens, J. Gross, and E. Moller (2000). Class Action Dilemmas: Pursuing Public Goals for Private Gain. Santa Monica, CA, RAND.

Hensler, D., and T. Rowe Jr. (2001). "Beyond 'It Just Ain't Worth It': Alternative Strategies for Damage Class Action Reform." Law & Contemp. Prob. 64:137.

Hersch, J., and W. Viscusi (2004). "Punitive Damages: How Judges and Juries Perform." J. Leg. Stud. 33:1.

Hoffman, L. (2006). "The Lawsuit Abuse Reduction Act: The Legislative Bid to Regulate Lawyer Conduct." Rev. of Lit. 2006; U. Texas Law, Public Research Paper No. 101.

Horowitz, J. (2010). "Rule 68: The Settlement Promotion Tool That Has Not Promoted Settlement." Denv. U. L. Rev. 87:485.

Horowitz, M. (1995). "Making Ethics Real, Making Ethics Work: A Proposal for Contingency Fee Reform." Emory L. J. 44:173.

Houseman, A. (1998). "Civil Legal Assistance for the Twenty-First Century: Achieving Equal Justice for All." Yale L. & Pol'y Rev. 17:369.

—— (2009). "Civil Legal Aid in the United States: An Update for 2009." Center for Law and Social Policy, July. www.clasp.org.

Houseman, A., and L. Perle (2007). "Securing Equal Justice for All: A Brief History of Civil Legal Assistance in the United States." Center for Law and Social Policy, January. www.clasp.org.

Howard, P. K. (1994). The Death of Common Sense: How Law Is Suffocating America. New York, Random House.

—— (2002). The Collapse of the Common Good: How America's Lawsuit Culture Undermines Our Freedom. New York, Ballantine Books.

—— (2006). "Making Civil Justice Sane." City Journal 16:64.

—— (2009). Life without Lawyers: Liberating Americans from Too Much Law. New York, W.W. Norton.

Hubbard, F. P. (2006). "The Nature and Impact of the Tort Reform Movement." Hofstra L. Rev. 35:437.

Huber, P. W. (1988). Liability: The Legal Revolution and Its Consequences. New York, Basic Books.

—— (1991). Galileo's Revenge: Junk Science in the Courtroom. New York, Basic Books.

Huber, P. W., and R. Litan (1991). The Liability Maze: The Impact of Liability Law on Safety and Innovation. Washington, DC, Brookings Institution Press.

Hyman, D., B. Black, and C. Silver (2014). "The Economics of Plaintiff-Side Personal Injury Practice." University of Texas Law School, Law and Economics Research Paper No. 512.

Hyman, D., and C. Silver (2006). "Medical Malpractice Litigation and Tort Reform: It's the Incentives, Stupid." Vand. L. Rev. 59:1085.

—— (2013). "Five Myths of Medical Malpractice." Chest 143:222.

Inselbuch, E. (2001). "Contingent Fees and Tort Reform: A Reassessment and Reality Check." Law & Contemp. Prob. 64:175.

Issacharoff, S., and G. Miller (2013). "An Information-Forcing Approach to the Motion to Dismiss." J. Leg. Anal. 5:437.

Iowa Legal Aid (2013). The Economic Impact of Iowa Legal Aid. Des Moines, IA, Iowa Legal Aid.

Jaffe, A. (2008). "Patent Reform: No Time Like the Present." I/S J. Law & Pol'y 4:59.

Joy, P. (2003). "The Relationship between Civil Rule 11 and Lawyer Discipline: An Empirical Analysis Suggesting Institutional Choices in the Regulation of Lawyers." Loy. L.A. L. Rev. 37:765.

Kagan, R. A. (2001). Adversarial Legalism: The American Way of Law. Cambridge, MA, Harvard University Press.

Kakalik, J., and N. Pace (1986). Costs and Compensation Paid in Tort Litigation. Santa Monica, CA, RAND Institute for Civil Justice.

King, J. H., Jr. (2004). "Pain and Suffering, Noneconomic Damages, and the Goals of Tort Law." SMU L. Rev. 57:163.

Koeltl, J. (2010). "Progress in the Spirit of Rule 1." Duke L. J. 60:536.

Koenig, T., and M. Rustad (1993). "The Quiet Revolution Revisited: An Empirical Study of the Impact of State Tort Reform of Punitive Damages in Products Liability." Justice System J. 16:21.

——— (2001). In Defense of Tort Law. New York, New York University Press.

Kozel, R., and D. Rosenberg (2004). "Solving the Nuisance-Value Settlement Problem: Mandatory Summary Judgment." Va. L. Rev. 90:1849.

Kritzer, H. M. (1998). "The Wages of Risk: The Returns of Contingency Fee Legal Practice." DePaul L. Rev. 47:267.

——— (2004). Risks, Reputations, and Rewards. Redwood City, CA, Stanford University Press.

Kritzer, H., A. Sarat, D. Trubek, K. Bumiller, and E. McNichol (1984). "Understanding the Costs of Litigation: The Case of the Hourly-Fee Lawyer." Law & Soc. Inq. 9:3.

La Fetra, D. J. (2003). "Freedom, Responsibility, and Risk: Fundamental Principles Supporting Tort Reform." Ind. L. Rev. 36:645.

Landes, W., and R. Posner (1987). The Economic Structure of Tort Law. Cambridge, MA, Harvard University Press.

Lee, C., and R. LaFountain (2011). "Medical Malpractice in Litigation in State Courts." National Center for State Courts, Court Statistics Project.

Lee, E., III, and T. Willging (2008). "The Impact of the Class Action Fairness Act on the Federal Courts: An Empirical Analysis of Filings and Removals." U. Pa. L. Rev. 156:1723.

——— (2010a). "Litigation Costs in Civil Cases: Multivariate Analysis." Federal Judicial Center, Report to the Judicial Conference Advisory Committee on Civil Rules.

——— (2010b). "Defining the Problem of Cost in Federal Civil Litigation." Duke L. J. 60:765.

Legal Services Corporation (2005). Documenting the Justice Gap in America: The Current Unmet Civil Legal Needs of Low-Income Americans. Washington, DC, Legal Services Corporation.

——— (2009). Documenting the Justice Gap in America: The Current Unmet Civil Legal Needs of Low-Income Americans, An Updated Report of the Legal Services Corporation. Washington, DC, Legal Services Corporation.

Leslie, C. (2012). "Antitrust Law as Public Interest Law." U. Cal. Irvine L. Rev. 2:885.

Logue, Kyle D. (Forthcoming). Insuring Legal Services for the Middle Class: Tax Subsidies for Pre-Paid Plans.

Luxardo, V. (2006). "Towards a Solution to the Problem of Illegitimate Patent Enforcement Practices in the United States: An Equitable Affirmative Defense of Fair Use in Patent." Emory Int'l L. Rev. 20:791.

Lyon, L., B. Toben, J. M. Underwood, and W. D. Underwood (2007). "Straight from the Horse's Mouth: Judicial Observations of Jury Behavior and the Need for Tort Reform." Baylor L. Rev. 59: 419.

Magliocca, G. (2007). "Blackberries and Barnyards: Patent Trolls and the Perils of Innovation." Notre Dame L. Rev. 82:1809.

Maryland Access to Justice Commission (2012). Annual Report. Annapolis, MD, Maryland Access to Justice Commission.

——— (2013). Economic Impact of Civil Legal Services in Maryland. Annapolis, MD, Maryland Access to Justice Commission.

McCann, M., W. Haltom, and A. Bloom (2001). "Java Jive: Genealogy of a Juridical Icon." U. Miami L. Rev. 56:113.

McFeely, D. (2008). "An Argument for Restricting the Patent Rights of Those Who Misuse the U.S. Patent System to Earn Money through Litigation." Ariz. St. L. J. 40:289.

McMillan, L. (2007). "The Nuisance Settlement Problem: The Elusive Truth and a Clarifying Proposal." Am. J. Trial Advoc. 31:221.

Mello, M. (2006). "Medical Malpractice: Impact of the Crisis and Effect of State Tort Reforms." Robert Wood Johnson Foundation, Research Synthesis Project.

Mello, M., R. C. Boothman, T. McDonald, J. Driver, A. Lembitz, D. Bouwmeester, B. Dunlap, and T. Gallagher (2014). "Communication-And-Resolution Programs: The Challenges and Lessons Learned from Six Early Adopters." Health Affairs 33:20.

Merritt, D., and K. Barry (1999). "Is the Tort System in Crisis? New Empirical Evidence." Ohio St. L. J. 60:315.

Metzloff, T. (1992). "Reconfiguring the Summary Jury Trial." Duke L. J. 41:806.

——— (1993). "Improving the Summary Jury Trial." Judicature 77:9.

Meurer, M. (2003). "Controlling Opportunistic and Anti-Competitive Intellectual Property Litigation." BC L. Rev. 44: 509.

Miller, A. (2003). "The Pretrial Rush to Judgment: Are the 'Litigation Explosion,' 'Liability Crisis,' and Efficiency Cliches Eroding Our Day in Court and Jury Trial Commitments?" NYU L. Rev. 78:982.

——— (2010). "From Conley to Twombly to Iqbal: A Double Play on the Federal Rules of Civil Procedure." Duke L. Rev. 60:1.

——— (2013). "Simplified Pleading, Meaningful Days in Court, and Trials on the Merits: Reflections on the Deformation of Federal Procedure." NYU L. Rev. 88:286.

Miller, G. (1986). "An Economic Analysis of Rule 68." J. Legal Stud. 15:93.

Miller, J. (1987). Citizen Suits: Private Enforcement of Federal Pollution Control Laws. New York, Wiley Law.

Moffitt, M. (2006). "Customized Litigation: The Case for Making Civil Procedure Negotiable." Geo. Wash. L. Rev. 75:461.

Moncrieff, A. (2009). "Federalization Snowballs: The Need for National Action in Medical Malpractice Reform." Colum. L. Rev. 109:845.

Murphy, J. (2002). "Engaging with the State: The Growing Reliance on Lawyers and Judges to Protect Battered Women." Am. U. J. Gender Soc. Pol'y & L. 11:499.

Nelson, L., M. Morrisey, and M. Kilgore (2007). "Damages Caps in Medical Malpractice Cases." Milbank Q. 85:259.

Newman, J. (1996a). "No More Myths About Prisoner Lawsuits." New York Times, January 3.

——— (1996b). "Pro Se Prisoner Litigation: Looking for Needles in Haystacks." Brook. L. Rev. 62:519.

Nockleby, J. (2007). "How to Manufacture a Crisis: Evaluating Empirical Claims Behind 'Tort Reform.'" Or. L. Rev. 86:533.

——— (2009). "Access to Justice: It's Not for Everyone." Loy. L.A. L. Rev. 42:859.

Olson, W. (1992). The Litigation Explosion. New York, Plume.

——— (2003). The Rule of Lawyers. New York, St. Martin's.

Osevala, A. (2012). "Let's Settle This: A Proposed Offer of Judgment Rule for Pennsylvania." Temple L. Rev. 85:185.

Ostrom, B., R. Hanson, and R. Cheesman (2003). "Congress, Courts, and Corrections: An Empirical Perspective on the Prison Litigation Reform Act." Notre Dame L. Rev. 78:1525.

Painter, R. W. (1995). "Litigating on a Contingency: A Monopoly of Champions or a Market for Champerty." Chi.-Kent L. Rev. 71:625.

——— (2000). The New American Rule: A First Amendment to the Client's Bill of Rights. Civil Justice Report, Center for Legal Policy at the Manhattan Institute. www.manhattan-institute.org.

Pate, R., and D. Hunter (2006). "Code Blue: The Case for Serious State Medical Liability Reform." Heritage Foundation, Backgrounder No. 1908. www.heritage.org.

Percelay, J. (2000). Whiplash: America's Most Frivolous Lawsuits. Kansas City, MO, Andrews McMeel.

Peters, P., Jr. (2008). "Health Courts?" B.U. L. Rev. 88:227.

Peterson, M., S. Sarma, and M. Shanley (1987). Punitive Damages: Empirical Findings. Santa Monica, CA, RAND.

Porter, N. (2008). "The Perfect Compromise: Bridging the Gap between At-Will Employment and Just Cause." Neb. L. Rev. 87:62.

Posner, R. (1986). "The Summary Jury Trial and Other Methods of Alternative Dispute Resolution: Some Cautionary Observations." U. Chi. L. Rev. 53:366.

Pound, R. (1906). "The Causes of Popular Dissatisfaction with the Administration of Justice." Am. Law. 14:445.

Prescott, J. (2010). "The Challenges of Calculating the Benefits of Providing Access to Legal Services." Fordham Urb. L. J. 37:303.

Puplava, J. (1997). "Peanut Butter and Politics: An Evaluation of the Separation-of-Powers Issues in Section 802 of the Prison Litigation Reform Act." Ind. L.J. 73:329.

Rauma, D. and R. Willging (2005). Report of a Survey of United States District Judges' Experiences and Views Concerning Rule 11, Federal Rules of Civil Procedure. Washington, DC, Federal Judicial Center.

Reda, S. (2012). "The Cost-and-Delay Narrative in Civil Justice Reform: Its Fallacies and Functions." Or. L. Rev. 90:1085.

Redish, M. (2003). "Class Actions and the Democratic Difficulty: Rethinking the Intersection of Private Litigation and Public Goals." U. Chi. Legal F. 71.

Rennie, D. (2012). "Rule 82 and Tort Reform: An Empirical Study of the Impact of Alaska's English Rule on Federal Civil Case Filings." Alaska L. Rev. 29:1.

Rhode, D. (2000). In the Interests of Justice: Reforming the Legal Profession. New York, Oxford University Press.

—— (2001). "Access to Justice." Fordham L. Rev. 69:1785.

—— (2004a). Access to Justice. New York, Oxford University Press.

—— (2004b). "Frivolous Litigation and Civil Justice Reform: Miscasting the Problem, Recasting the Solution." Duke L. J. 54:447.

—— (2004c). "Access to Justice: Connecting Principles to Practice." Geo. J. Legal Ethics 17:369.

—— (2009). "Whatever Happened to Access to Justice?" Loy. L.A. L. Rev. 42:869.

—— (2011). "Senior Lawyers Serving Public Interests: Pro Bono and Second-Stage Careers." Prof. Lawyer 21:1.

Robbennolt, J., and C. Studebaker (2003). "News Media Reporting on Civil Litigation and Its Influence on Civil Justice Decision Making." Law & Human Behavior 27:5.

Robertson, C., and D. Yokum (2012). "The Effect of Blinded Experts on Jurors' Verdicts." J. Emp. Leg. Stud. 9:765.

Roosevelt, K., III (2003). "Exhaustion Under the Prison Litigation Reform Act: The Consequence of Procedural Error." Emory L. J. 52:1771.

Roots, R. (2002). "Of Prisoners and Plaintiffs' Lawyers: A Tale of Two Litigation Reform Efforts." Willamette L. Rev. 38:210.

Rubenstein, W. (2006). "Why Enable Litigation? A Positive Externalities Theory of the Small Claims Class Action." U. Mo. Kansas City L. Rev. 74:3.

Rubin, P., and J. Shepherd (2007). "Tort Reform and Accidental Deaths." J. Law & Econ. 50:221.

Rustad, M. (1992). "In Defense of Punitive Damages in Product Liability: Testing Tort Anecdotes with Empirical Data." Iowa L. Rev. 78:1.

—— (1998). "Unraveling Punitive Damages: Current Data and Further Inquiry." Wis. L. Rev. 1998:15.

—— (2005). "The Closing of Punitive Damages' Iron Cage." Loy. L.A. L. Rev. 38:1297.

Saks, M. (2007). "Reducing Variability in Civil Jury Awards." Law & Human Behavior 21:243.

—— (2010). "The Impact of Counsel: An Analysis of Empirical Evidence." Seattle J. for Soc. Sci. 9:56.

Sandefur, R., and A. Smyth (2011). "First Report of the Civil Justice Infrastructure Mapping Project." American Bar Foundation. www.americanbarfoundation.org

Saxton, J. (1996). Improving the American Legal System: The Economic Benefits of Tort Reform. Washington, DC, Joint Economic Committee Study, United States Congress.

Scherer, A. (2006). "Why People Who Face Losing Their Homes in Legal Proceedings Must Have a Right to Counsel." Cardozo Pub. L. Pol'y & Ethics J. 3:699.

Schiller, E., and J. Wertkin (2000). "Frivolous Filings and Vexatious Litigation." Geo. J. Legal Ethics 14:909.

Schlanger, M. (2003). "Inmate Litigation." Harv. L. Rev. 116:1555.

—— (2006). "What We Know and What We Should Know about American Trial Trends." J. Disp. Resol. 2006:35.

Schlanger, M., and G. Shay (2008). "Preserving the Rule of Law in America's Jails and Prisons: The Case for Amending the Prison Litigation Reform Act." U. Pa. J. Const. L. 11:139.

Schneider, E. (2010). "The Changing Shape of Federal Civil Pretrial Practice: The Disparate Impact on Civil Rights and Employment Discrimination Cases." U. Pa. L. Rev. 158:517.

Schwab, S., and K. Claremont (2008). "Employment Discrimination Plaintiffs in Federal Court: From Bad to Worse?" Harv. Law & Pol. Rev. 3:103.

Schwartz, V., and C. Silverman (2005). "Common-Sense Construction of Consumer Protection Acts." U. Kan. L. Rev. 54:1.

Schwarzer, W. (1992). "Fee-Shifting Offers of Judgment: An Approach to Reducing the Cost of Litigation." Judicature 76:147.

Schwinn, S. (2008). "Faces of Open Courts and the Civil Right to Counsel." Balt. L. Rev. 37:21.

Scott, N. (2001). "Don't Forget Me: The Client in a Class Action Lawsuit." Geo. J. Legal Ethics 15:561.

Seabury, S., N. Pace, and R. Reville (2004). "Forty Years of Civil Jury Verdicts." J. Emp. Leg. Stud. 1:1.

Sebok, A. J. (2007). "Dispatches from the Tort Wars." Texas L. Rev. 85:1465.

Selmi, M. (2001). "Why Are Employment Discrimination Cases So Hard to Win?" La. L. Rev. 61:555.

Shelton, D. (2006). "Rewriting Rule 68: Realizing the Benefits of the Federal Settlement Rule by Injecting Certainty into Offers of Judgment." Minn. L. Rev. 91:865.

Sherman, E. (1998). "From 'Loser Pays' to Modified Offer of Judgment Rules: Reconciling Incentives to Settle with Access to Justice." Tex. L. Rev. 76:1863.

Silver, C. (2002). "Does Civil Justice Cost Too Much?" Tex. L. Rev. 80:2073.

Silver, C., and D. Hyman (2009). "Access to Justice in a World without Lawyers: Evidence from Texas Bodily Injury Claims." Fordham Urb. L. J. 37:358.

Simon, R., Jr. (1985). "Riddle of Rule 68." Geo. Wash. L. Rev. 54:1.

Sloan, F., and L. Chepke (2010). Medical Malpractice. Boston, MIT Press.

Smith, K., and K. Thayer (2014). "An Assessment of the Economic and Societal Impacts of Civil Legal Services Programs Funded by the York County Bar Foundation." The Resource for Great Programs. www.pabar.org.

Solimine, M., and B. Pacheco (1997). "State Court Regulation of Offers of Judgment and Its Lessons for Federal Practice." Ohio St. J. on Disp. Resol. 13:51.

Solomon, J. (2010). "What Is Civil Justice?" Loy. L.A. L. Rev. 44:317.

State Bar of Wisconsin (2007). Bridging the Justice Gap: Wisconsin's Unmet Legal Needs. Madison, WI, Access to Justice Committee, State Bar of Wisconsion.

Steinberg, J. (2015). "Demand Side Reform in the Poor People's Court." Conn. L. Rev. 47:741.

—— (2016). "Informal, Inquisitorial, and Accurate: An Empirical Look at a Housing Court Experiment." J. Law & Soc. Inq.

Stienstra, D., J. Bataillon, and J. Cantone (2011). Assistance to Pro Se Litigants in U.S. District Courts: A Report on Surveys of Clerks of Court and Chief Judges. Washington, DC, Federal Judicial Center. www.fjc.gov.

Studdert, D., T. Brennan, and E. Thomas (2000). "Beyond Dead Reckoning: Measures of Medical Injury Burden, Malpractice Litigation, and Alternative Compensation Models from Utah and Colorado." Ind. L. Rev. 33:1643.

Sumner, A. (2003). "Is the Gummy Rule of Today Truly Better than the Toothy Rule of Tomorrow? How Federal Rule 68 Should Be Modified." Duke L. J. 52:1055.

Swank, D. (2004). "The Pro Se Phenomenon." BYU J. Pub. L. 19:373.

Taylor, P. (2005). "The Difference Between Filing Lawsuits and Selling Widgets: The Lost Understanding that Some Attorneys' Exercise of State Power Is Subject to Appropriate Regulation." Pierce L. Rev. 4:45.

Thornburg, E. (2008). "Judicial Hellholes, Lawsuit Climates, and Bad Social Science: Lessons from West Virginia." W. Va. L. Rev. 110:1097.

Trubek, D., A. Sarat, W. Felstiner, H. Kritzer, and J. Grossman (1983). "The Costs of Ordinary Litigation." UCLA L. Rev. 31:72.

Tyler, T. (1988). "What is Procedural Justice? Criteria Used by Citizens to Assess the Fairness of Legal Procedures." Law & Soc'y Rev. 22:103.

Vairo, G. (1998). "Rule 11 and the Profession." Fordham L. Rev. 67:589.

Van Wormer, N. (2007). "Help at Your Fingertips: A Twenty-First Century Response to the Pro Se Phenomenon." Vand. L. Rev. 60:983.

Vidmar, N. (1993). "Empirical Evidence on the Deep Pockets Hypothesis: Jury Awards for Pain and Suffering in Medical Malpractice Cases." Duke L. J. 43:217.

—— (1995). Medical Malpractice and the American Jury: Confronting the Myths About Jury Incompetence, Deep Pockets, and Outrageous Damage Awards. Ann Arbor, University of Michigan Press.

Vidmar, N., and V. Hans (2007). American Juries: The Verdict. New York, Prometheus Books.

Vidmar, N., and M. Holman (2010). "The Frequency, Predictability, and Proportionality of Jury Awards of Punitive Damages in State Courts in 2005: A New Audit." Suffolk U. L. Rev. 43:855.

Vidmar, N., K. MacKillop, and P. Lee (2006). "Million Dollar Medical Malpractice Cases in Florida: Post-Verdict and Pre-Suit Settlements." Vand. L. Rev. 59:1343.

Vidmar, N., and M. Rose (2001). "Punitive Damages by Juries in Florida: In Terrorem and in Reality." Harv. J. on Legis. 38:487.

Viscusi, W. K. (1988). "Pain and Suffering in Product Liability Cases: Systematic Compensation or Capricious Awards?" Internat'l Rev. of L. Econ. 8:203.

—— (1991). Reforming Products Liability. Cambridge, Harvard University Press.

—— (2001). "The Challenge of Punitive Damages Mathematics." J. Leg. Stud. 30:313.

——. (2002). "Punitive Damages: How Jurors Fail to Promote Efficiency." Harv. J. on Legis. 39:139.

—— (2004). "The Blockbuster Punitive Damages Awards." Emory L. J. 53:1404.

White, M. J. (2003). Understanding the Asbestos Crisis. NBER Summer Institute in Law & Economics, University of California, San Diego.

Willging, T., and E. Lee, III (2010). In Their Words: Attorney Views About Costs and Procedures in Federal Civil Litigation. Washington, DC, Federal Judicial Center.

Winslow, J. (2001). "The Prison Litigation Reform Act's Physical Injury Requirement Bars Meritorious Lawsuits: Was It Meant To?" UCLA L. Rev. 49:1655.

Wistrich, A., and J. Rachlinski (2013). "How Lawyers' Intuitions Prolong Litigation." S. Cal. L. Rev. 86:101.

Woolf, L. (1996). Access to Justice: Final Report to the Lord Chancellor on the Civil Justice System in England and Wales. London: Her Majesty's Stationery Office.

Worcel, S., M. Finigan, and T. Allen (2009). "Civil Right to Counsel Social Science Study Design Report." Final Report to the Northwest Justice Product and the Civil Right to Counsel Leadership and Support Initiative. www.npcresearch.com.

Yoon, A., and Baker, T. (2006). "Offer-of-Judgment Rules and Civil Litigation: An Empirical Study of Automobile Insurance Litigation in the East." Vand. L. Rev. 59:153.

Zalesne, D. (1999). "Sexual Harassment Law: Has it Gone Too Far, or Has the Media?" Temp. Pol. & Civ. Rights L. Rev. 8:351.

INDEX

Page numbers in *italics* indicate figures; page numbers with a t indicate tables.

Galanter, M., 7
general civil cases, defined, 16, 18
general jurisdiction, 20, 22, 245n4
Gideon right, 225, 229
good-governance, 40
grievances. *See* professional discipline

Hadfield, G., 7–8
Haltom, W., 7
"Handbooks on Recoverable Costs," 169
Hans, V. P., 7, 113
harassment: Rule 11, 141; Section 1927, 175;
    sexual harassment cases, 2; vexatious
    litigation statutes, 146–47
harms: legal *vs.* non-legal, 12; non-
    economic, 30; social harms from civil
    litigation, 28, 82–85; temporary *vs.*
    permanent, vii, viii
Hawaii and vexatious litigation statutes,
    146
health courts, 187–88, 190–95, 244
hearsay in expedited jury trials, 211–12,
    214
Helland, E., 103, 113
Hersch, J., 113
high/low damages, 215–16, 217–18
Holman, M., 110
homelessness, 41–42, 126
hotlines, legal, 198
housing cases: judges' participation, 180;
    limits on LSC-funded organizations,
    89

illegal immigration cases, 89, 125
Illinois and counsels for pro se represen-
    tation, 157, 232–33, 244
ILR (Institute for Legal Reform), 93–94
impact litigation, 79, 86, 89
inaccessibility. *See* access
income. *See* low-income populations;
    moderate-income populations
income tax incentives, 227
injunctive relief, 32, 33, 43, 62

injuries. *See* harms
Institute for Legal Reform (ILR), 93–94
insurance: expedited jury trials, 215–17;
    income tax incentives, 227; and over-
    representation of business, 128–29
Insurance Journal, 97–98, 102
intellectual property cases, 2, 81, 86
intent, 15
intentional torts: damages, 108, 109, 110;
    plaintiff success rates, 106; punitive
    damages, 109, 110; volume, 22
interest on lawyer trust accounts
    (IOLTA), 125
internalization of costs. *See* pay to impose;
    pay to lose
IOLTA funds, 125

"Jester's Courtroom," 95
joinder of claims, 23, 37, 79
Judge and Jury (Helland and Tabarrok),
    103
judges: bench trials, 111–13; calendar
    management, 180–81; class action
    case screening, 179–80; correction of
    punitive damages, 32, 100, 111; and
    costs, 162, 177–81, 222, 239; damages,
    32, 100, 103, 111, 112–13; expedited jury
    trials, 212, 213–14; health courts, 191;
    jurisdiction stretching, 82; medium
    claims courts, 205, 206, 207–8, 209–10;
    plaintiff success rates, 111–12; punitive
    damages, 32, 100, 103, 111, 113; referrals,
    231–33; reliability, 82; Rule 11 usage,
    140–41, 179; small claims courts, 195,
    200–203; survey on need for reform,
    114–15; tailoring processes, 219–20, 221;
    workload, 178
judgments. *See* default judgments; offers
    of judgment; summary judgments
judicial hellholes, 82, 94
juries: *vs.* bench trials, 112; damages, 3,
    76–77, 99–100, 103, 108, 110, 111, 112–13;
    expert, 191, 194; health courts, 191, 194;

ABOUT THE AUTHOR*

Steven P. Croley is a partner with Latham & Watkins LLP. He recently served in President Barack Obama's Administration on the Domestic Policy Council, as Deputy White House Counsel, and as General Counsel of the U.S. Department of Energy. He previously served as a Special Assistant U.S. Attorney in the Eastern District of Michigan, representing the United States in affirmative and defensive civil matters. Prior to that, he represented individual clients. Following a judicial clerkship, he began his legal career as a law professor at the University of Michigan Law School, where he specialized in administrative law, civil procedure, and torts, and in 2010 was named the Harry Hutchins Collegiate Professor of Law.

---

* All author proceeds from this book are donated to Legal Services of South Central Michigan.